Carving & Painting a
PINTAIL DRAKE
with Jimmie Vizier

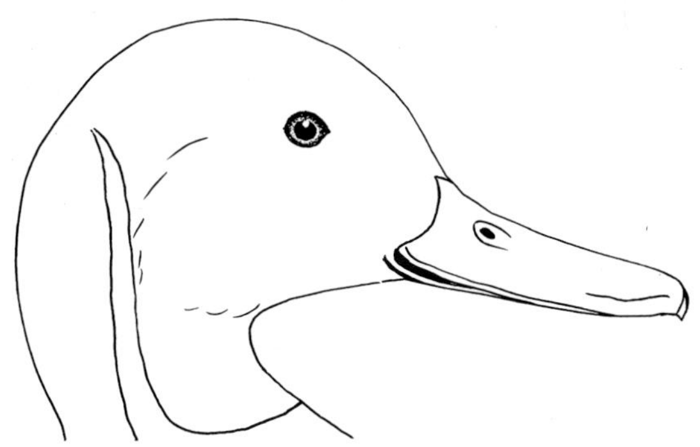

Curtis J. Badger

STACKPOLE BOOKS

Copyright © 1999 by Stackpole Books

Published by
STACKPOLE BOOKS
5067 Ritter Road
Mechanicsburg, PA 17055
www.stackpolebooks.com

All rights reserved, including the right to reproduce this book or portions thereof in any form or by any means, electronic or mechanical, including photocopying, recording, or by any information storage and retrieval system, without permission in writing from the publisher. All inquiries should be addressed to Stackpole Books, 5067 Ritter Road, Mechanicsburg, PA 17055.

Printed in China

First Edition

10 9 8 7 6 5 4 3 2 1

Cover design by Wendy Reynolds

All photographs by Curtis J. Badger unless otherwise credited.

Library of Congress Cataloging-in-Publication Data

Badger, Curtis J.
Carving and painting a pintail drake with Jimmie Vizier / Curtis J. Badger. — 1st ed.
p. cm.
ISBN 0-8117-2701-7
1. Decoys (Hunting). 2. Wood-carving—Technique. 3. Decoys (Hunting)—Painting. 4. Northern pintail in art. I. Vizier, Jimmie. II. Title.
TT199.75.B33 1999
745.593'6—dc21 98-8288
CIP

Contents

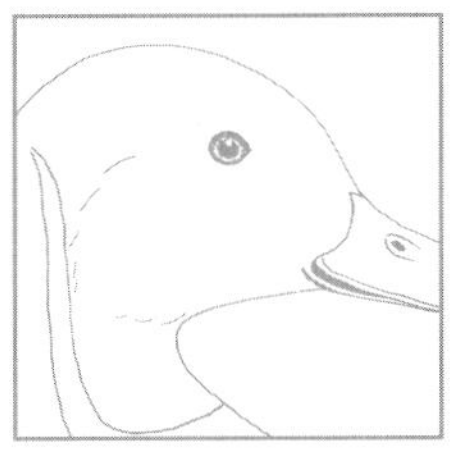

CHAPTER ONE

Jimmie Vizier—An Artist in the Cajun Tradition

Jimmie Vizier has spent more than half of his sixty-six years at sea, and although he has retired from his most recent career as captain of a seagoing tugboat, he is never far from the water. Jimmie lives in Galliano, Louisiana, in Bayou Lafourche, a short distance from the Intracoastal Waterway and close to the Mississippi River and the Gulf of Mexico, where time in the boat is now considered recreation, not work. When Jimmie gets behind the controls of a boat, he is more often in search of redfish, speckled sea trout, or Louisiana shrimp.

Jimmie grew up in nearby Cut Off, a few miles farther south down the bayou, just this side of Grand Isle, where his family once had a hunting and fishing camp. There Jimmie learned to handle a shotgun, to put wild ducks on the table for the family dinner, and to carve decoys in the Cajun style of his father, Odee Vizier, and uncle, Clovis, who was perhaps the best of the Lafourche carvers.

Jimmie Vizier today carries on what is not only a family tradition, but one of a community, a parish, a people. He makes decoys in the traditional manner, meant that they are made to float in the water, to toll a dawn flight of pintails, to have function as well as form. He is among the best in the world at this genre of wildlife art.

The only immersion most of Jimmie's carvings get comes at one of the wildfowl carving competitions around North America, where gunning decoys are judged the old-fashioned way, as they bob about in a tank of water. True to their roots, Jimmie's decoys are keeled and weighted, thoroughly tested, and guaranteed to self-right and float without yawing or pitching. After all, they have a substantial pedigree to uphold. Odee and Clovis, whose work is prized by collectors today, would be proud of Jimmie, who turned out to be a pretty fair carver.

There is little superficial resemblance between Jimmie's meticulous carvings and those of Clovis and Odee. Their decoys were carved from cypress root, light as balsa, sleek bodied as the root itself. They were roughed out with a hatchet, whittled with a pocketknife, rounded with a wood rasp, and painted with the most appropriate colors available.

Odee was a fisherman and hunter who traded a few decoys for groceries and sold some for spending money, which, with ten kids in the family, was always in short supply. Clovis, whom everyone called Cadiz, carved decoys while Odee was fishing or trapping muskrats. Local hunters bought the decoys, as did a few sports from the city. Today his carvings turn up regularly in antique galleries and folk art auctions.

Cadiz and Odee made handsome little decoys, their work often influenced by the size and shape of the cypress root available. They were limited only by their materials and tools—hatchets and pocketknives will take you only so far.

Jimmie also carves with hatchets and knives, but he doesn't let traditional restraints such as tools limit or influence his work. He squares his carving blocks with a jointer, cuts out the head and body blocks with a band saw, uses flexible-shaft grinders to shape the carvings, and paints his decoys with a broad palette of Jo Sonja acrylic pigments.

So a Jimmie Vizier pintail is both similar to and different from one that might have been carved a generation ago by Cadiz or Odee. Jimmie's is highly detailed and expressive, with textured feathers, finely blended paints, and meticulous vermiculation. Theirs, by contrast, might seem crude to the unpracticed eye. But put them on the water at dawn in a Bayou Lafourche swamp, hunker down with your 12-gauge double and your black Lab, and they will function just as well. The function has not changed, only the medium.

Jimmie was the eighth of ten Vizier children. The family lived for most of the year in a floating camp on Bayou Lafourche. They moved camp to follow the seasons. In summer they would fish for shrimp and blue crabs; in winter they would move into the marshes to trap muskrats, gather oysters, and shoot ducks. At age twelve, Jimmie's chore was to go out to the marsh at the end of the day with the dog and the old hammer double, and bring home enough gadwalls and pintails to feed the family the next day.

In retirement, Jimmie still has the look of a seafarer. He has a pencil-thin mustache, gray now, and deep-set green eyes that have seen the worst of it from the Gulf of Mexico to the North Sea. Photos of Jimmie show him in his captain's hat and in his Marine uniform. He has a tattoo on his left arm, a souvenir of a weekend long forgotten.

A 16-foot outboard sits in the driveway of the Vizier home in Galliano, ready should Jimmie feel the need again to have salt spray in his face. But his days no longer center around tides and shipping schedules. Instead, he rises in the morning, has a cup of instant coffee, feeds Smokey, his black Lab, and heads to his carving shop, a frame building on the southeast corner of his property.

Business centers around gunning decoys, handsome birds that are meticulously wrought, yet capture some undefinable essence of a bird, just as the old ones did. Jimmie's success in carving competitions is impressive, especially for a man who spent his prime years towing huge oil rigs across the North Sea for Brown and Root Corporation. Now that he has retired, his list of ribbons is growing, as is the list of collectors waiting to get one of his carvings. As this book was going to press, Jimmie had just won best-of-show honors at both the Northern Nationals and the Midwest Decoy Contest.

The current wait for a Vizier carving is one to two years, unless one happens upon a bird at a fund-raising auction for Ducks Unlimited or the Ward Museum, nonprofit groups Jimmie has supported for years. Not only is his work in demand, but Jimmie feels himself increasingly drawn to travel, especially when it involves fishing and hunting. He begins the waterfowl season in Canada in September and ends it in Louisiana in January; few decoys get carved during that time.

Jimmie left school after the sixth grade to help support a large family, but he has gotten his education through real-world experience—first the hunting camps and the shrimp boats, then the Marine Corps, Korea, work aboard oceangoing tugs, and finally, ownership with his brother Tommy of Vizier Towing, which operated a fleet of tugs around the world.

"It was assumed in the Cajun world that a boy would leave school and help support the family as soon as he got big enough," says Jimmy. "My father ran a shrimp boat, and when I got big enough to pull a line, that's what I did. I went to work."

Jimmie's departure from Bayou Lafourche came courtesy of the U.S. Marines, which Jimmie chose over taking his chances with the Army in the draft. After the Marines, he planned to return to Lafourche and resume the semisubsistence lifestyle of shrimping, hunting, fishing, and as a diversion, decoy carving. But the shrimp boats fell on hard times, work on the water was hard to come by, and Jimmie again looked to leaving the bayou. He and Marion Cheramie, a Lafourche girl, were married in 1957, and soon a family was on the way. Jobs were available on tugboats, and since Jimmie knew the water well, he quickly got a job.

In time, Jimmie and Tommy went from working as hired hands to being the ones doing the hiring. Jimmie got his coveted captain's license, no small achievement for a man with abbreviated formal schooling, and he and Tommy invested in an oceangoing tugboat, a 125-footer built right at home in Lafourche. Offshore oil exploration was getting under way, and contracts for towing oil platforms for manufacturers such as Brown and Root soon had the young Vizier company on a growth spurt.

Brown and Root was very active in the North Sea, and Vizier Towing followed it there, sailing the *Taroze* from Lafourche to New York to Bremerhaven, Germany, a journey that took twenty-three days. For a time, Jimmie and Tommy alternated months operating the tug off England and Scotland, flying back to Lafourche between shifts. Later, Jimmie moved his young family to England, and as a result, his three daughters, Myra, Jessica, and Mitzi, are Cajuns with a British accent.

The Vizier company grew to include two tugs, and then three. It was exhausting, often dangerous, work, even for experienced seamen like Jimmie and Tommy. Not only were there the physical challenges of towing huge oil structures in rough weather, but there were also the issues of hiring crew members, meeting schedules, negotiating contracts, and being away from family for long stretches.

In 1988 Jimmie decided that he'd had enough. He and Marion and the family moved back to Galliano, to their comfortable house, Jimmie's studio, their friends, and his hunting and fishing buddies. With time on his hands for the first time in years, Jimmie began carving again.

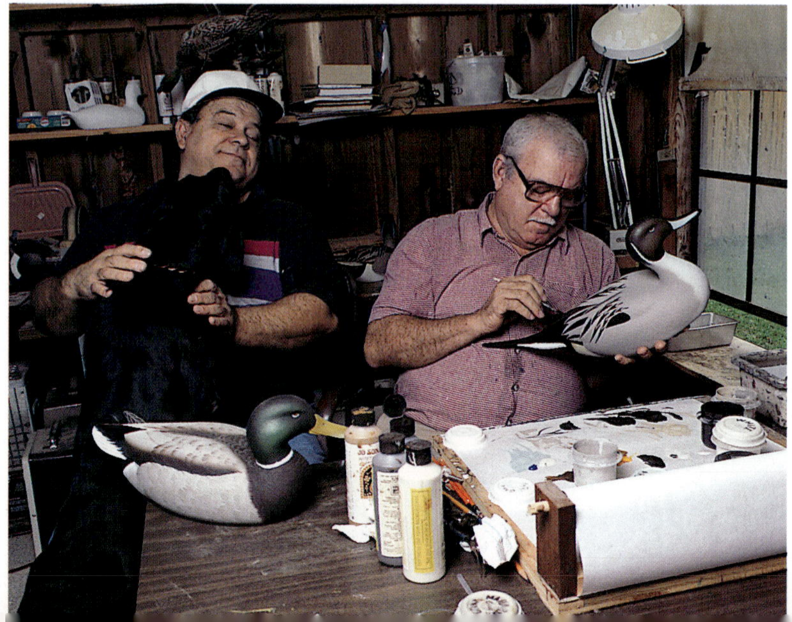

Jimmie and his friend, neighbor, and frequent carving companion, Tan Brunet, who dropped by for a visit and is greeted by Smokey. Tan is a five-time World Champion carver, and his sons, Jett and Jude, have each won the award twice.

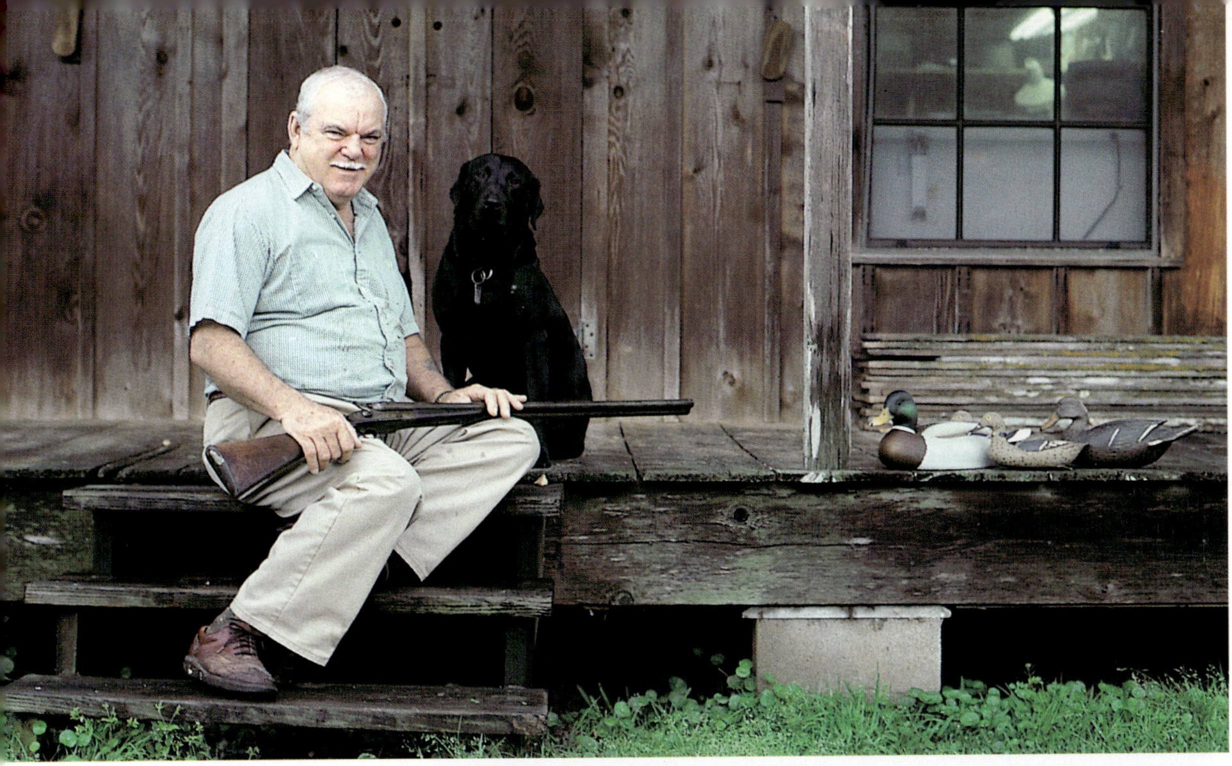

Jimmie and his black Lab, Smokey, at Jimmie's carving shop in Galliano, Louisiana.

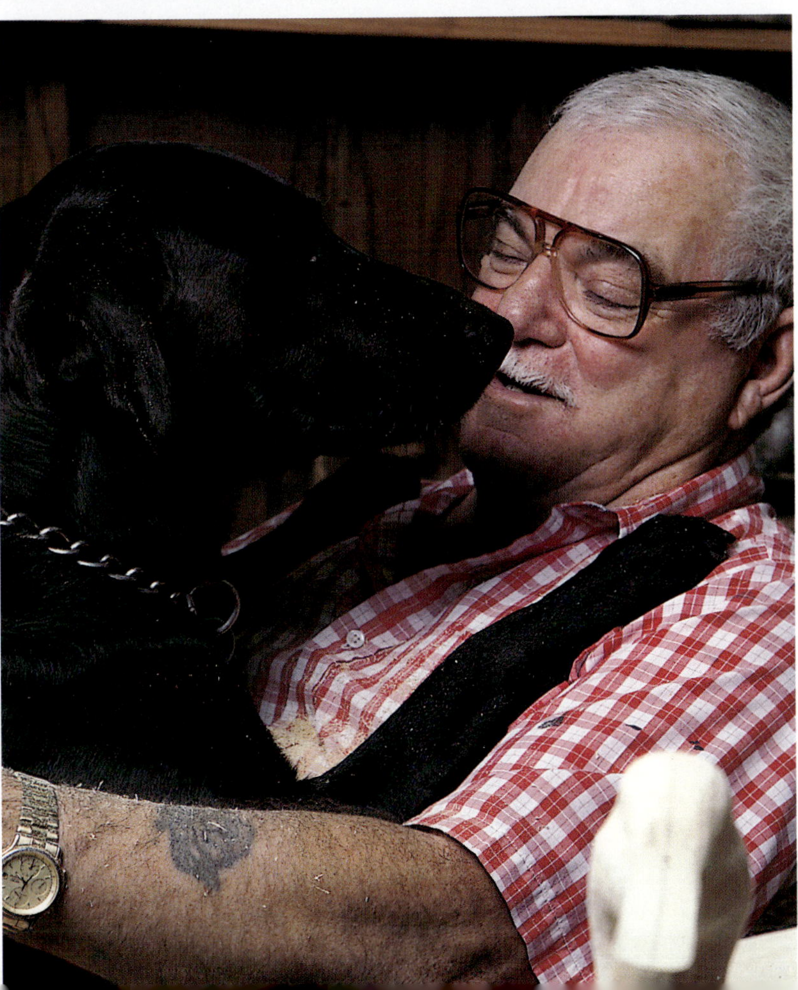

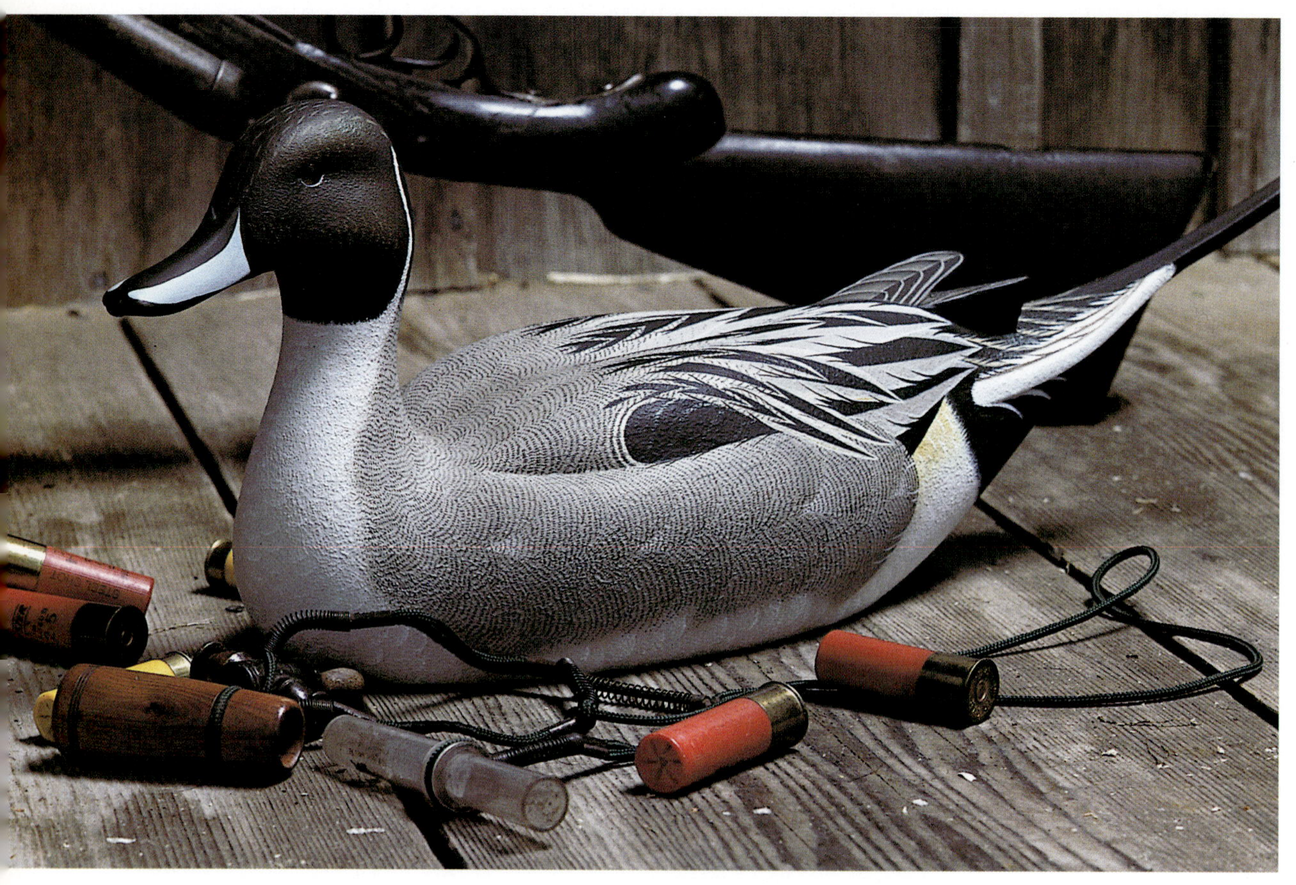

The finished pintail drake. The shotgun is one Jimmie hunted with in Bayou Lafourche when he was a child.

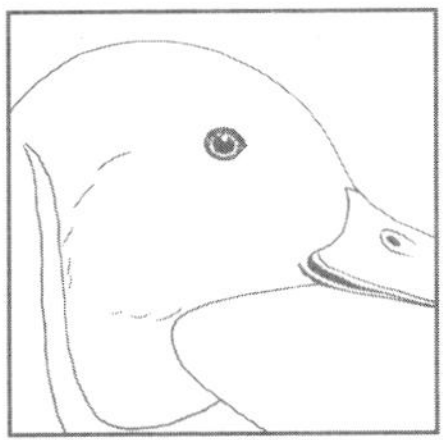

CHAPTER TWO

About the Pintail

The pintail, a common bird with uncommonly good looks, has been one of the favorite subjects of North American wildfowl artists for years. It's one of North America's most abundant and widespread ducks, found in nearly every state and province. This sleek and graceful duck has nicely curved lines that naturally lend themselves to classical compositions, with its long, curved neck and upswept tail, gentle C-curve of white along the head, the drake's long scapular feathers that cascade across the sidepockets. The pintail provides a textbook study in pleasing composition; render it accurately in a carving and you can't go wrong. J. W. Long, writing in *American Wild-fowl Shooting* (1879), called the pintail "the most graceful and symmetrically formed of the whole duck tribe." Can't argue with that.

Long, who hunted pintails in the American West, observed that "upon the breaking up of winter, they arrive in countless numbers, taking possession, as it were, of the overflowed prairies and cornfields where they feed upon the previous season's waste and unharvested grain and the grassy seeds which, floating upon the surface of the water, become drifted together into large patches. Here they soon become exceedingly fat and their flesh fine flavored."

Pintails have long been a favorite of hunters as well as artists. Jimmie Vizier grew up hunting pintails and gadwalls in the marshes of southern Louisiana, and while learning to carve from his father and uncle, he came to appreciate both the artistic and gastronomic virtues of the pintail.

These widespread ducks are known by a variety of colloquial names. Sprig or sprig-tail is one of the most common. American pintail, northern pintail, Bahama pintail, kite-tail, sharp-tail, spike-tail, picket-tail, and spring-tail are all regional names for the pintail, *Anas acuta,* which means "pointed duck," referring to the drake's tail. Henry W. Henshaw, chief of the U.S. Biological Survey, writing in *The Book of Birds* (1914), noted that the pintail is locally known in Britain as the sea pheasant because of its long neck and pointed tail.

The pintail is one of North America's fastest ducks. Henshaw wrote that he once witnessed one in California being chased by a prairie falcon. The race went on for about a half mile, Henshaw said, and the falcon was closing the gap. The pintail suddenly circled toward Henshaw, and the falcon, fearing the human, reluctantly gave up the chase.

Pintails nest in the northern United States, the Canadian prairies, and the tundra region of arctic Alaska and Hudson Bay. The nest is usually a depression or hollow built in the tundra, sometimes far from water, or in sedge and hay meadows or lightly used pastureland.

Pintails arrive on the nesting grounds in early April in the southern portions of the summer range and in early May in the tundra regions. Eggs are laid in clutches of six to ten from May to July. The female incubates the cream-colored eggs, which hatch in twenty-three to twenty-five days. First flight comes thirty-eight to fifty-two days after hatching, according to John K. Terres's *Audubon Society Encyclopedia of North American Birds.*

Pintails, like all dabbling ducks, are shallow-water feeders, with a diet of vegetative matter and small fish and shellfish. The pintail subsists mainly on the seeds of grasses, pondweeds, and sedges, but also eats snails, small crabs, crayfish, minnows, and aquatic insects. The diet of the hen likely varies according to the egg-laying and nesting cycle and the accompanying need for protein and calcium.

The pintail is one of the few North American waterfowl to winter in Hawaii, with flocks routinely making the 2,000-mile flight from the Aleutian Islands to Hawaii. Terres writes that one pintail, banded at the Bear River Refuge in Utah, was recovered in the Hawaiian Islands eighty-two days later. It could be that pintails are not only some of our most graceful and abundant waterfowl, but also among the smartest.

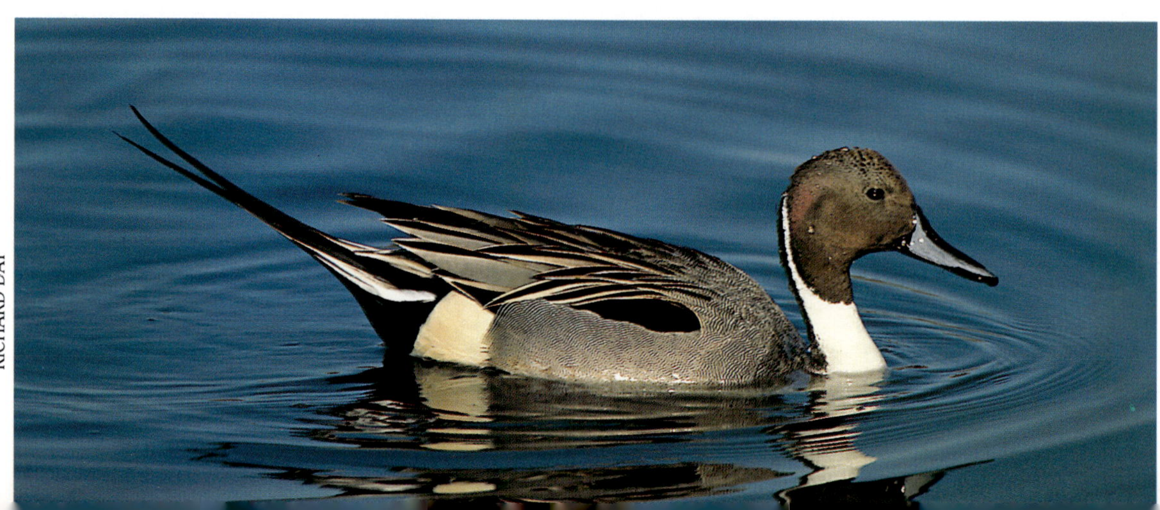

RICHARD DAY

The pintail drake is one of North America's most elegant waterfowl. Note the long, sweeping tail feathers, which give the bird its name. Note also the graceful curve of the neck, which is emphasized by the bold white stripes that run from the neck to the back of the head. The graceful lines of the pintail make it a favorite among artists.

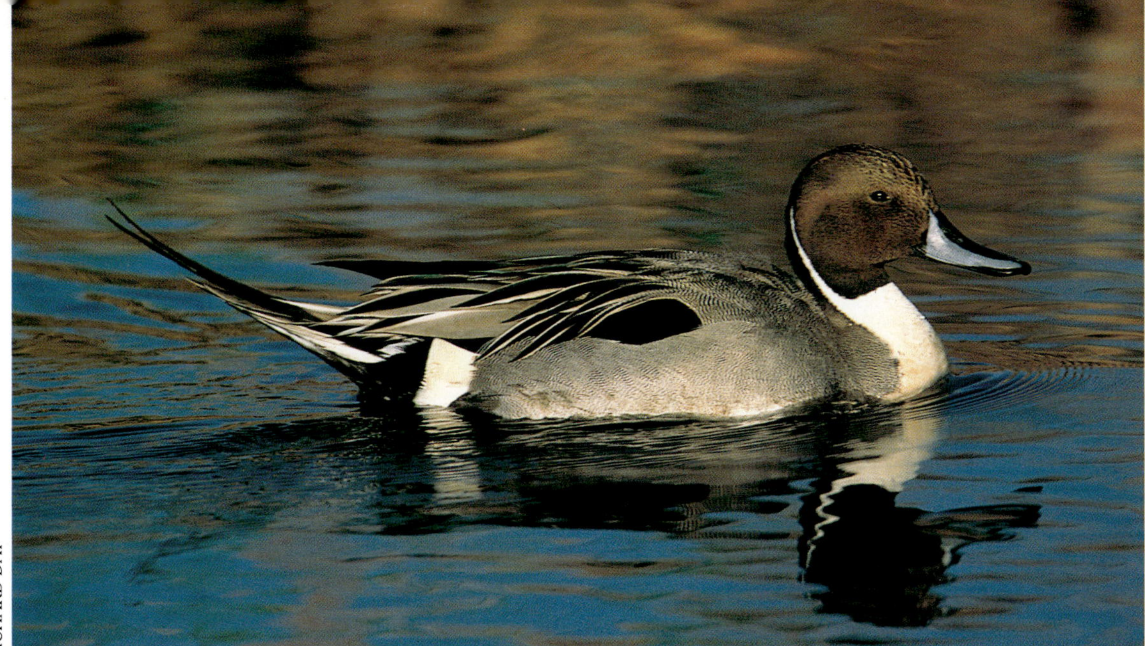

RICHARD DAY

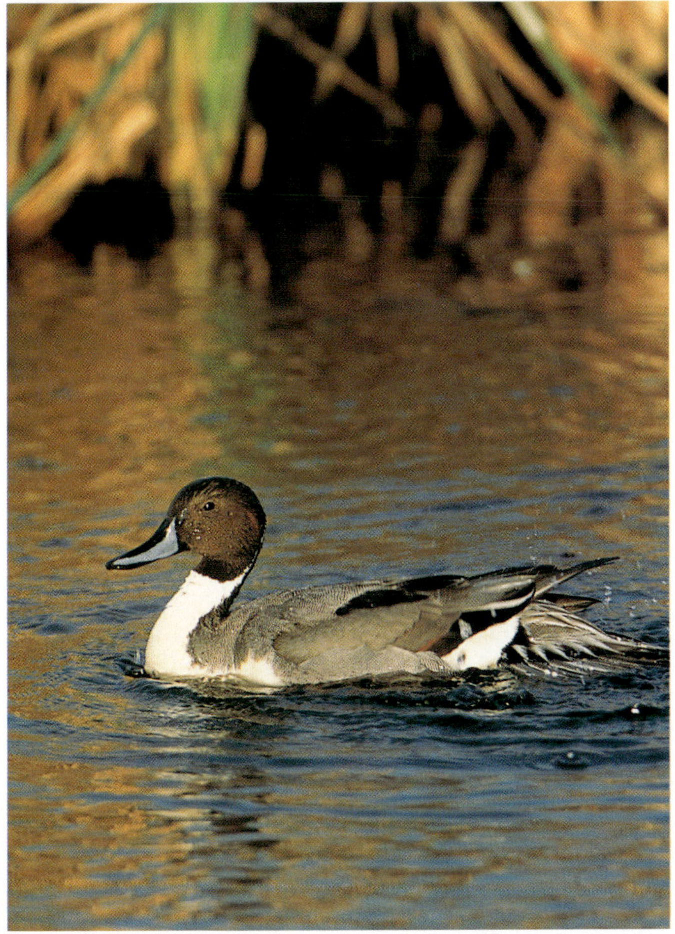

RICHARD DAY

The sides of the pintail drake are covered by irregular lines called vermiculation, which from a distance produce a shade of medium gray. Jimmie will carefully paint each line; this photo will give you a good idea of how the lines are configured. Note that they are smaller and farther apart near the belly of the bird and denser and tighter near the back.

This photo provides a good look at the graceful neck of the pintail. Note how the curve of the neck is reflected by the white area of the neck and head. Even the bill of the pintail has a slight curve, complementing that of the forehead. This photo also provides a good look at the speculum and the long primary flight feathers.

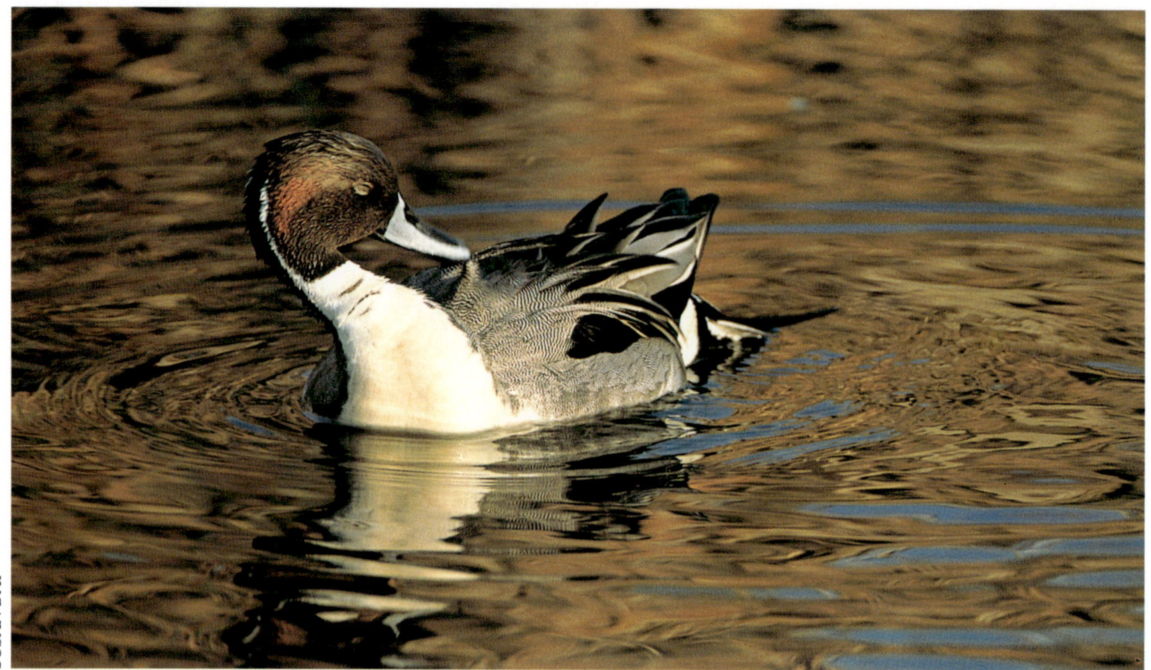

SUSAN DAY

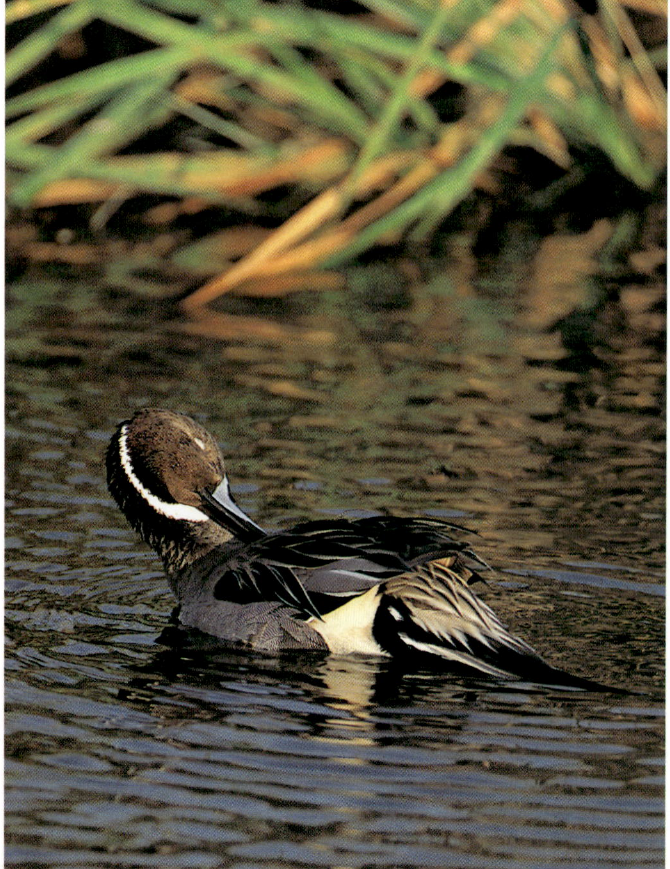

SUSAN DAY

If you choose to carve and paint a pintail in a preening position, this photo will be invaluable. This front quarter view provides a good look at the breast and neck, which is turned and extended as the bird lifts a feather on its back. Note also the vermiculated detail and the long primary feathers.

Another preening photo, this time from the rear quarter, provides good detail of the flight feathers and those that lie across the tail. This photo also provides good reference for painting the white line along the neck and head. Note that the edges are irregular and that the line narrows somewhat at the back of the head.

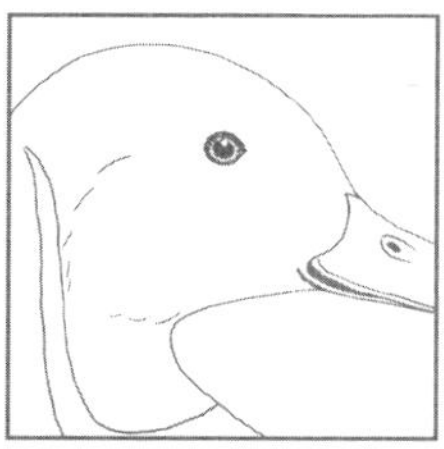

CHAPTER THREE

Roughing Out the Body and Head

Jimmie carves with tupelo gum and begins with two blocks, one for the body and one for the head. The wood should be clear, with no knots, splits, or checks. The block for the body is 5 by 7 by 15 1/2 inches. The block for the head is 6 inches long by 4 1/2 inches high by 2 1/8 inches thick. The thickness dimension of the block for the head is slightly more than the finished width of the head will be. This allows for some sanding, but it will make the carving process easier to have the head the proper width from the start.

Both blocks are run through a jointer before they are cut out on the band saw. This ensures that they will be square and that when the pattern is cut out on the band saw, the edges will be parallel.

Jimmie traces the top and side patterns of the body onto the block of tupelo. The block is just slightly larger than the finished bird in all three dimensions. The line at the neck where the head will be mounted is parallel to the waterline, ensuring that when the head is mounted it can be turned at any angle and will be straight. If that line were not parallel to the waterline, the head would be unnaturally tilted when turned.

Jimmie cuts out the patterns on the band saw, then rounds off the carving with a small hatchet. A flexible-shaft grinding tool is used to do the preliminary shaping of the body and head. Jimmie uses a number of power tools, from a jointer to a band saw to a grinder, but only the last is really necessary for this carving project. Grinders are available at hobby stores and woodworking shops. Although a carving could be done just with knives, grinders make the process quicker, easier, and more accurate. A good-quality grinder with a variety of cutting bits should be one of your first investments when setting up a carving shop. If you do not have a jointer or band saw, a woodworking shop could square the workpiece and cut out the patterns for you. If you do the work yourself, be sure to abide by the safety precautions supplied by the manufacturer of the equipment. Power tools are great time-savers, but they can be dangerous when used improperly.

It is also important to have some sort of dust-removal system in your carving shop. Tools such as high-speed grinders generate a lot of fine wood particles, which are dangerous to the respiratory system. Commercial dust-removal systems are widely available, or you can make your own using a fan or vacuum system. Jimmie carves at an open window and uses a large fan to exhaust airborne particles.

In roughing out the carving, Jimmie will primarily use his Foredom flexible-shaft grinder. Later, for more detailed work, he will use a Gesswein high-speed grinder, which operates at a higher RPM than the Foredom, along with a variety of knives. Knives are important, especially for the detailed work that will come later in the carving process. Jimmie makes his own knives using surplus blades bought in bulk. The advantage to making your own, he says, is that you can design blade and handle shapes for particular tasks. Jimmie uses knives extensively for fine carving and shaping, and he keeps them very sharp.

He begins the roughing-out process by first drawing a centerline on the block of tupelo, then sketching side and top profiles of the body. He next draws the side profile of the head onto the smaller piece of tupelo. The patterns are then cut out on the band saw, and the carving process begins.

Jimmie marks the center of the block that will be used for the body of the pintail. A centerline is drawn and will be maintained throughout the carving process.

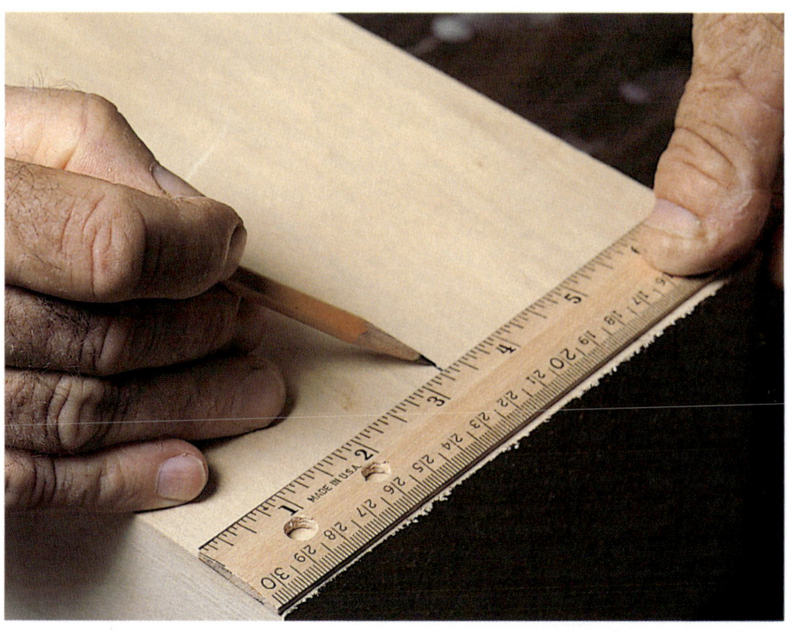

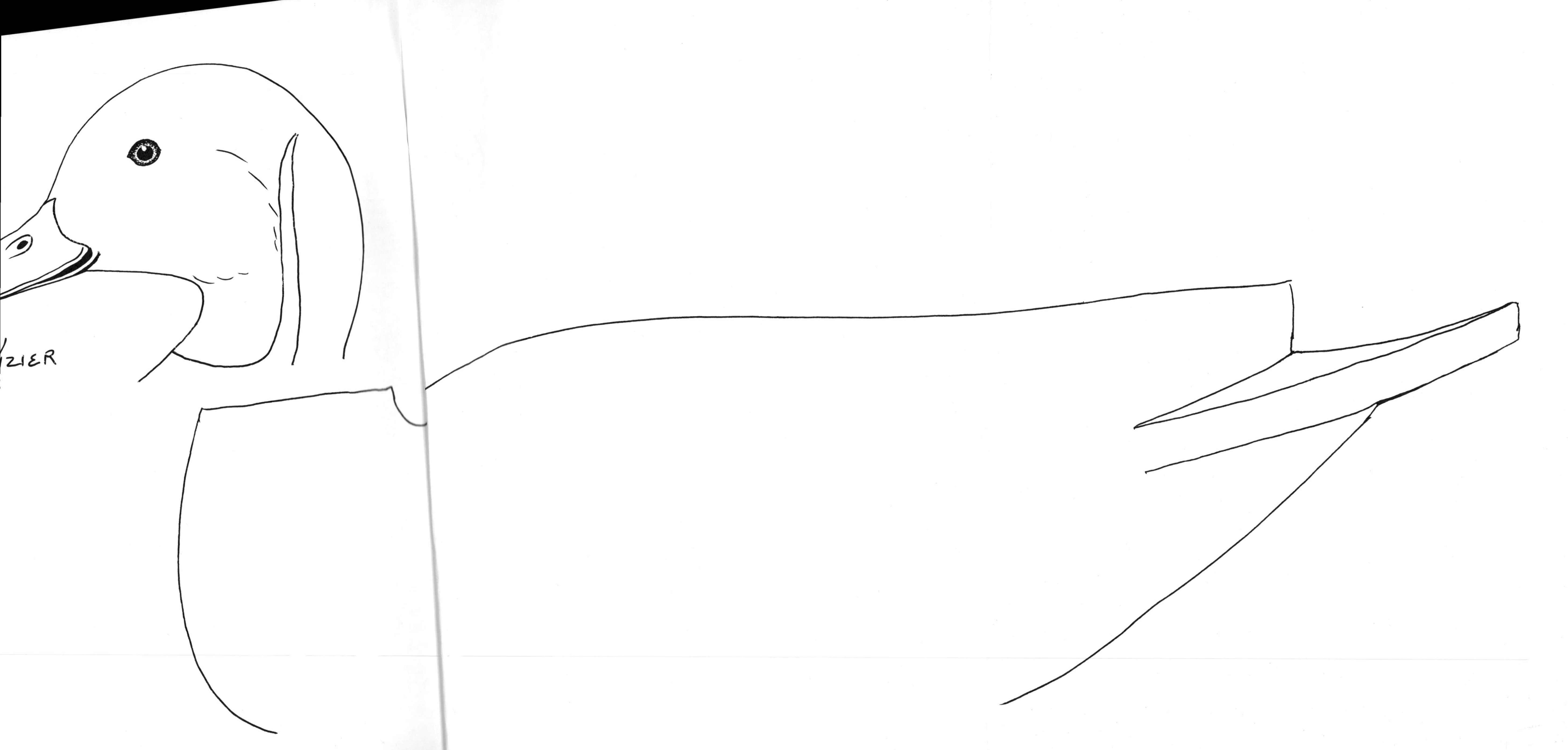

Tail is P.V.C pipe

Jimmie Vizier
1998

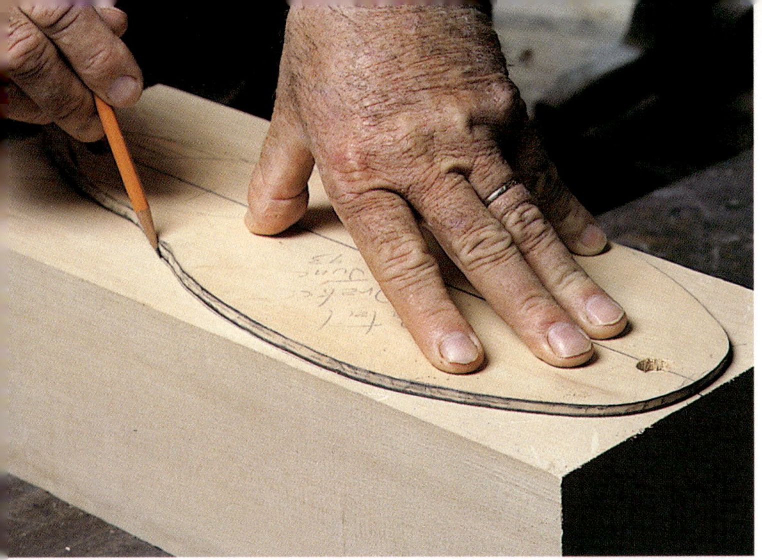

The top profile is drawn first. The pencil line represents the outer dimensions of the body of the bird. The block of tupelo is just slightly larger than the pattern.

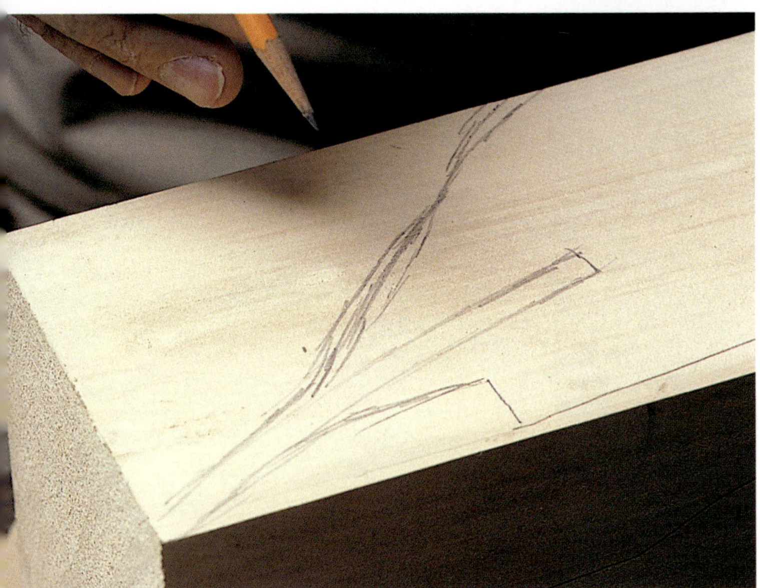

The side profile is drawn next, which Jimmie does freehand. Here he sketches the tail and rump. The long tail feather distinctive of the pintail will be inserted later. Jimmie prefers to design each bird individually, and although he uses a basic pattern, he changes various details as he sketches. In this bird, for example, the primary feathers will cross over the rump. That detail will be sketched now and carved later.

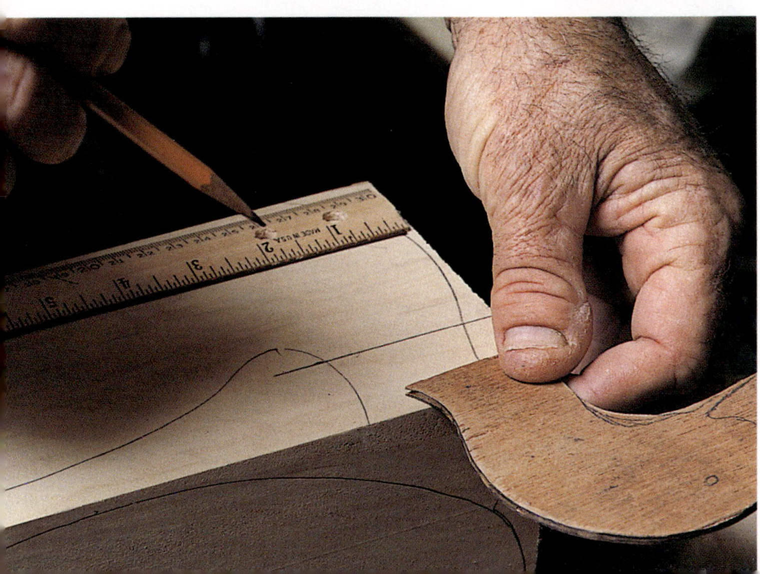

It's important to have the shelf where the head is mounted parallel to the waterline. That way, the head can be turned to any angle and will not be unnaturally tilted; the eyes will also remain parallel to the waterline. The line Jimmie draws now represents the shelf where the head will be mounted.

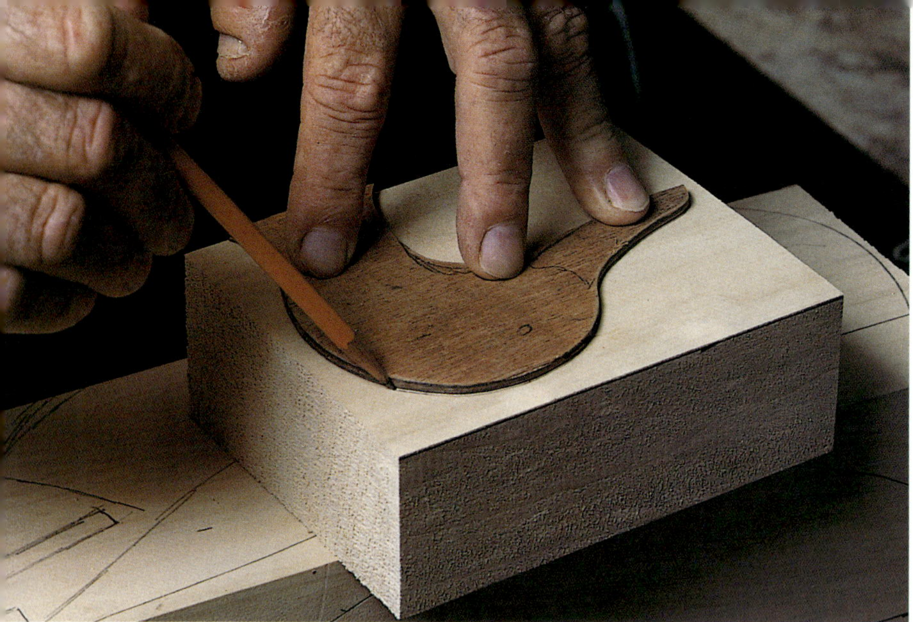

The side profile of the head is sketched. The width of the workpiece is just slightly greater than the finished width of the head will be, so a top profile is not needed. Jimmie uses a needle to transfer the eye position from the pattern to the workpiece at this point.

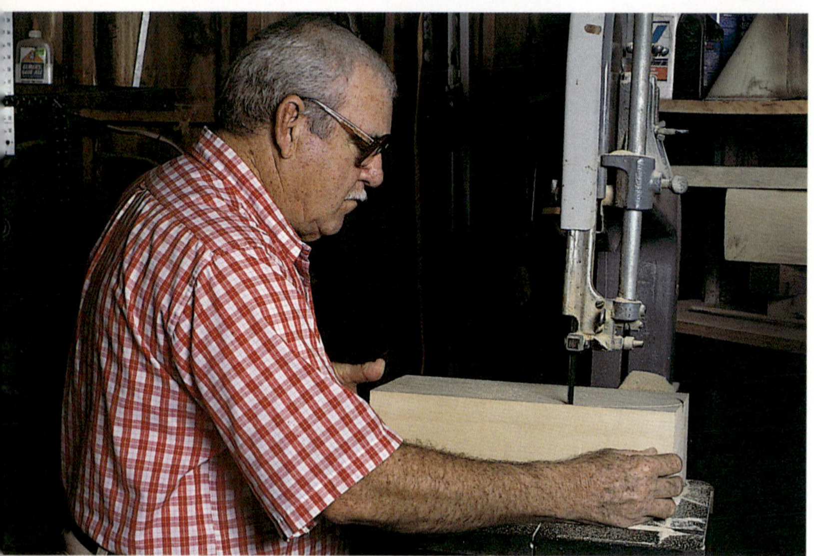

The body is cut out on the band saw. Safety is a primary concern at this stage. Jimmie has had many years of experience with the band saw and other power tools. If you are not experienced with such tools, have the pattern cut out at a professional woodworking shop.

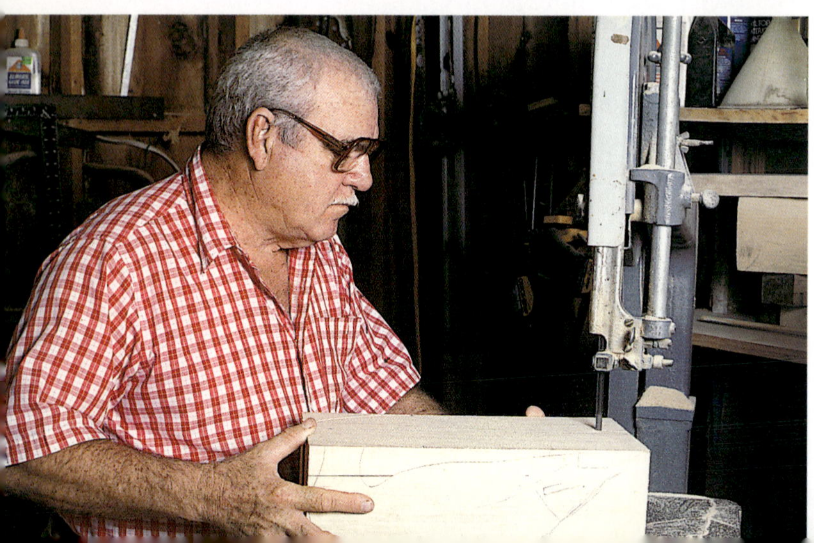

As Jimmie cuts out the top pattern, he will leave a small area uncut on both sides of the body. These will keep the side profiles intact so that they can be cut next.

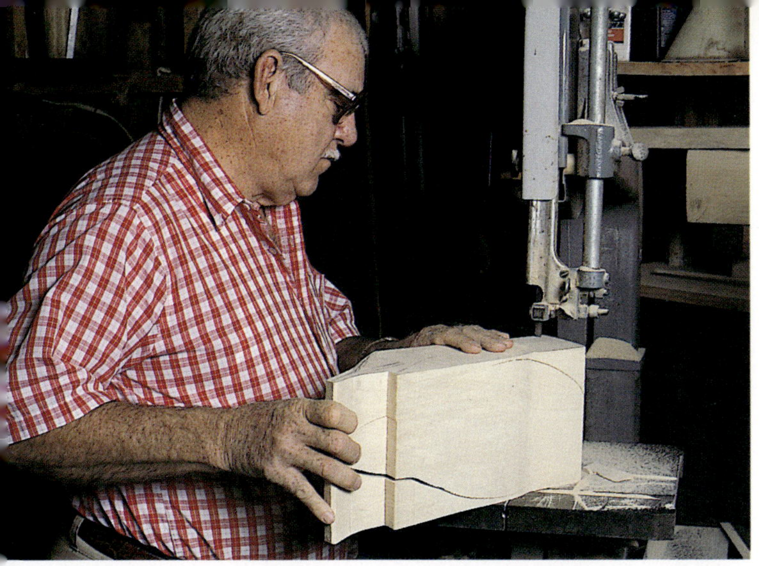

The side profile is cut, following the pencil lines sketched earlier. Leaving the side patterns intact makes this step easier; otherwise, they would have to be reattached with glue or nails.

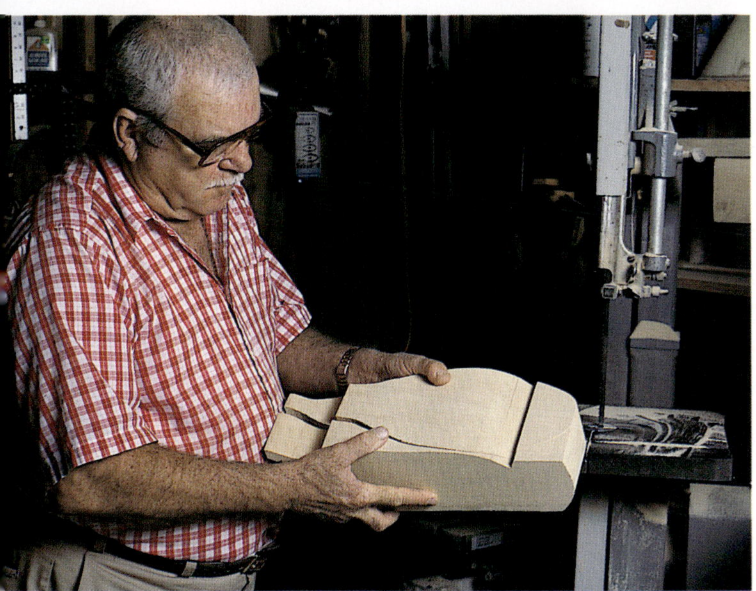

With the side profiles cut, Jimmie breaks away the waste pieces of wood. The body is now roughed out and will be shaped with the hatchet, grinder, and knife.

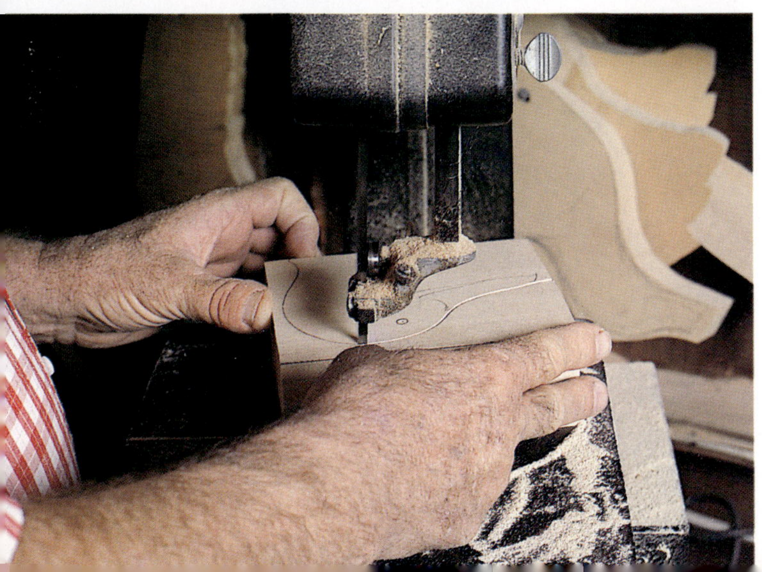

A smaller band saw is used to cut out the head profile. Again, if you don't have a band saw, you can have this step done at a woodworking shop. Note the needle mark that locates the eye position.

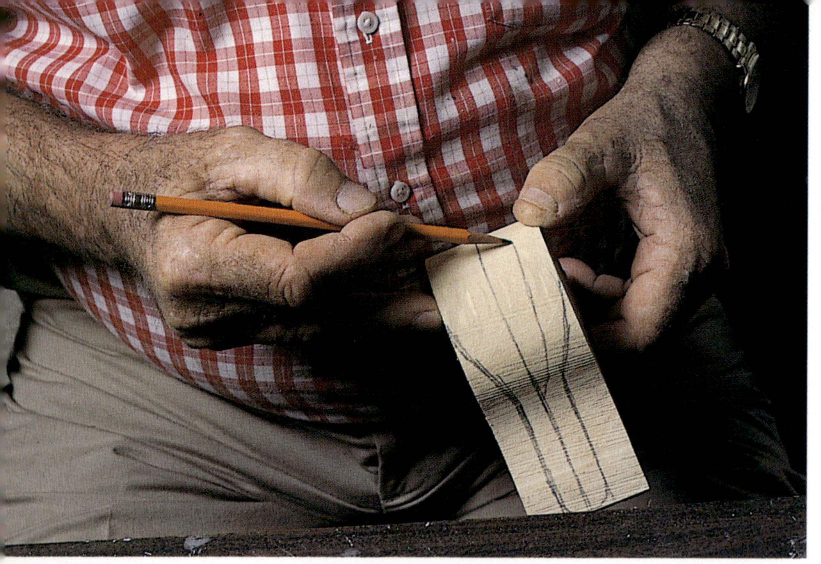

With the head and body patterns cut out, Jimmie will use the pencil to sketch various elements such as the major body contours, the bill, and the location of the wings. Here he sketches the bill by first drawing a centerline, then measuring off that line to delineate the bill and the position where it meets the head. He also sketches the top contour of the head.

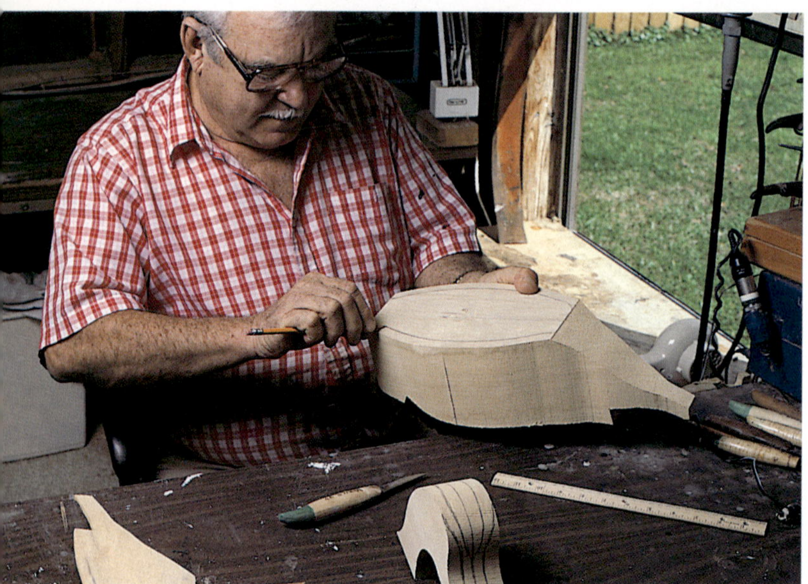

The contour of the body is sketched by holding a pencil approximately 1/2 inch from the edge of the wood and tracing a line around the perimeter of the body.

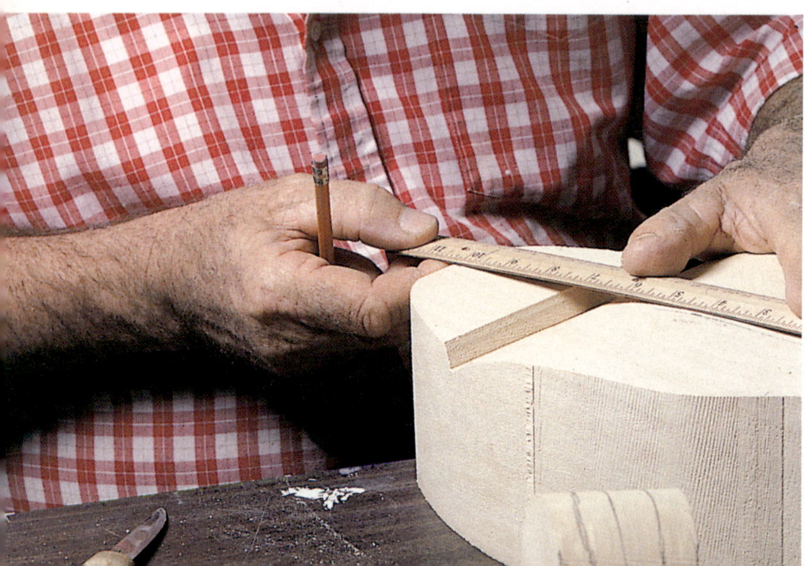

The centerline is reestablished on the body and is sketched with the pencil. This line will be maintained throughout the carving process.

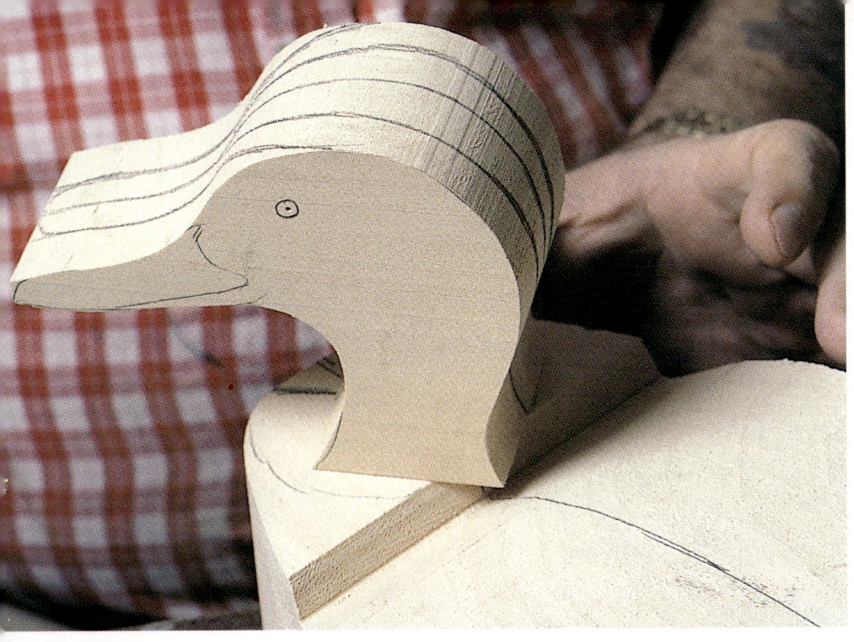

The head is set atop the shelf where it will later be mounted. The head will be turned at an angle, and Jimmie draws a line on the body representing the angle of the head and bill.

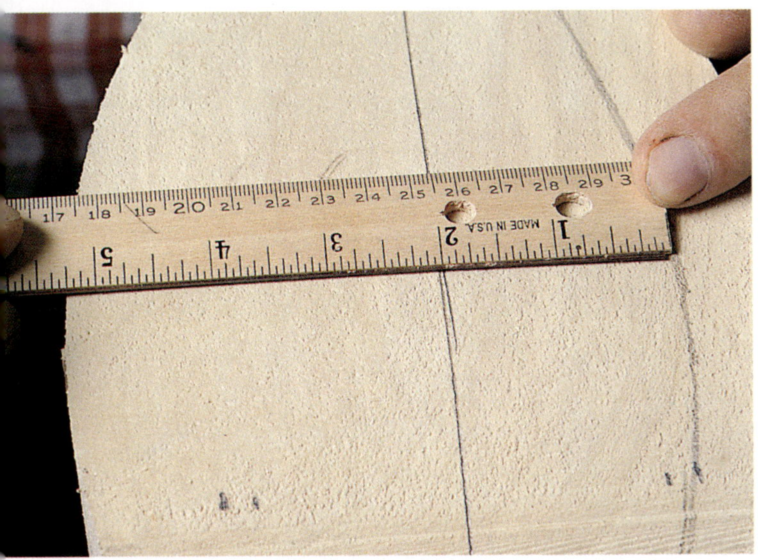

Jimmie measures off the centerline to make sure the body contour is symmetrical. The outside line should be 2 inches from the center at this point.

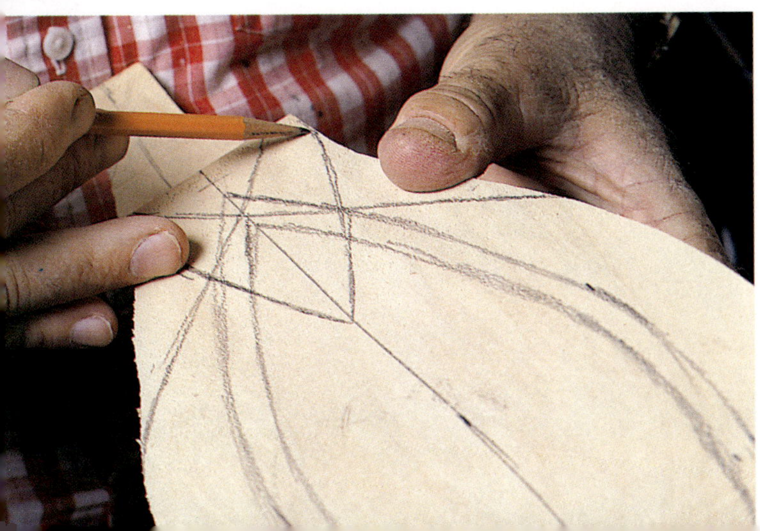

Jimmie does some preliminary sketching of the flight feathers. The primaries will cross over the tail of the bird, and Jimmie sketches in this detail now. He also sketches the outline of the tail and draws two lines about 1/2 inch apart that will guide him in thinning down the tail. Jimmie works a great deal with the pencil at this stage, using it to plan feather layout and other features.

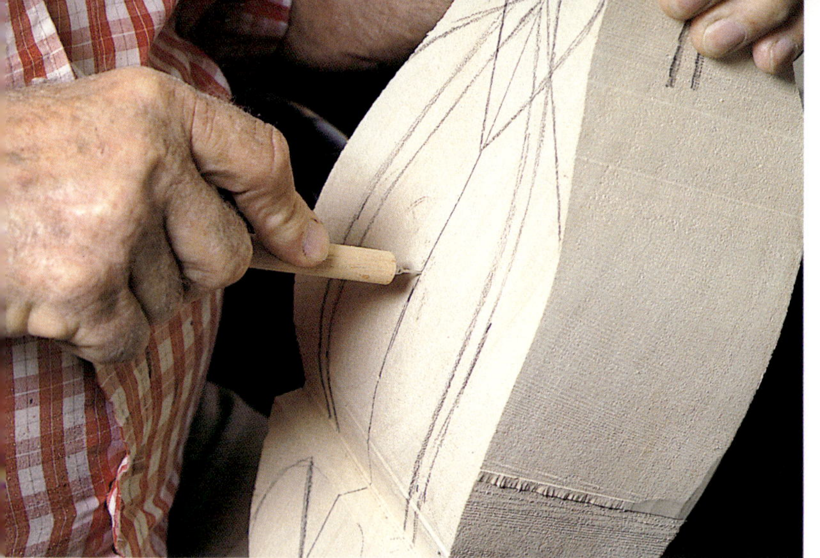

The centerline is all-important. The pencil mark that delineates it will be removed now and then during carving and sanding, so Jimmie presses a sharp gouge into the wood at several locations along the centerline to make sure he will be able to easily relocate it.

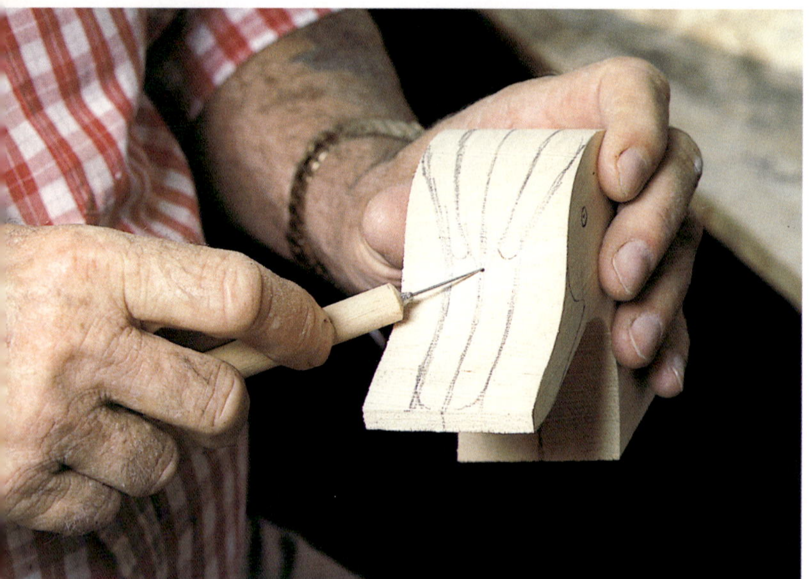

This process is also used on the head. When Jimmie needs to redraw the centerline, all he has to do is locate the holes left by the gouge. The gouge should be held at a 90-degree angle to the wood when making the hole.

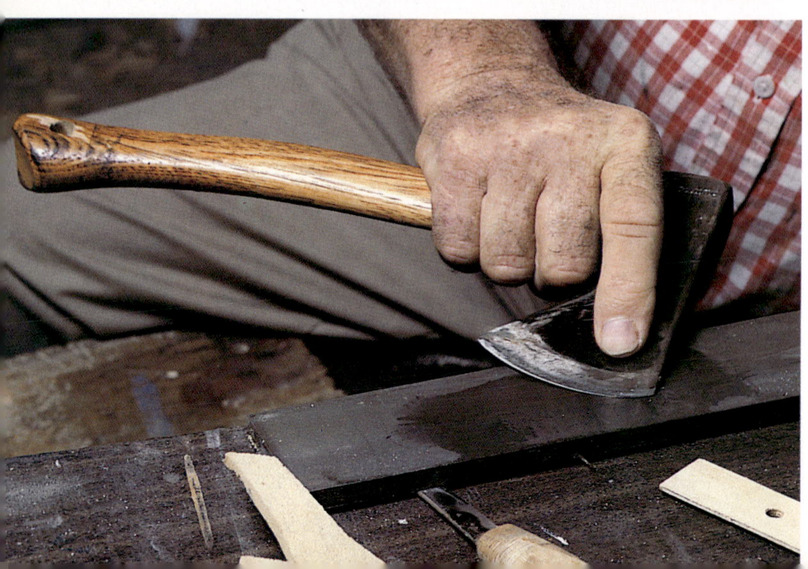

Jimmie learned to carve from his father and uncle, who used only simple hand tools such as a hatchet, rasp, and pocketknife. He does the preliminary roughing out the old-fashioned way, with a hatchet. The hatchet is still an important tool to him, and he keeps it razor sharp.

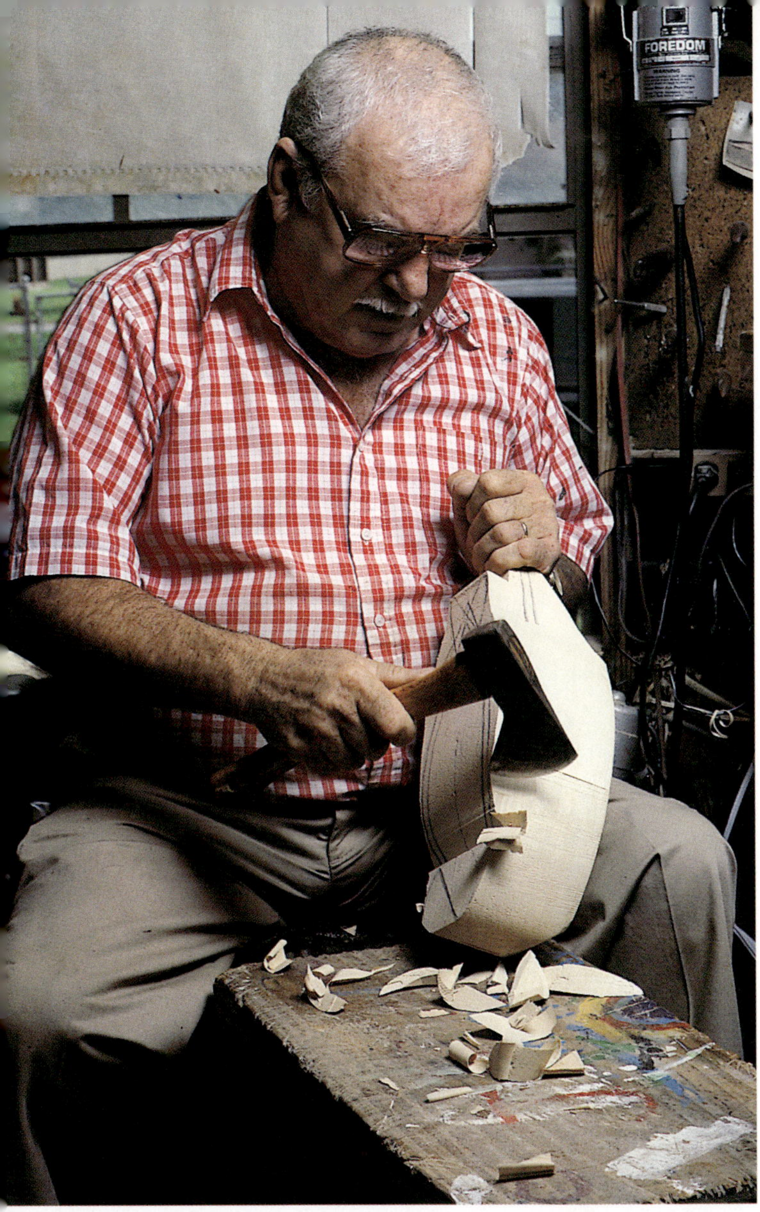

The sharp little hatchet makes quick work of rounding off the contours. Jimmie has used a hatchet for carving decoys for some fifty years; those with less experience might prefer to go directly from the band saw to the flexible-shaft grinder.

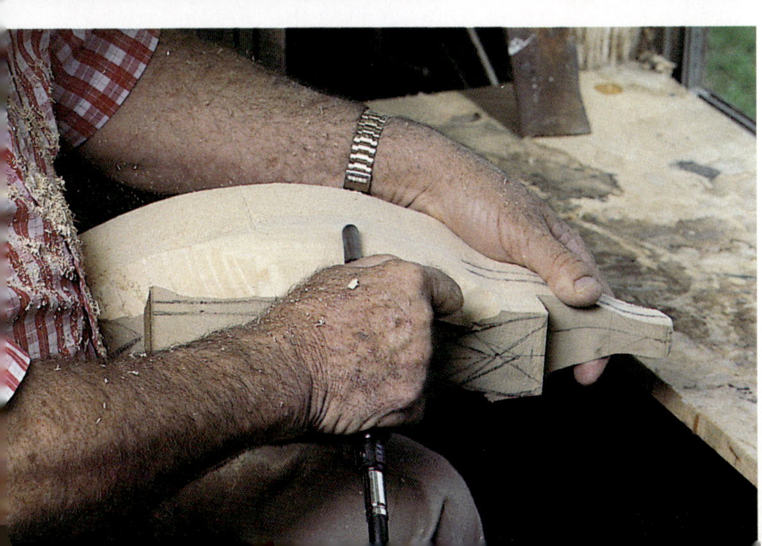

Once the body has been roughed out with the hatchet, Jimmie goes to the power tools to remove excess wood. This rasplike cutter is used on a Foredom flexible-shaft grinder.

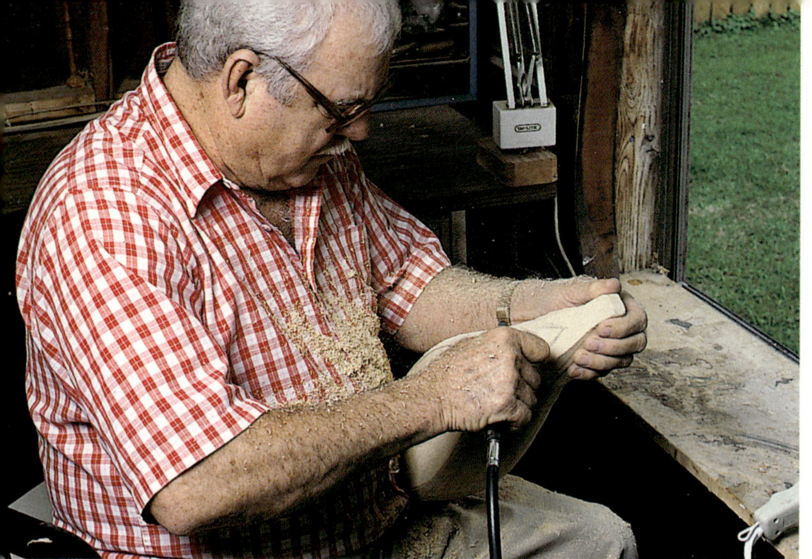

Jimmie carves in front of an open window. A large ventilation fan in his shop forces dust particles out the window. When carving, you should always use some sort of dust-removal system or wear a mask to filter out particulates.

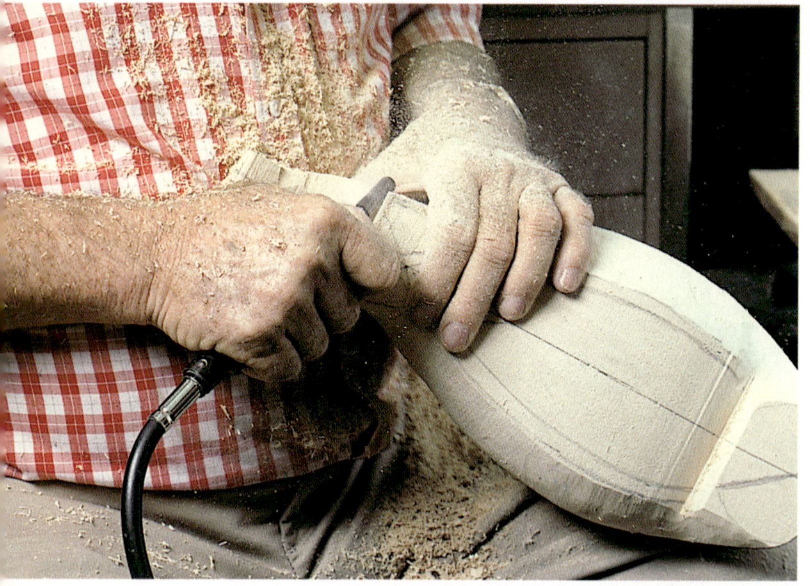

Jimmie essentially is removing the sharp corners at this stage, cutting down the contours to the pencil guidelines he drew earlier.

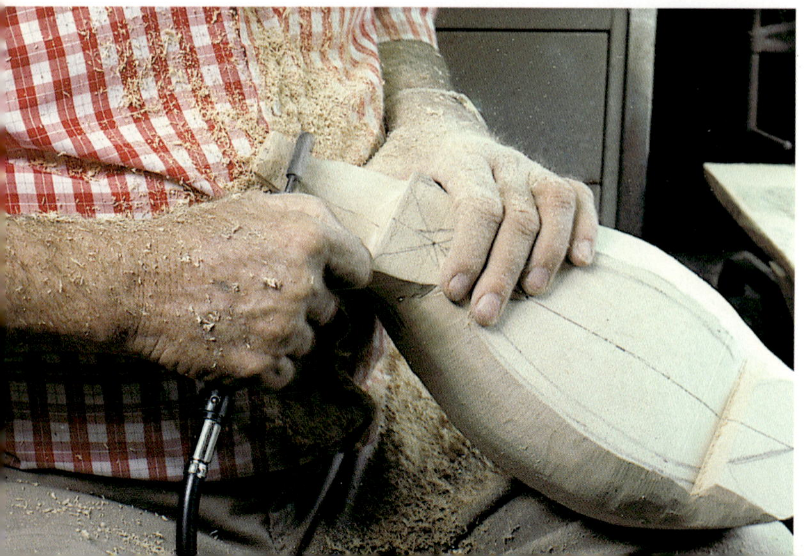

Here Jimmie does the preliminary shaping of the tail, beginning the process of thinning it down. The sharp, curved tail will be inserted later.

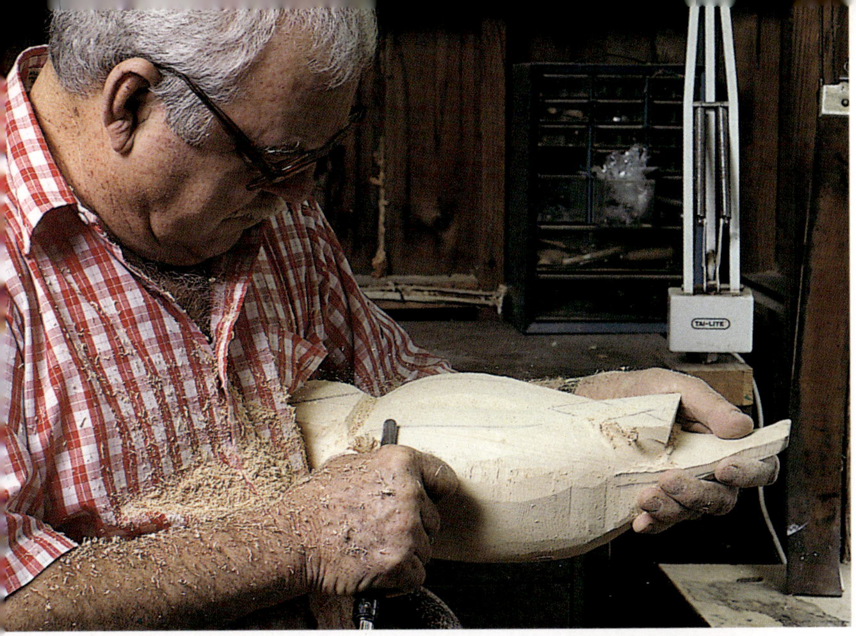

Jimmie rounds off the sides of the body, cutting back to the pencil line he drew 2 inches off-center. At this stage, he is simply removing wood as quickly as he can. Details will be added later.

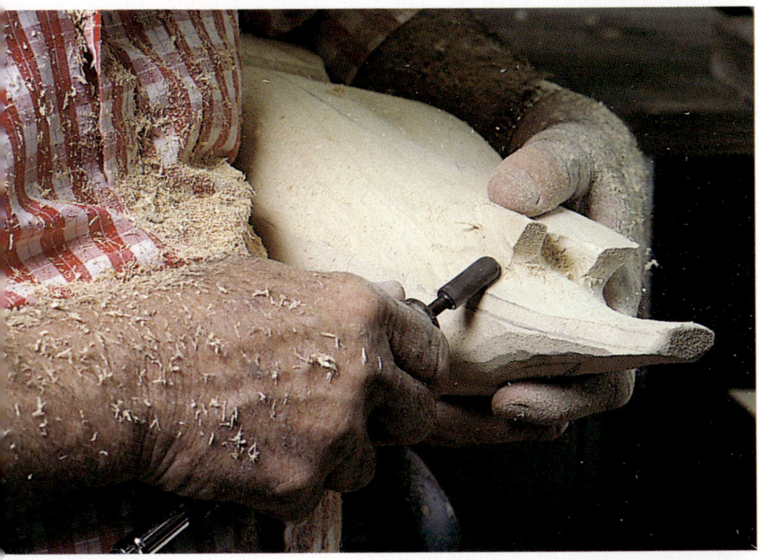

Now he uses the Foredom to thin down the tail, following the pencil lines he drew earlier. Since this is a gunning decoy, made to be handled, the tail feathers will be carved with considerable thickness.

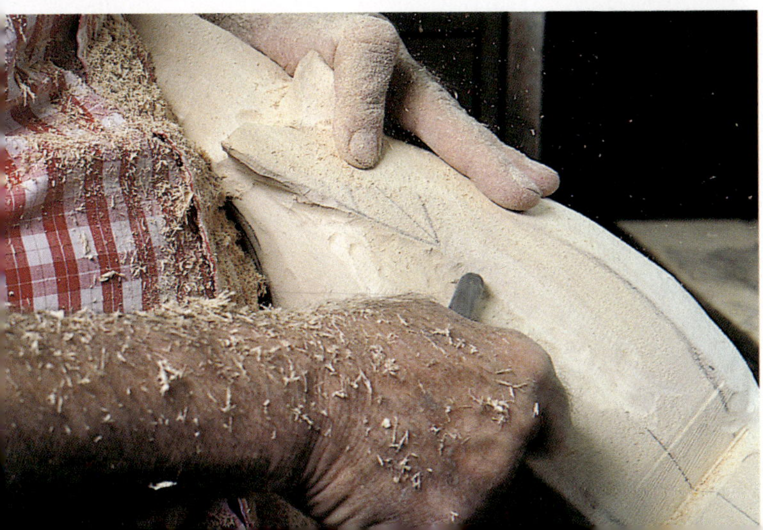

The same tool is used to do the preliminary carving of the wings, again following the pencil sketches. Jimmie begins shaping the primary flight feathers here; they are overlapped as they cross the tail.

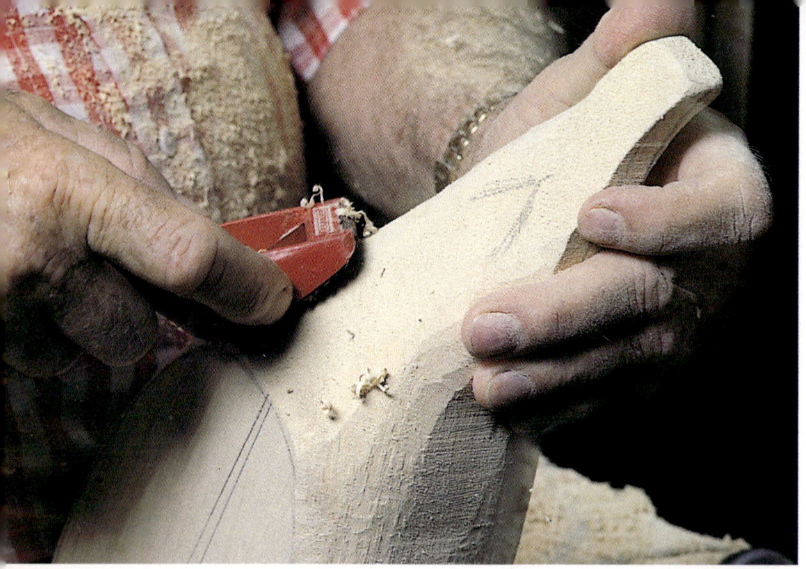

Once the preliminary roughing out of the body is done, Jimmie uses a Stanley Surform rasp to round off the contours of the body and remove tool marks left by the grinder.

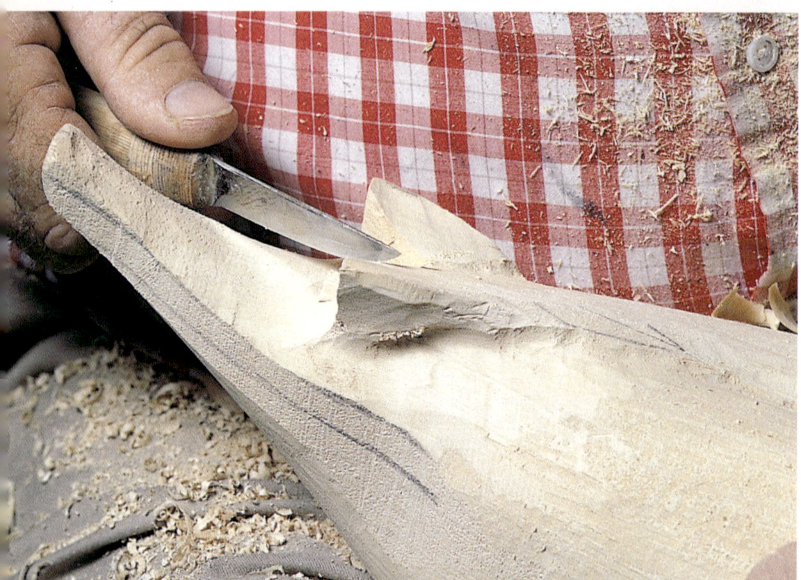

Some preliminary shaping of the primary flight feathers is now done with the knife. Jimmie undercuts the feathers slightly and removes wood between them where the wings overlap.

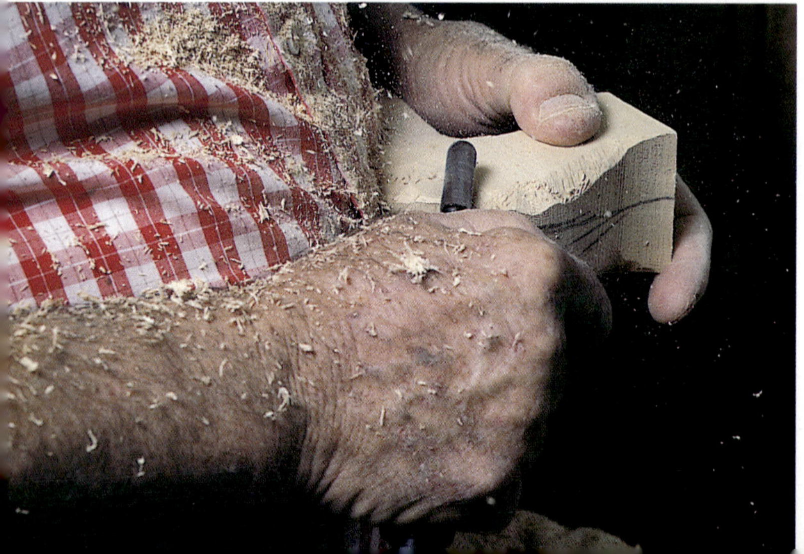

The body is pretty well roughed out at this stage, and now it's time to bring the head to the same point. As with the body, roughing out is done with the grinder and the knife.

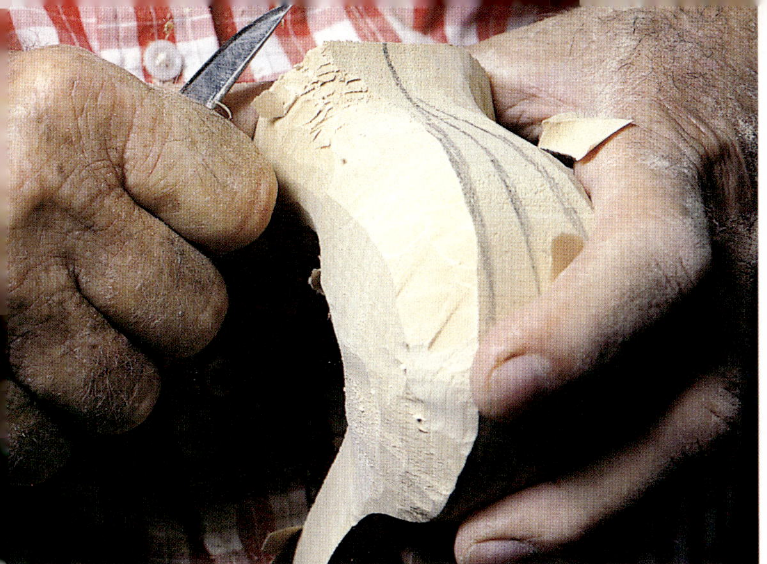

Jimmie creates contours, removing wood using the pencil lines as a guide. He switches back and forth from the grinder to the knife, depending upon the area to be shaped.

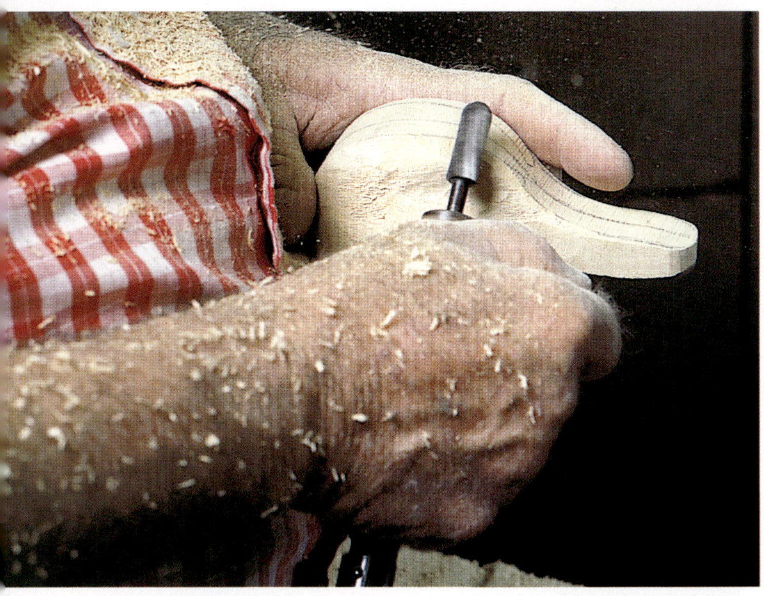

In roughing out the head, it's important to keep the centerline, which represents the outer dimensions of the head.

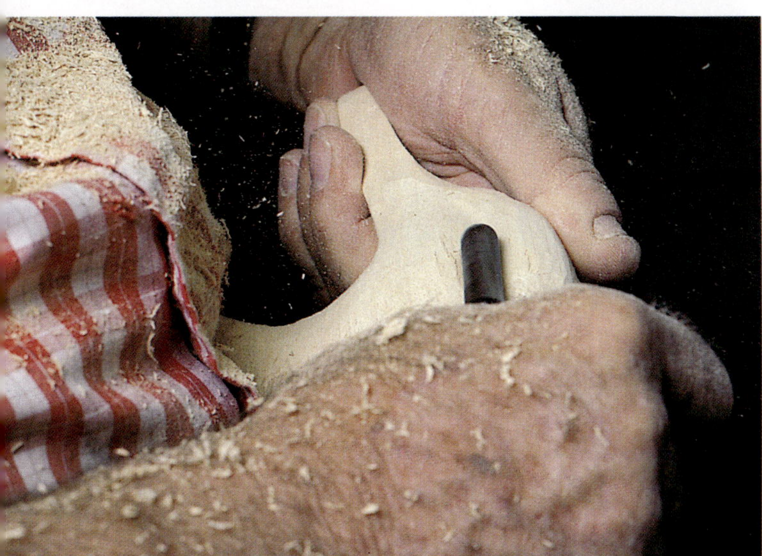

The final step in roughing out the head is the preliminary shaping of the eye channels. Jimmy uses the sketched eyes as reference, being careful to keep the channels on each side symmetrical.

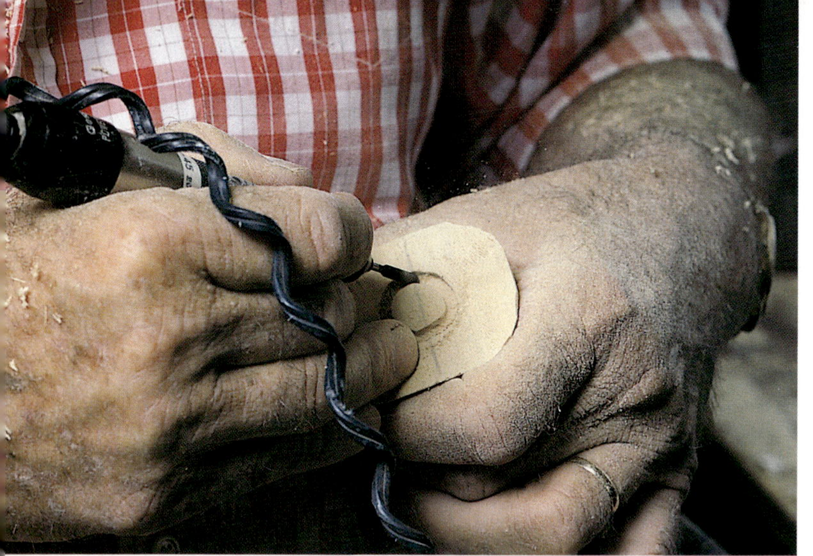

Jimmie will temporarily attach the head to the body in order to carve the neck and breast area. He later will remove the head to carve it and insert the eyes. To attach the head, he uses the high-speed grinder to create a small island of wood, which will be epoxied to the body and later broken off.

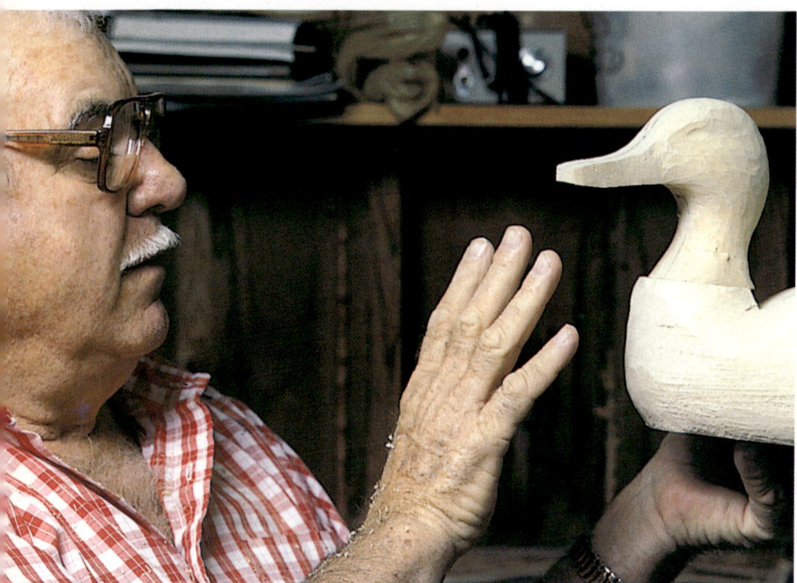

Jimmie places the head on the body, adjusts the angle, and inspects it carefully.

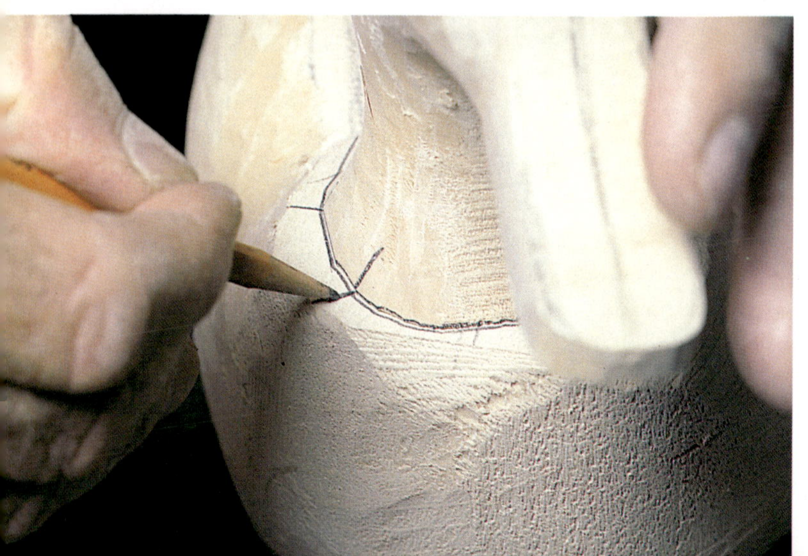

When he is satisfied with the angle at which the head is turned, he uses a pencil to put registration marks on the neck and body.

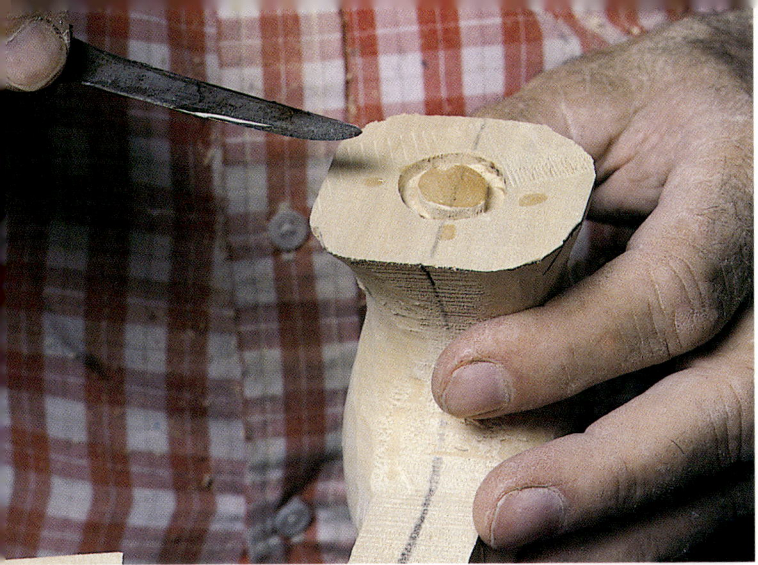

The head is attached with two-part epoxy. This center part will be glued and will break off later when Jimmie removes the head to carve it. A small amount of adhesive is placed around the wooden island.

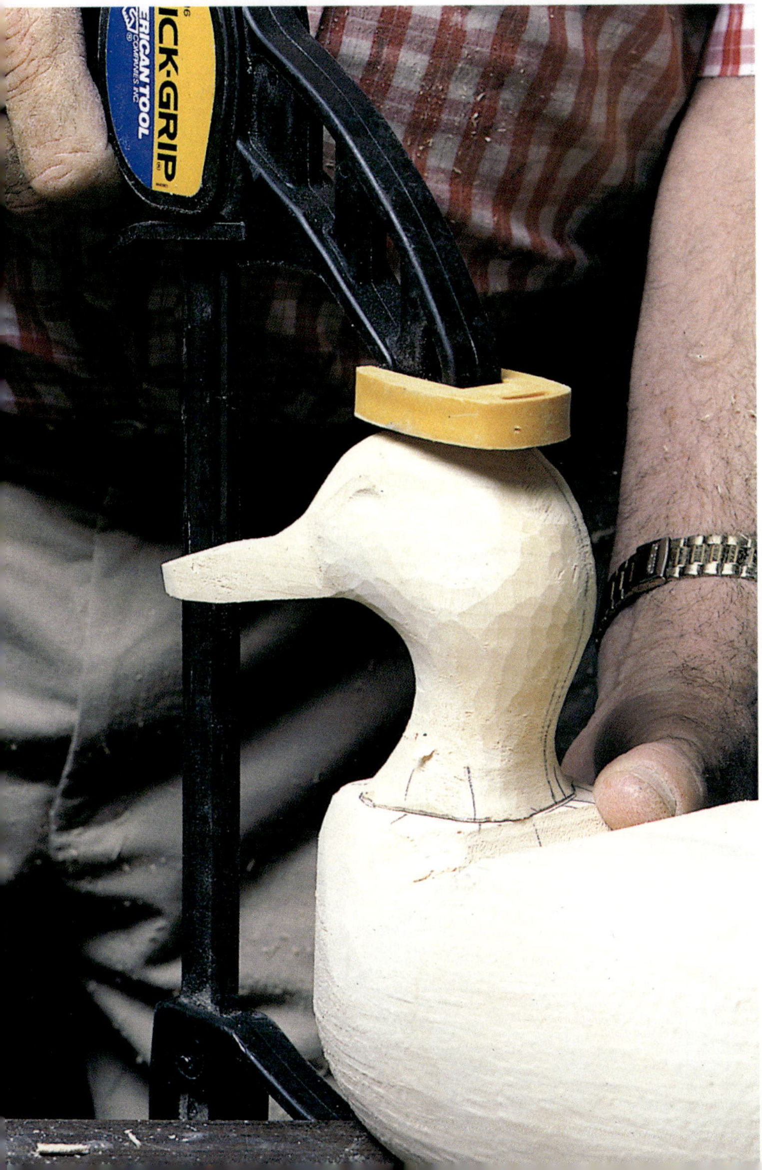

The head is held in place with a clamp while the epoxy dries, a process that will take about fifteen minutes.

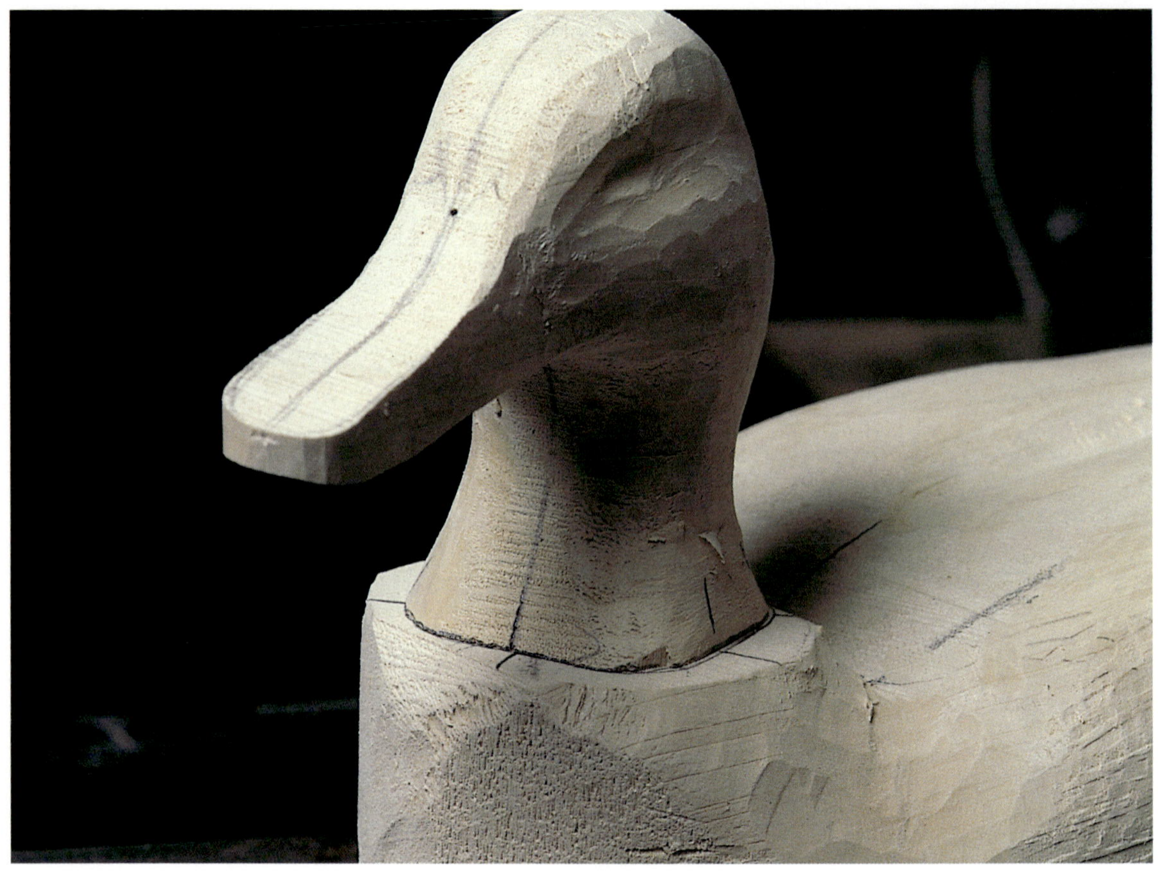

The head and body are now roughed out, and the head is temporarily attached to the body. The next step is to carve the breast, sidepockets, and wings and to add detail.

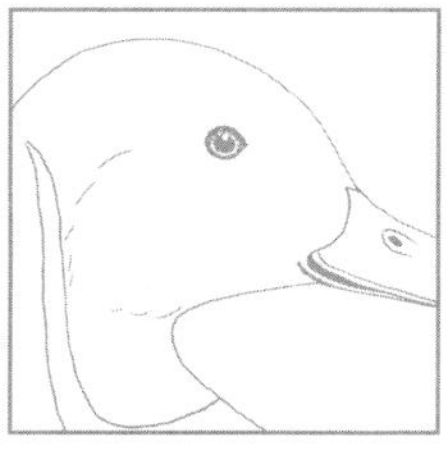

CHAPTER FOUR

Carving the Feather Groups and Inserting the Tail

In this chapter, Jimmie will shape the neck and breast area, lay out and carve the primary feathers and the sidepockets, and insert the tail, which is made of PVC pipe.

Reference material is very important, and unless you are very familiar with pintail drakes, you'll need something to go by when laying out the various feather groups and when painting the bird. It's a good idea to study everything you can get your hands on—photos, videos, field guides, magazines, live birds, taxidermy mounts—whatever you can find that provides accurate and reliable information. Use a pencil to sketch detail onto the carving, and be sure it's accurate and visually pleasing before you go to work with the cutting tools. It's easy to erase a pencil line, but not so easy to recarve a feather. Although Jimmie has carved many pintails over the years, he still sketches detail in pencil before carving it.

In the following steps, Jimmie will add definition to the overlapping primary feathers, and he will carve the sidepockets, those areas on the sides of the pintail that will be vermiculated later during the painting process. This chapter is a bridge that takes us from the roughing-out process to the task of creating fine detail, a vital step in adding lifelike realism to the bird.

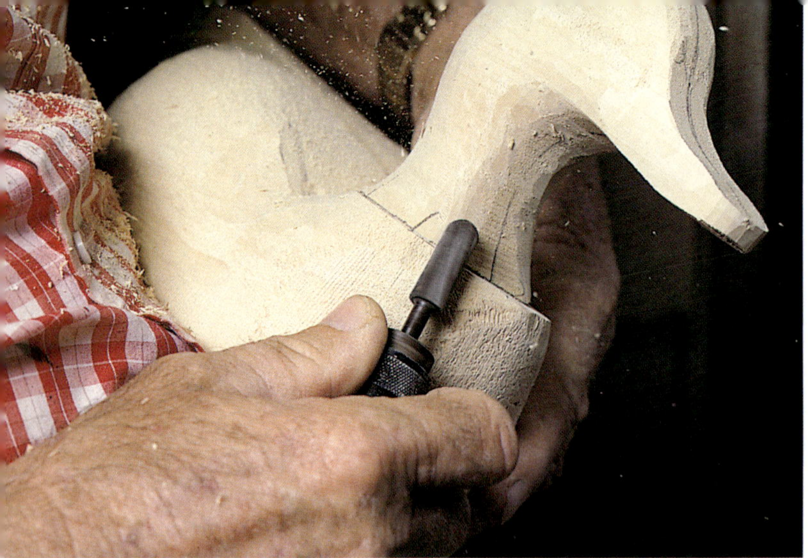

With the head temporarily attached to the body, Jimmie uses the flexible-shaft grinder to shape the neck and breast area. Carving here must be done with the head attached, but detailed carving of the head is easier when it can be held in the hand, so Jimmie will remove it later to carve it and add detail to the eyes and bill.

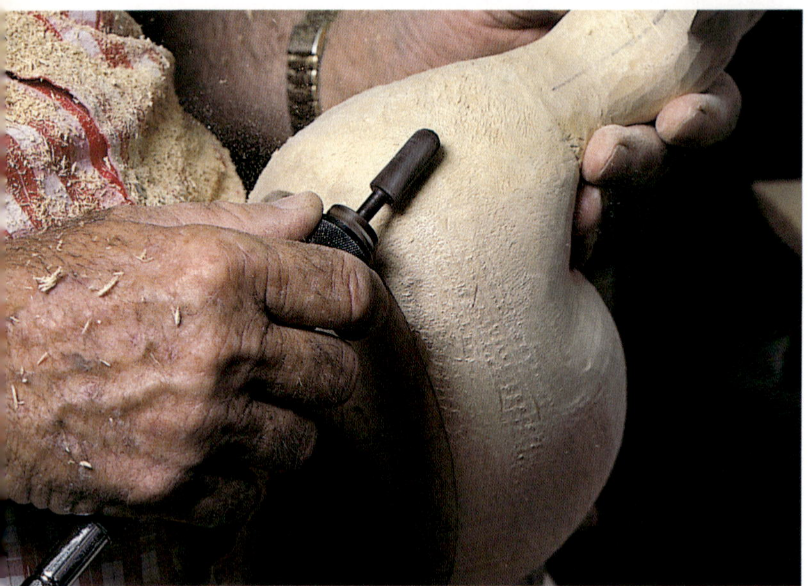

Consult your reference material and you will notice that the pintail has a very long neck. When sitting on the water like this bird will be, its neck is at the front of the breast, somewhat tucked into the breast feathers. That's the area Jimmie is carving here, narrowing the breast where the neck meets it.

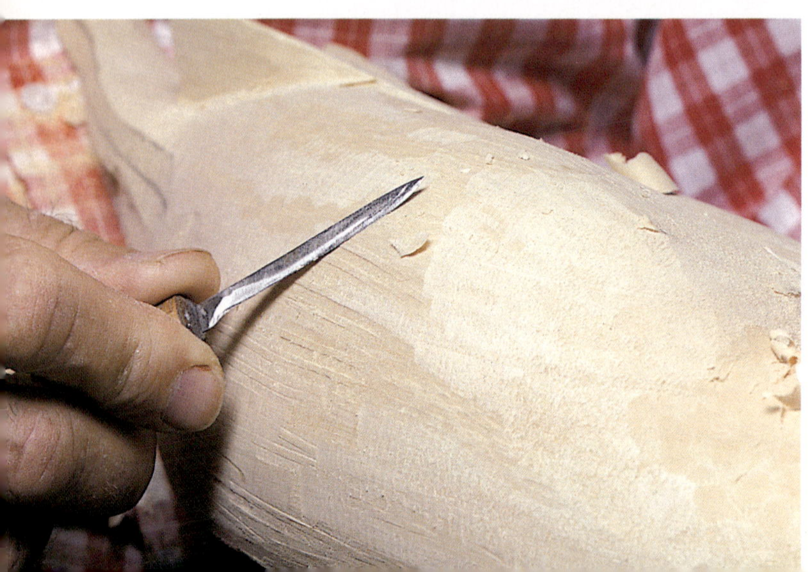

Before laying out and carving the feather groups, Jimmie does some fine-tuning to the basic shape of the pintail, using a slender-bladed knife he made to remove a small amount of wood.

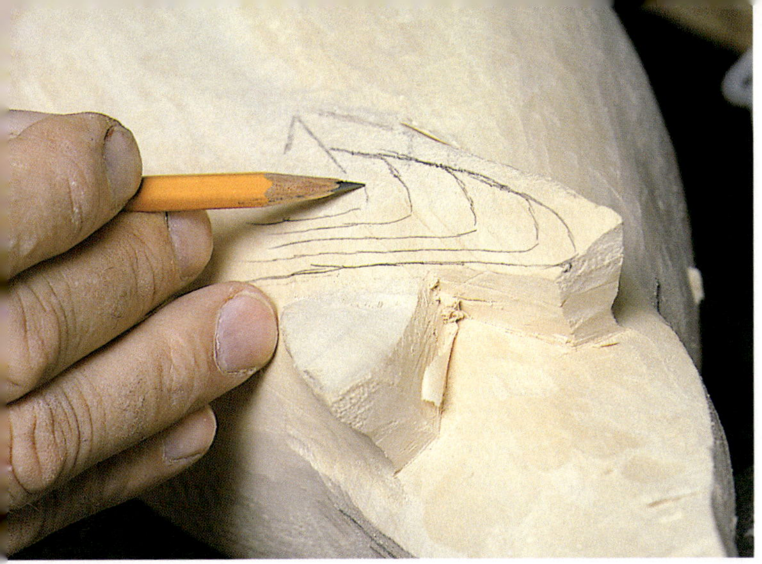

Jimmie lays out the primary feathers of the wings with a pencil, making sure they lie at a natural angle. It's a good idea to look at photos of pintails or live birds and notice how the wings lie when the bird is at rest. The primary feathers will be crossed on this bird, and it's important to have their lines follow the same angle as the rest of the wing.

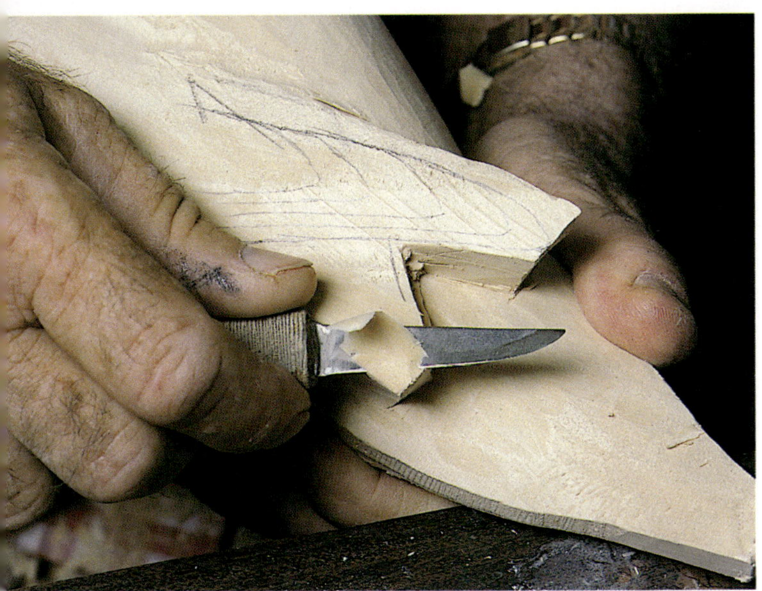

The primary feathers are carved with the knife. The left wing rests atop the right one, and Jimmie begins carving that separation in this step.

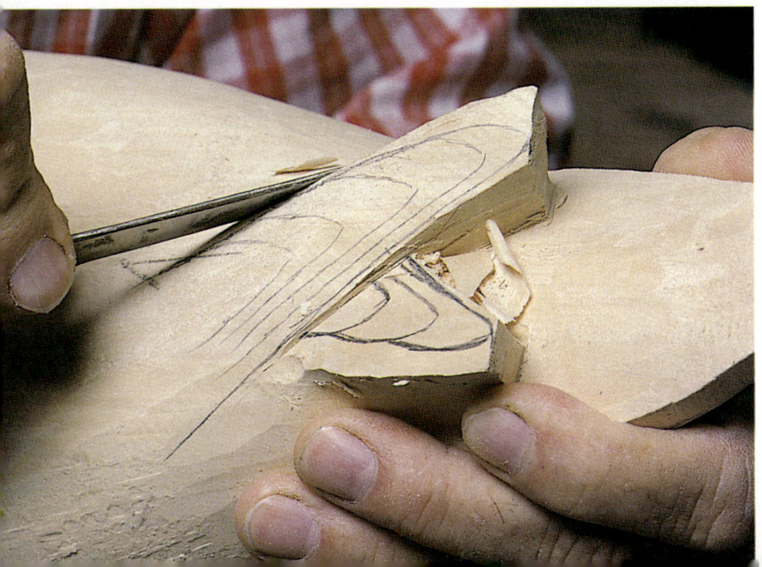

Jimmie follows the outline of the left primary feathers here, separating them from those on the right wing. This process could be done with a grinder, if you prefer.

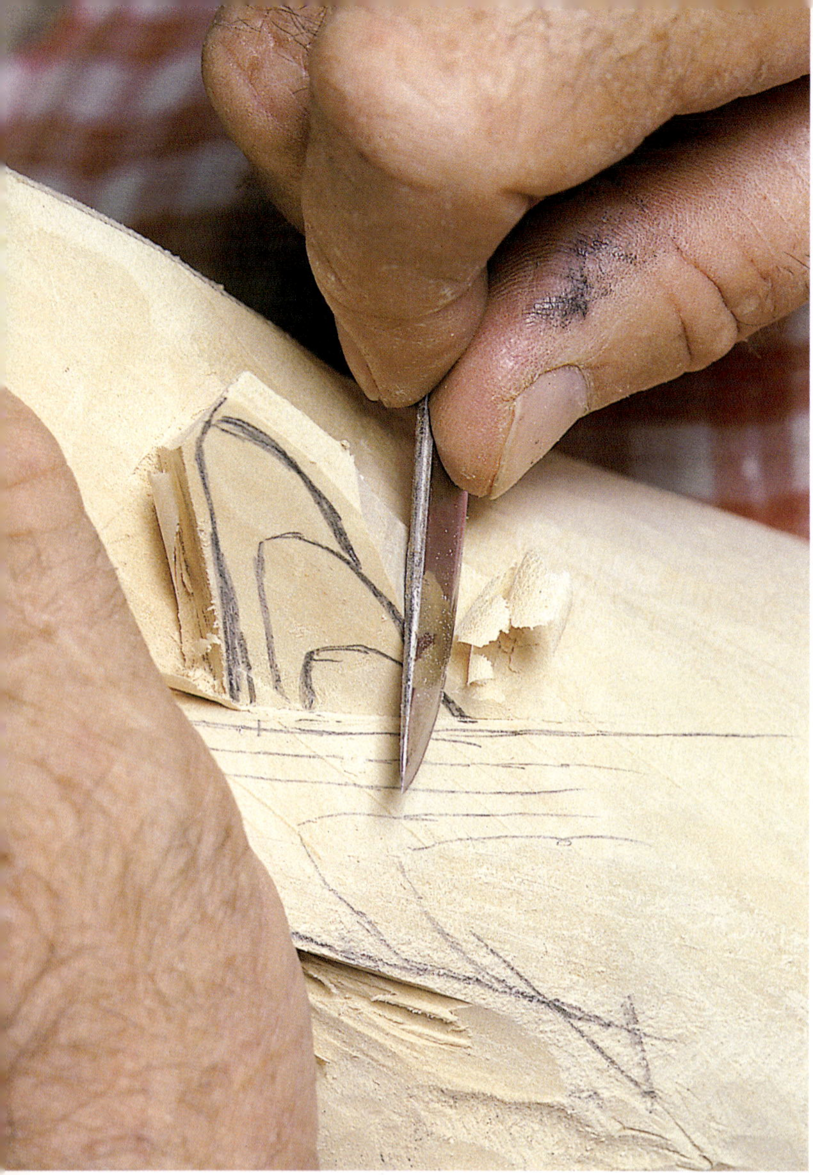

The underlying wing feathers are now being defined, separated from the body of the bird.

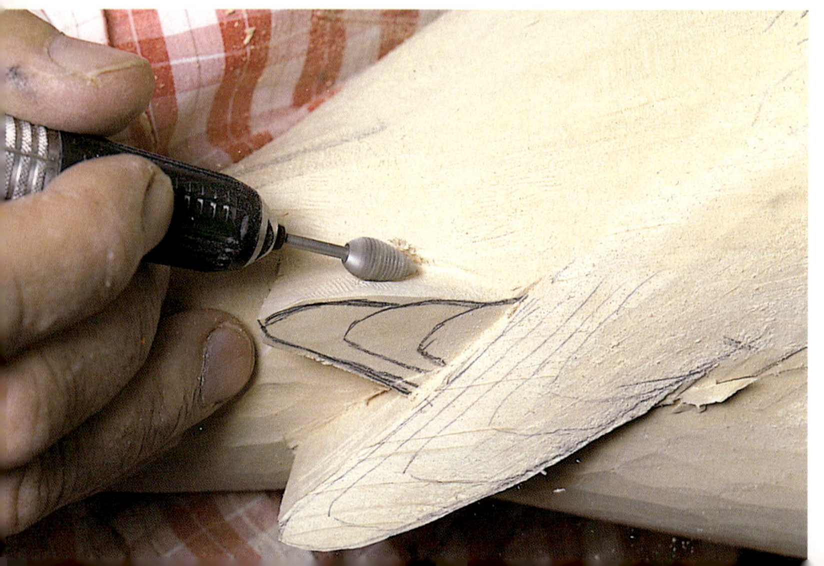

With the general shape of the primary feathers complete, Jimmie uses the grinder to smooth the area and to undercut the primary groups somewhat.

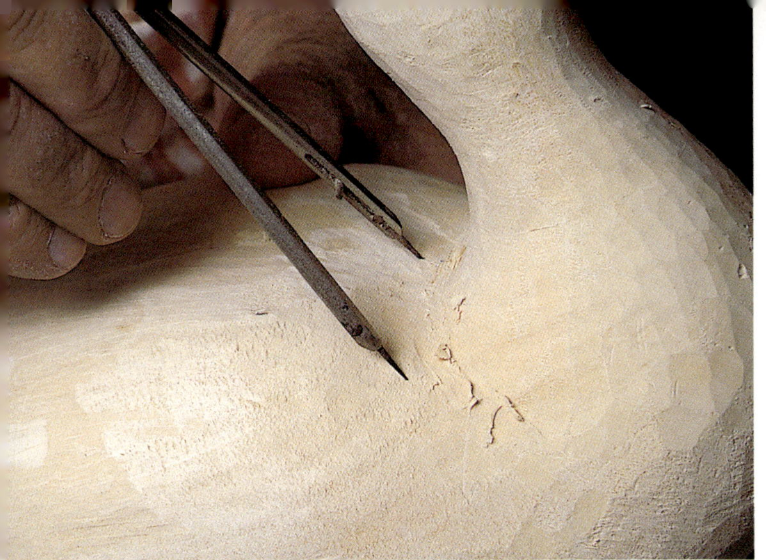

Jimmie is now ready to lay out the sidepocket areas, but before doing so, he uses the dividers to determine their margins and to ensure that they are symmetrical. He measures here from the center of the back to the front edge of the sidepocket on the right side and will then transfer that measurement to the left side, ensuring that the areas are symmetrical.

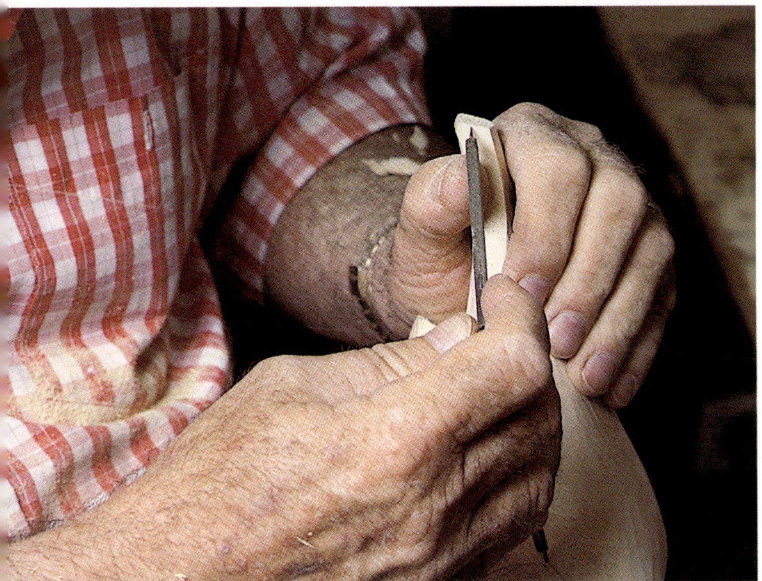

The rear margins of the sidepockets are measured from the tip of the tail, again making sure that the measurements are the same on both sides.

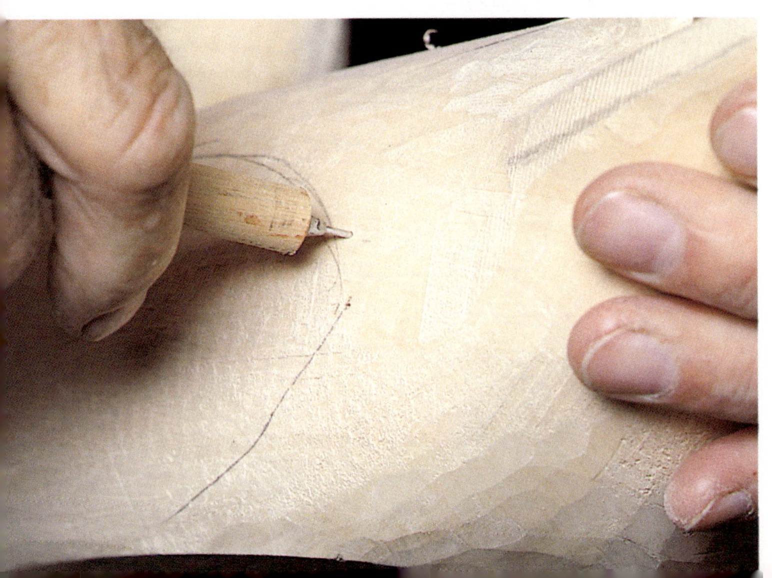

Once the sidepocket areas are established, Jimmie "locks in" the margins by again using the small gouge to press a hole into the wood. When wood is removed later, along with the pencil markings, the small holes will delineate the margins of the sidepockets.

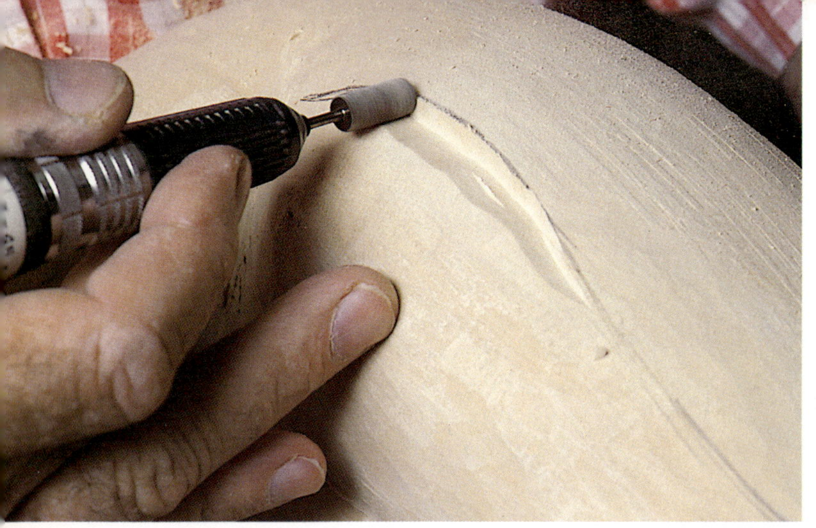

The Foredom grinder is used with a straight cylinder to carve a line along the top margins of the sidepockets on both sides of the pintail. Jimmie does not cut the groove along the rear portions of the sidepockets, because this is where the scapular feathers will drape down. Take a look at the finished photos for this detail.

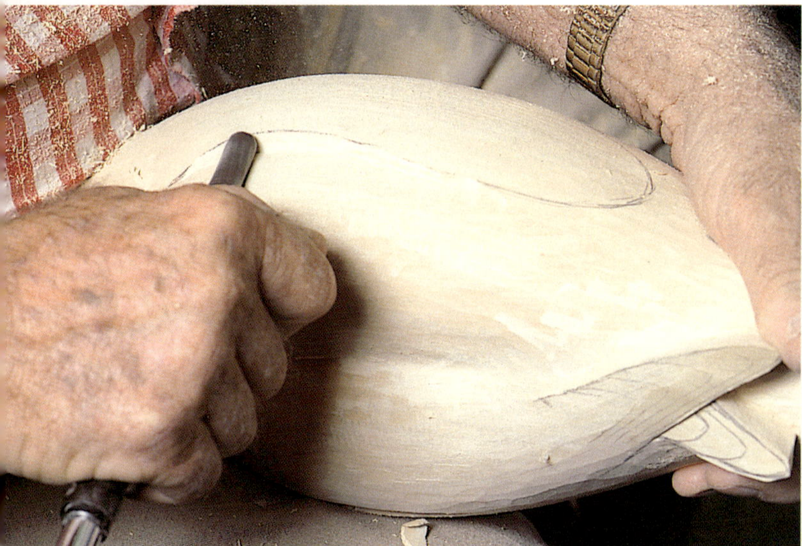

Jimmie cuts a fairly deep line and then carves back to it using the sides of the cylinder, making the line more subtle. This process separates the wings from the sides of the bird, giving definition to each.

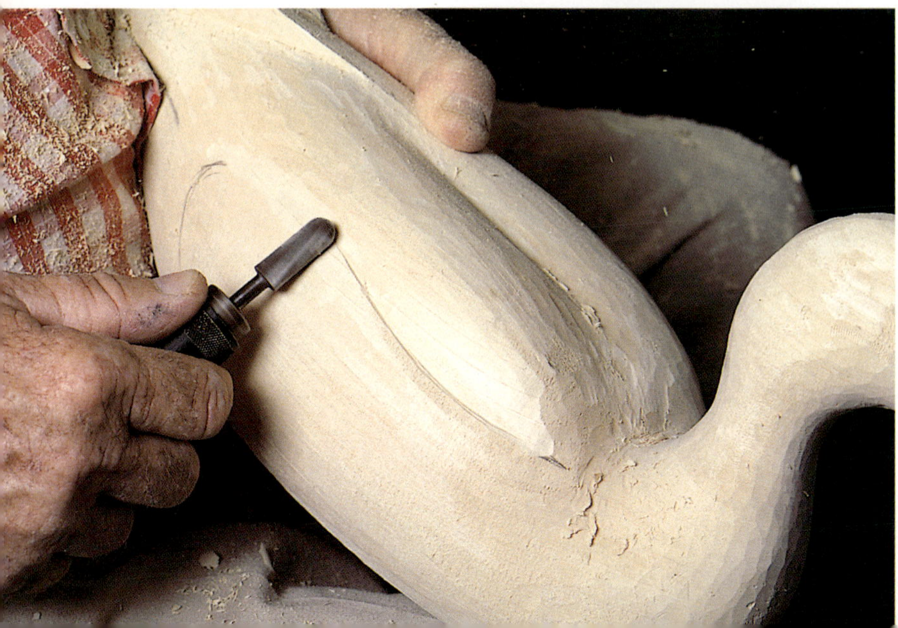

The Foredom is used with a tapered cutter to round off the top edges of the sidepockets, creating a very gentle contour that separates the sidepockets from the wings.

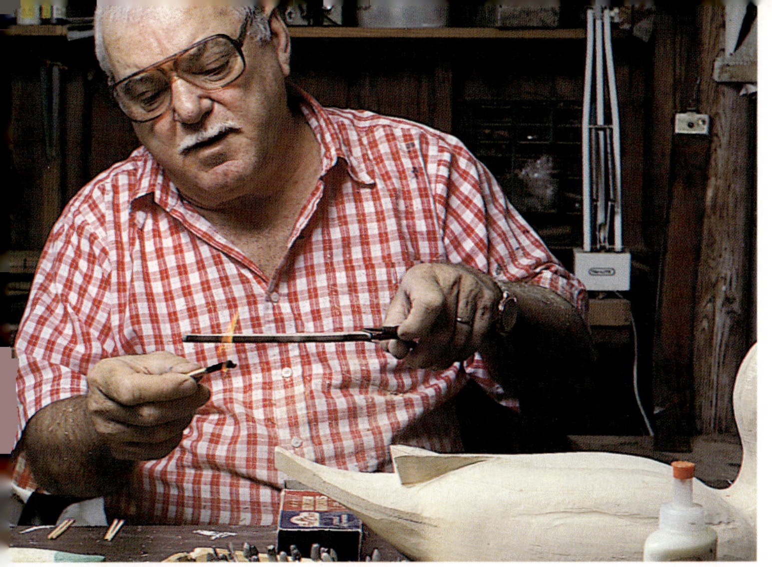

The tail feather is made of a piece of PVC plastic cut from a 4-inch-diameter pipe. Jimmie heats the plastic and then bends it to follow the gentle contour of the tail.

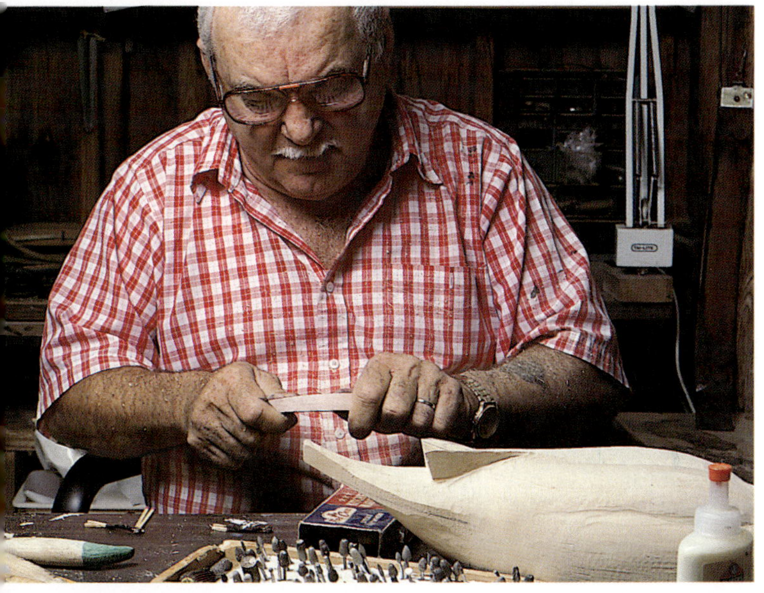

Bending and fitting the tail to the carved bird is largely a matter of trial and error. Jimmie likes to exaggerate the curve of the tail somewhat. "I like the look of a pintail that has a high head and a strongly curved tail feather," he says. "If you enter the bird in competition, that really catches the judge's eye."

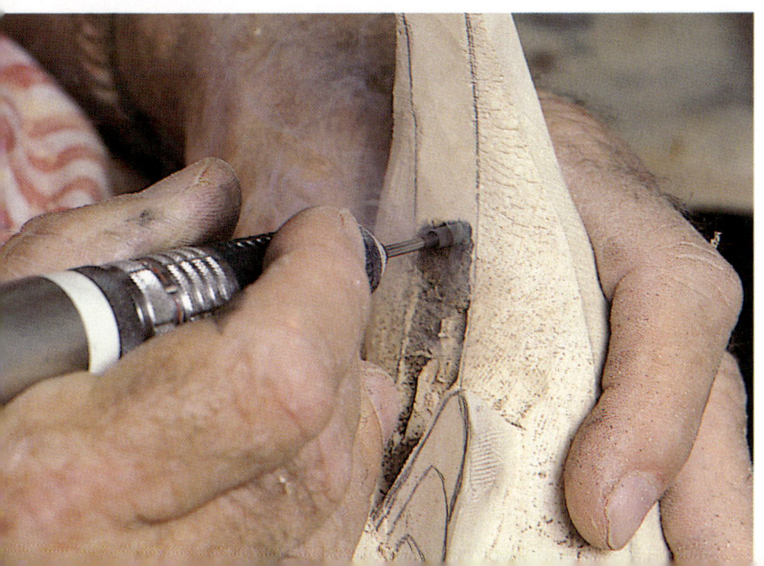

The tail is approximately 1/2 inch wide and 8 inches long at this stage, but its length will be reduced after it is mounted onto the carving. Jimmie traces the outline of the tail on the wood, then uses the straight cylinder to cut out a notch.

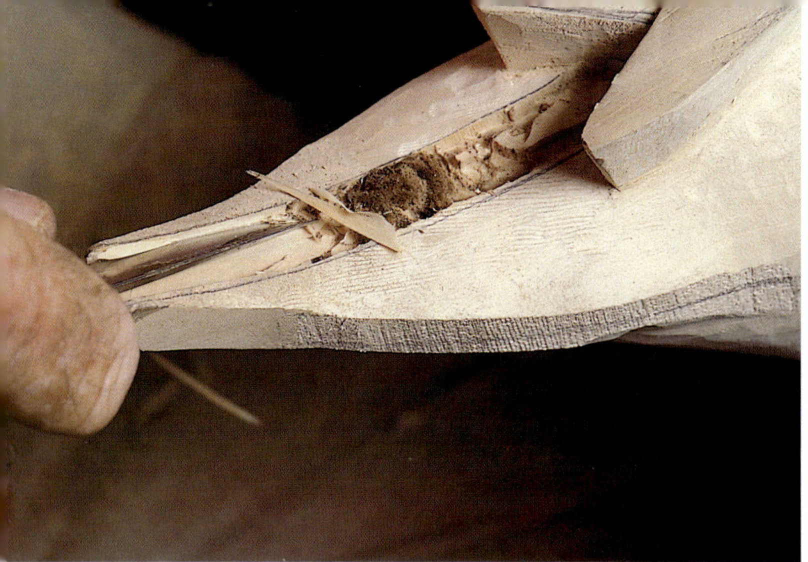

Jimmie uses the knife to clean out the notch where the tail will be mounted. The plastic tail is used for reasons of sturdiness. This carving is, after all, a gunning decoy, and if it were to actually see duty in a duck blind, a wooden tail would be very fragile. The plastic tail, however, although it looks very thin and graceful, is virtually unbreakable when epoxied in place.

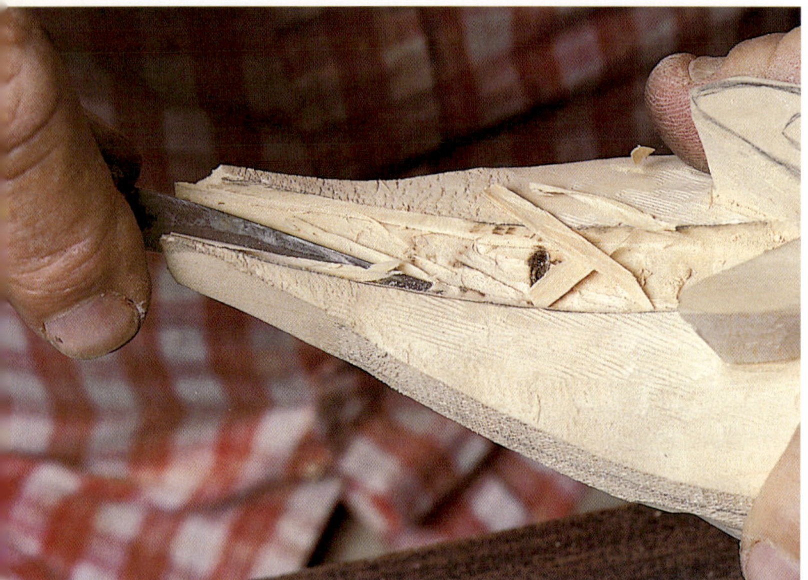

Fitting the tail takes quite a few trials, especially since it's curved. Jimmie keeps removing wood until the tail fits snugly and is flush with the surrounding wood. Any gaps will be filled by epoxy.

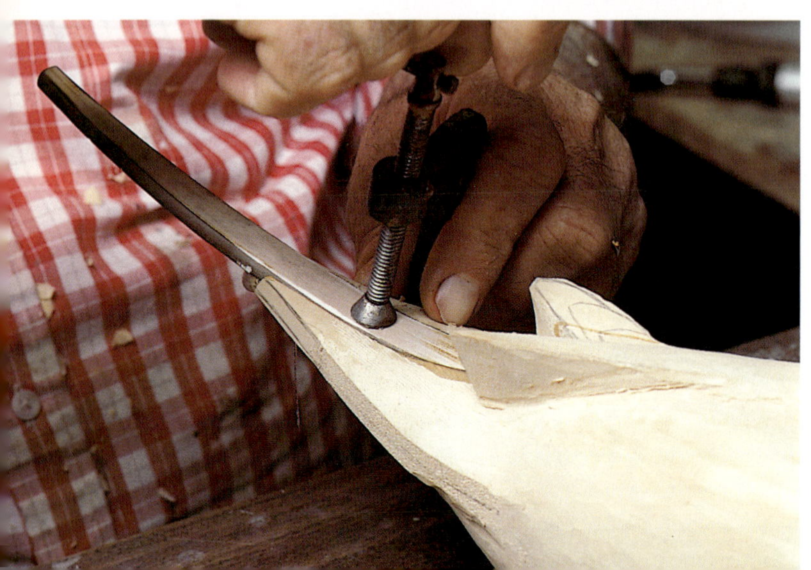

Two-part epoxy is applied to the notch, the plastic tail is pressed into place, and a C-clamp is used to hold it in position. The PVC pipe can be carved, and Jimmie will later shape it and reduce its length somewhat.

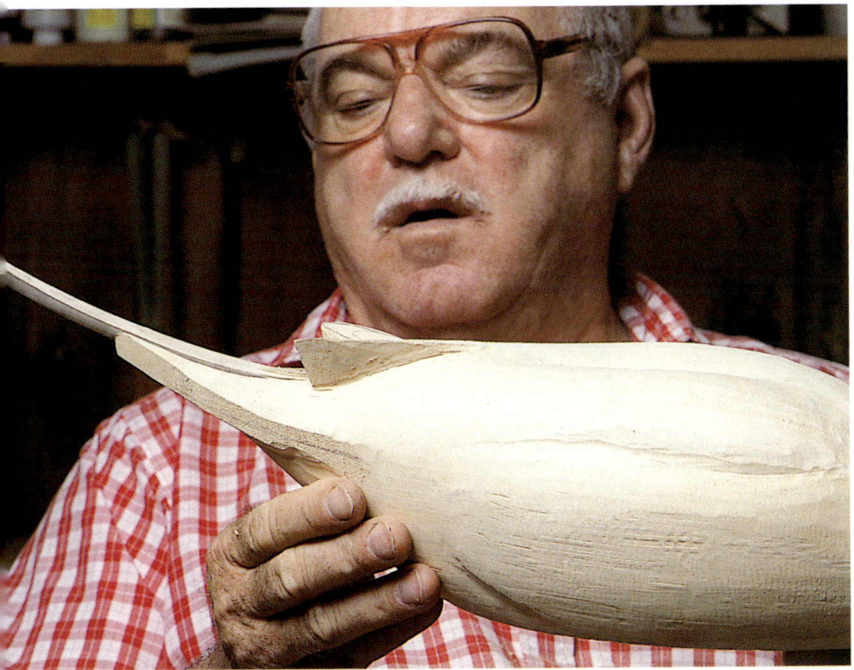

In a few minutes the epoxy has dried, and the clamp is removed. The plastic tail, with its gentle upward curve, provides a pleasing, graceful look.

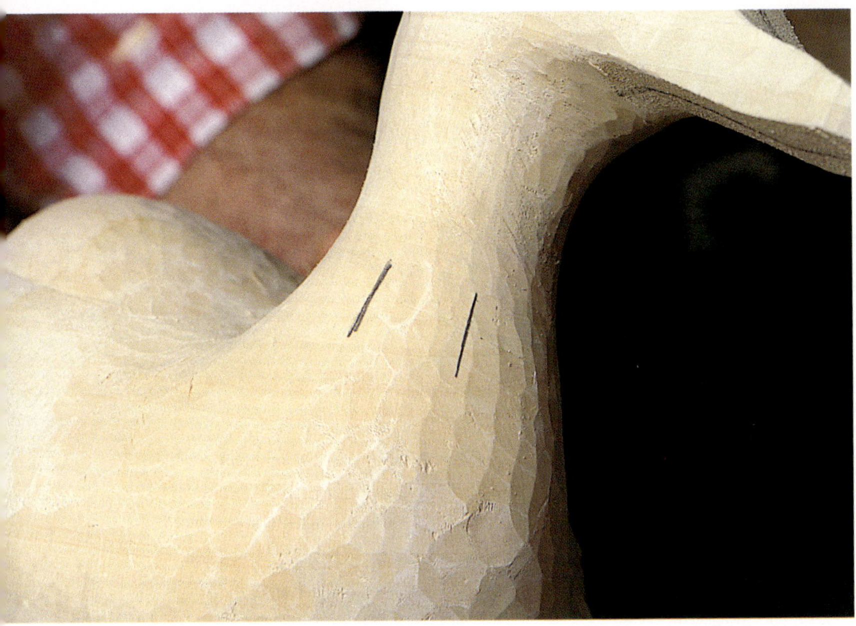

The body has now been carved to its finished dimensions. The wings, primary feathers, sidepockets, and tail have been defined, and now it's time to carve the head. To make the job easier, Jimmie will remove it from the body and reattach it later. The pencil marks will serve as reference, ensuring that the angle at which the head is turned will remain the same.

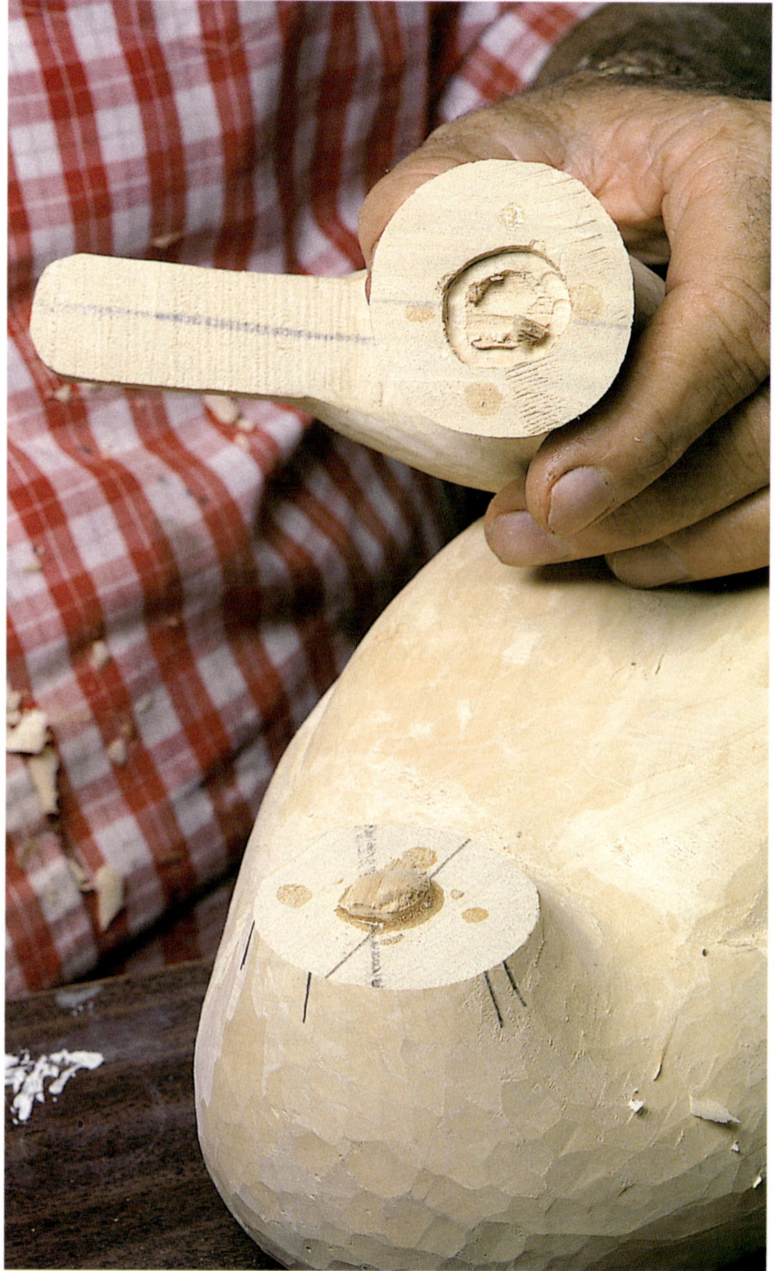

The head was glued only at the little island of wood in the center, and it breaks off easily. Jimmie will next carve bill detail, insert the eyes, and then replace the head on the body.

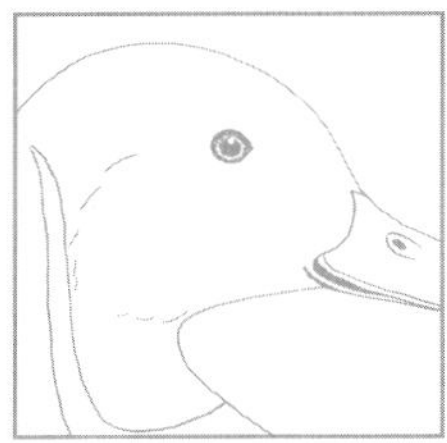

CHAPTER FIVE

Carving the Head

Jimmie will carve the head with a small knife and the high-speed grinder with several different cutters. He will drill eye holes and insert 10-millimeter light brown glass eyes, using wood filler as a base. Bill detail will be carved, the separation between the upper and lower mandibles will be defined, and the head will be sanded smooth before it is reattached to the body.

One of Jimmie's first steps in carving the head is drilling the holes in which the glass eyes will be inserted. Although the eyes will not be put in until later, drilling the holes now locks in the position and makes it easier to ensure that the eyes will be symmetrical. Jimmie used a needle to locate the eye position when cutting out the pattern in chapter 3, and in this chapter he uses the high-speed grinder to drill the two holes. The horizontal eye channels will be shaped after the holes are drilled.

It's important to have good reference material when carving the head and bill. You can study photos, taxidermy mounts, and live birds, and carving supply dealers even have cast study bills you can use for measurements and detail.

This is a gunning bird, however, so the bill will not have as much detail as that of a decorative carving. Jimmie will carve the separation between the mandibles, the lines that separate the bill from the head, and the nail, or little bump at the tip of the bill. He will not carve the nostrils.

Probably the most important element in this chapter is symmetry: One eye must not be higher or lower than the other, and the eye channels must be parallel and in alignment. Some time spent sketching will help make sure everything is symmetrical.

The head of the bird is where the life is, the personality, so take your time, study your reference material, and plan your carving with the pencil before going to work with the knife. When the eyes are inserted and the head is reattached to the body, the pintail will begin to come alive.

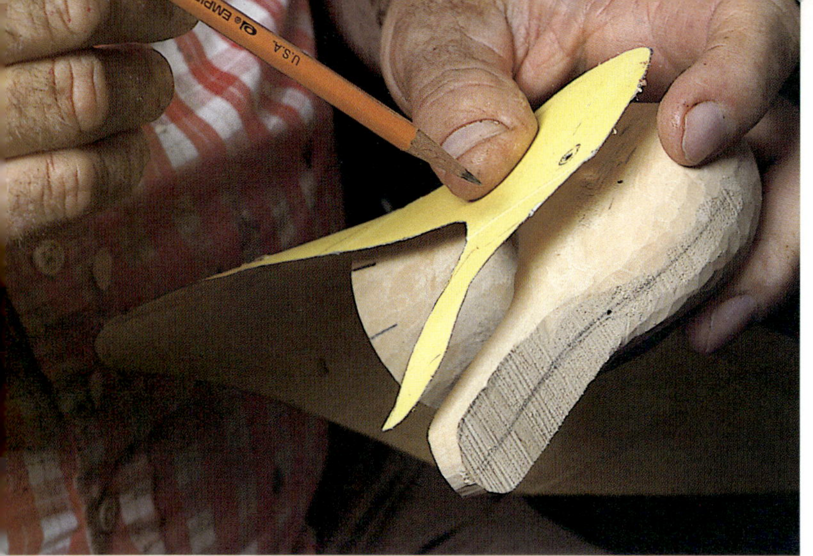

The first step in carving the head is to drill holes where the glass eyes will later be inserted. To make sure the eye position is correct, Jimmie checks the alignment using the head pattern.

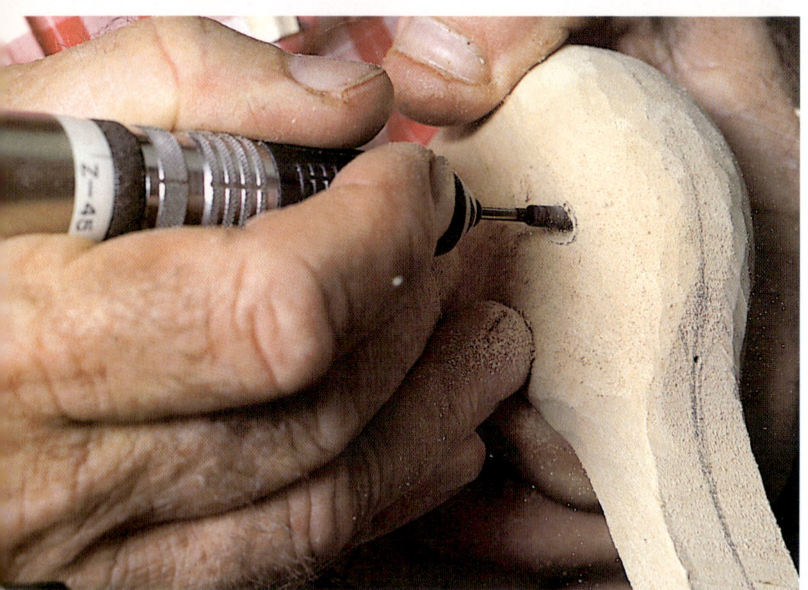

The high-speed grinder is used to drill the eye holes. The eye channel and cheek area will be carved before the eyes are inserted, but this step establishes the eye positions, making the shaping of the head easier and more accurate. The hole is slightly smaller than the 10-millimeter diameter of the glass eye at this point. It will be enlarged later when the eye is fitted.

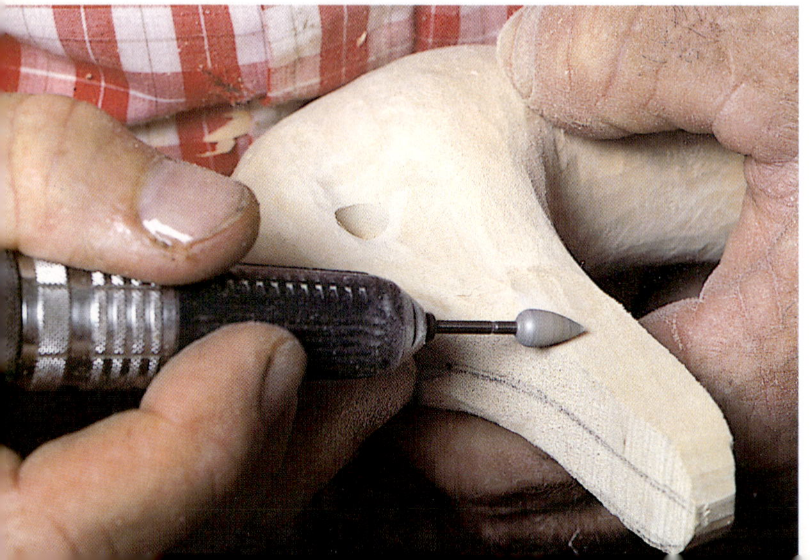

The high-speed grinder is used for some preliminary shaping of the bill. At this stage, Jimmie is simply reducing the hard edges and creating contours, much as he did when carving the body. Note the centerline down the bill and head.

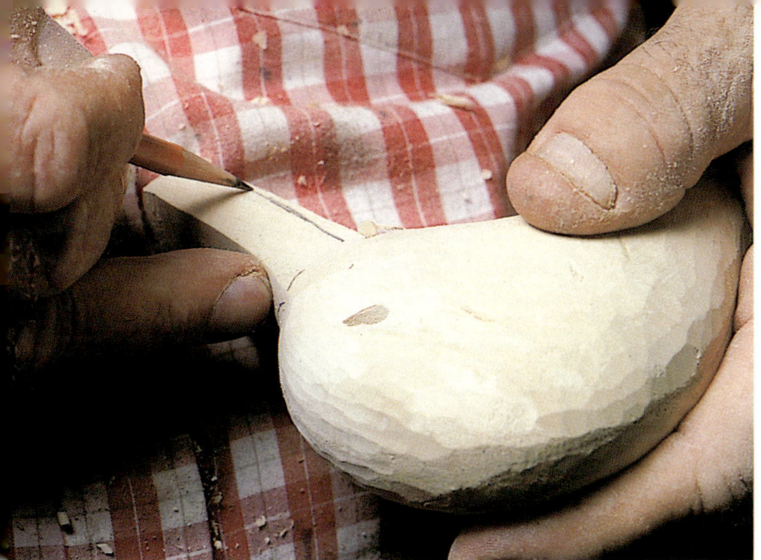

A pencil is used to sketch the separation between the upper and lower mandibles. Good reference material is important here. Consult photos, mounts, or molded study bills.

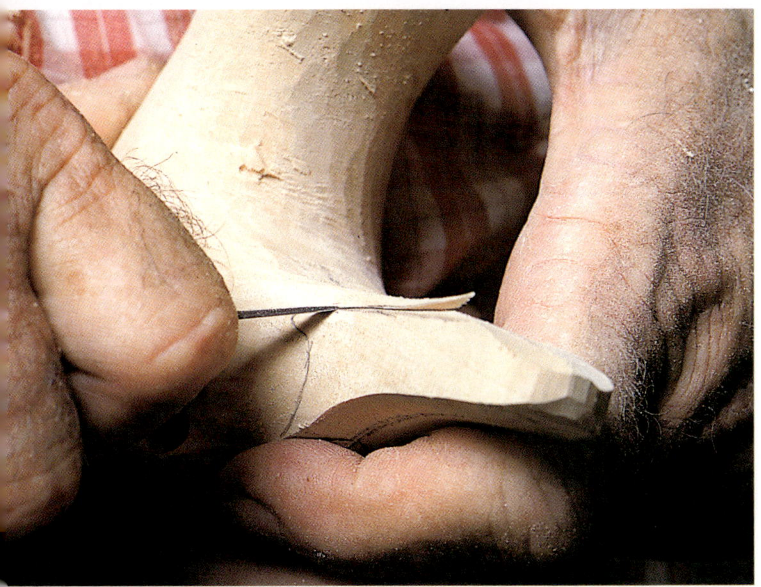

To carve the separation between the mandibles, Jimmie uses the knife, first making a cut perpendicular to the side of the bill.

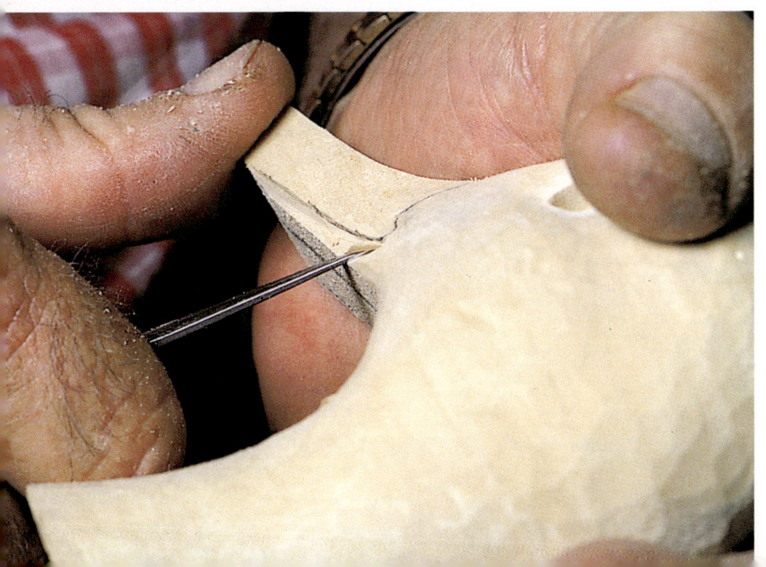

A second cut at a right angle to the first removes the wood, thus defining the lower mandible. The lower mandible is smaller than the upper one and fits into it. Only the portion near the base of the bill shows.

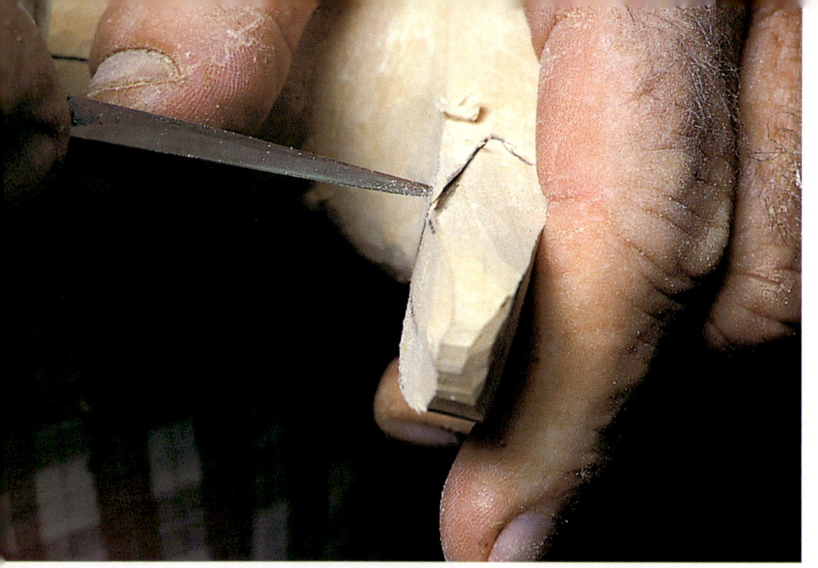

A similar carving procedure separates the bill from the head. Jimmie first sketches the separation with the pencil, then cuts along the pencil line with the knife.

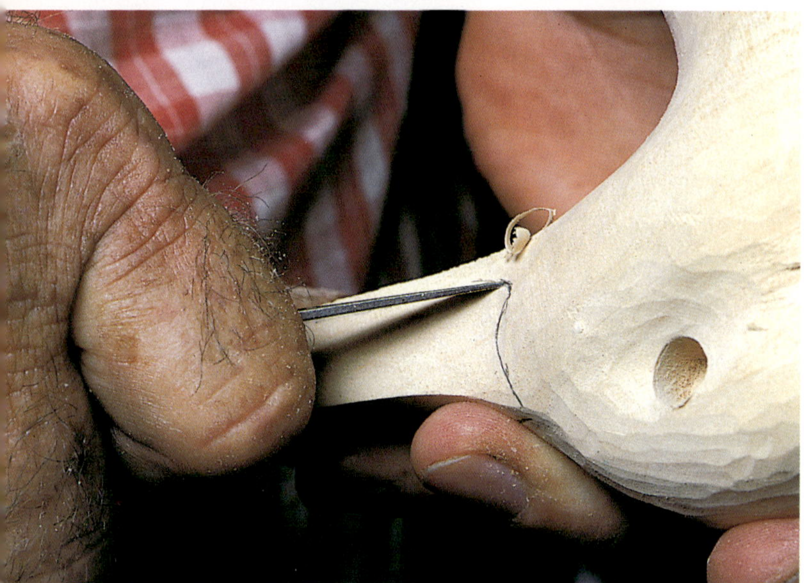

Jimmie then cuts back to the line along the bill, and the separation between the bill and head is defined.

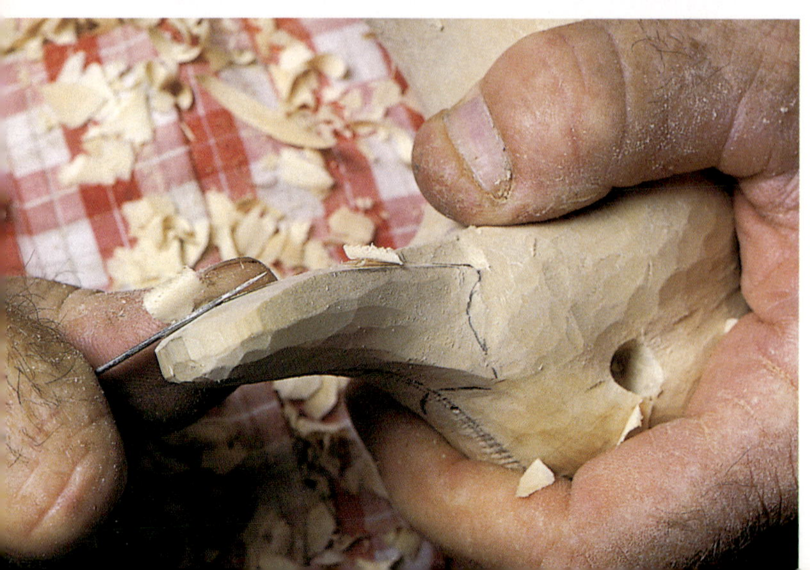

The knife is used for the preliminary shaping of the bill, reducing its thickness. Note that the bill has a slight upward curve.

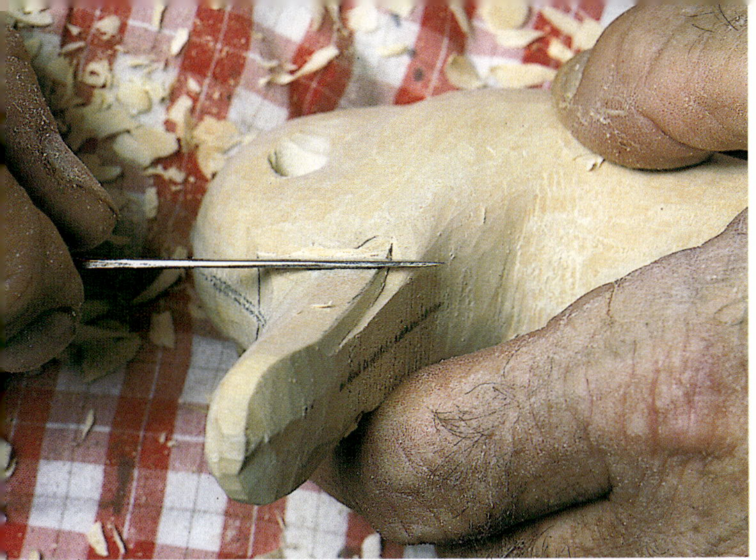

The width of the bill also is reduced slightly, helping to visually separate it from the head. Consult reference material for size, shape, and detail.

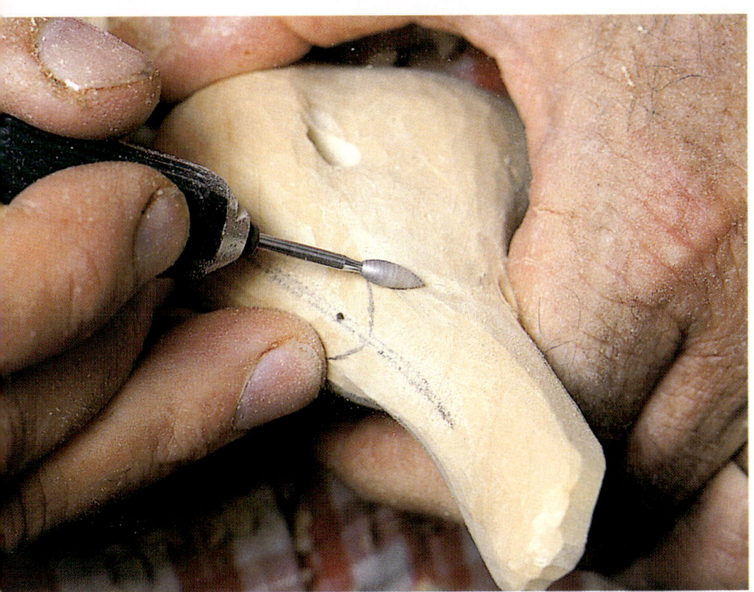

Once the bill has been roughed out with the carving knife, Jimmie turns to the high-speed grinder and a diamond stone to smooth the area and refine the shape.

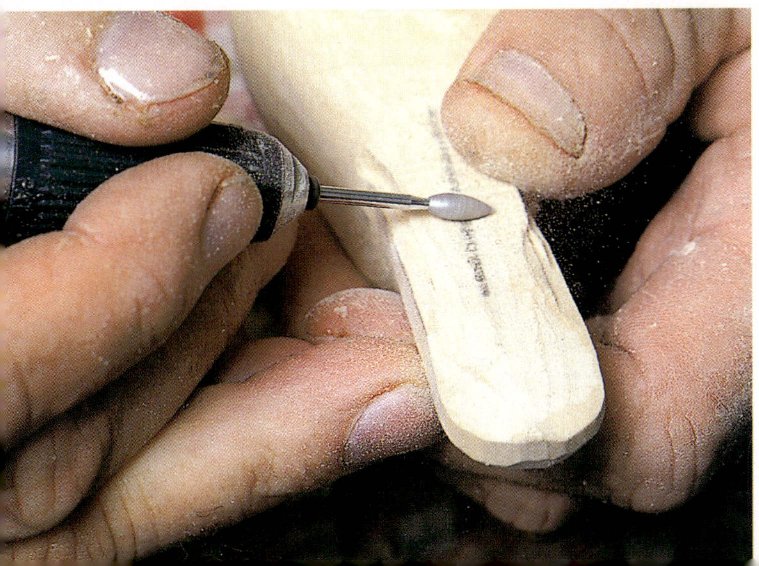

The grinder is used to curve the top of the upper mandible. Jimmie is careful to leave wood along the centerline, sloping the curve downward from that line.

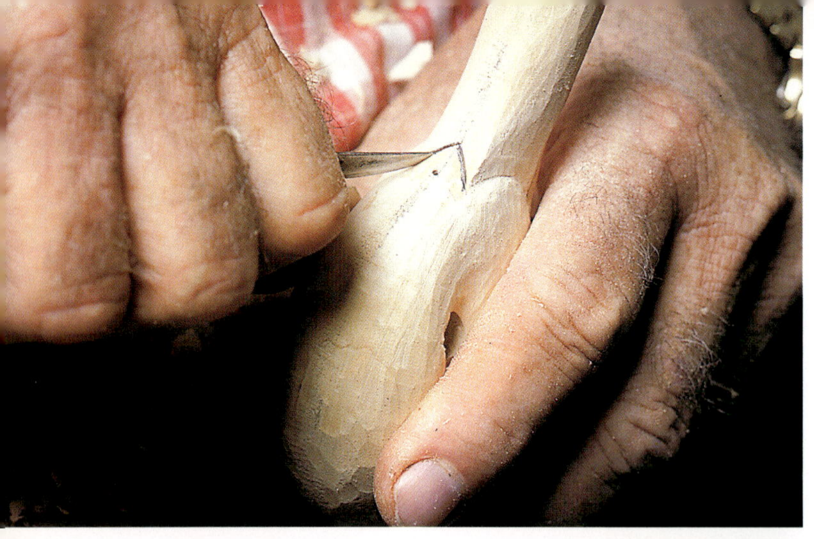

The top of the upper mandible is separated from the head in the same manner as the sides were. Jimmie sketches the separation in pencil, then cuts along the pencil line with the knife, first holding the blade at a 90-degree angle to the wood, and then cutting back to that line along the surface of the bill.

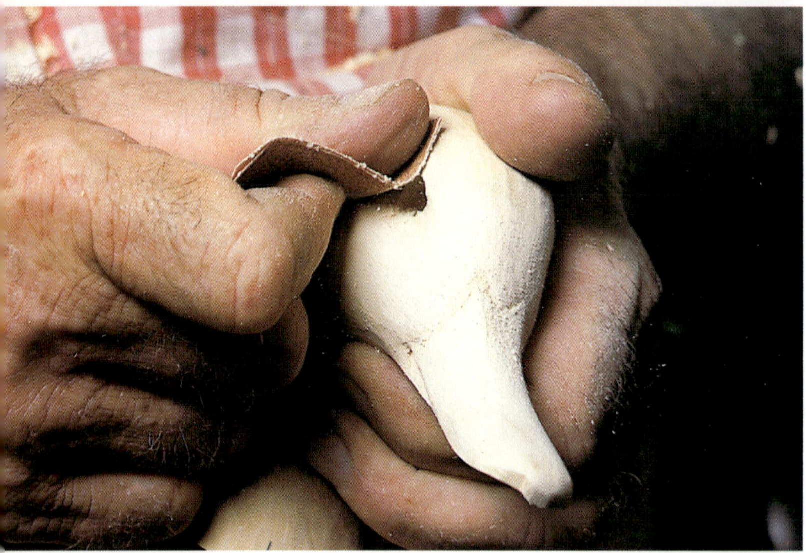

Once the preliminary shaping of the head is complete, Jimmie sands it and inserts the eyes before doing the final carving.

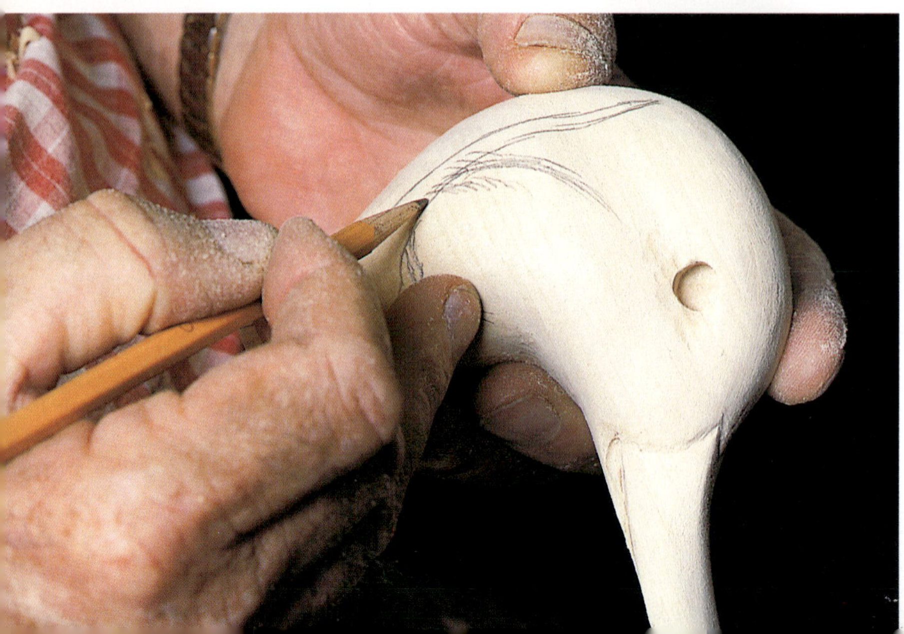

Jimmie frequently sketches on the surface of the wood during the carving process. Here, with the head sanded, he sketches in where the white vertical line will go on the side of the head. He plans feather detail that will be painted on later, with a few of the brown feathers of the head overlapping the white vertical line.

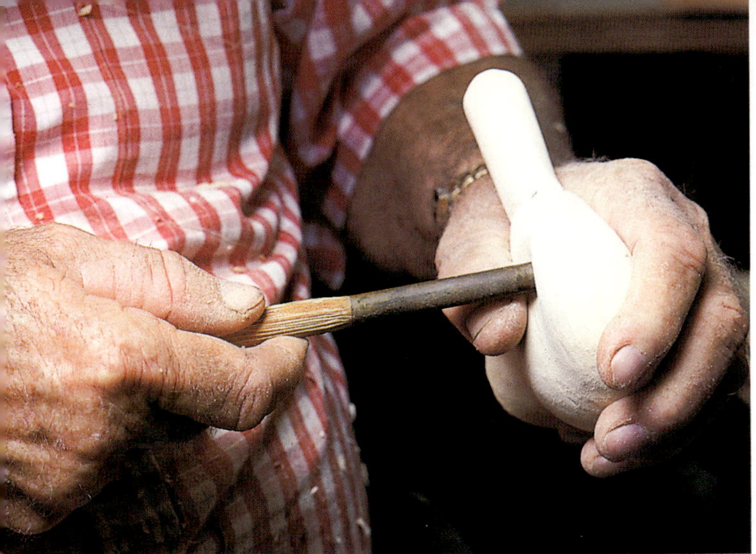

Jimmie uses a 10-millimeter sharpened cylinder to enlarge the eye sockets to accommodate the glass eyes.

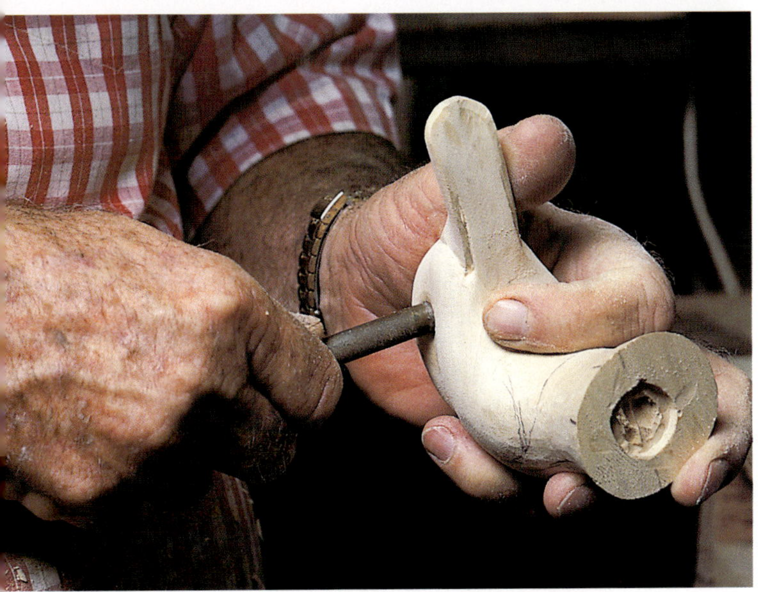

The cylinder is mounted on a wooden handle, making it easy to press into the wood. Because he originally made the eye holes slightly smaller than the finished diameter, Jimmie is able to fine-tune the position slightly, ensuring that the eyes will be symmetrical.

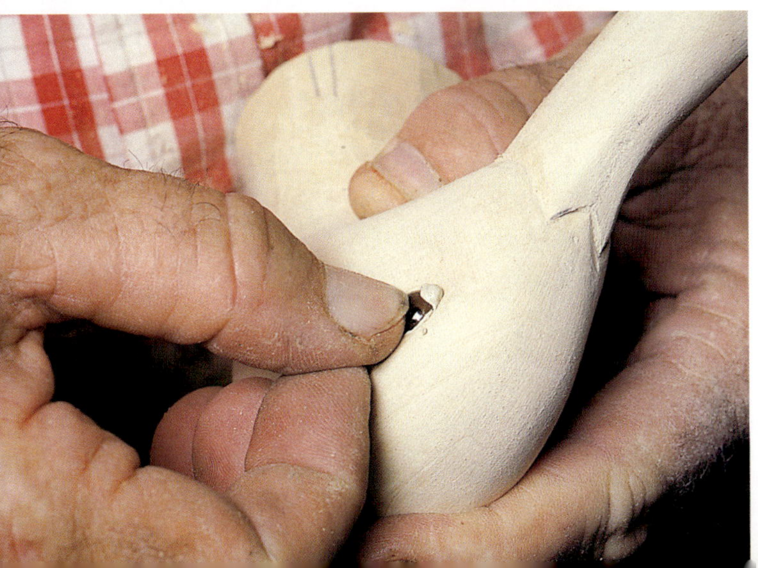

He applies Just Like Wood, a wood filler manufactured by 3-M, to the sockets, and then presses the 10-millimeter light brown glass eyes into place.

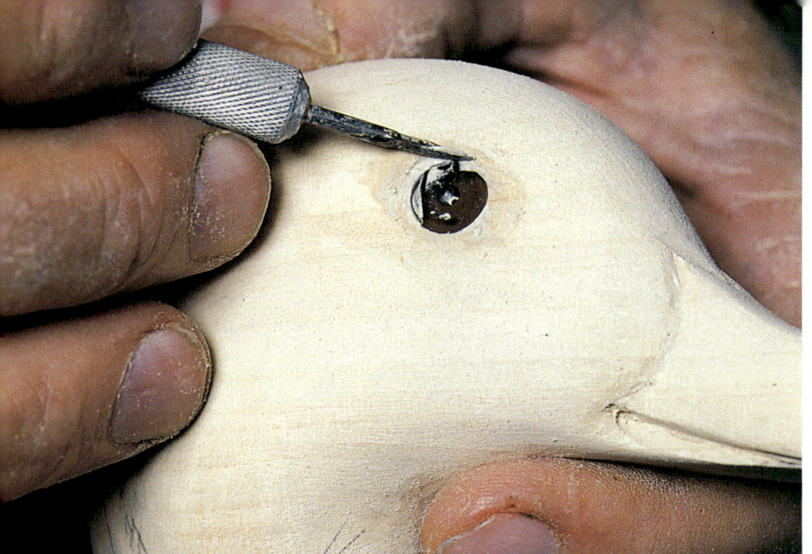

He uses a pick to smooth out the filler, shaping it around the glass eyes. When the compound dries, it will be sanded, carved, and cleaned off the eye.

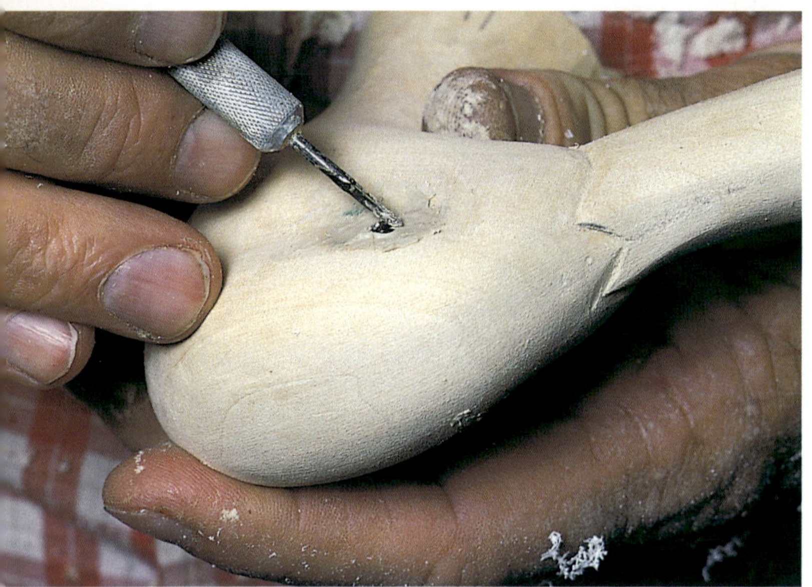

The same procedure is used in inserting the left eye. Filler is pressed into the eye socket, the glass eye is inserted, and the excess filler is scraped away.

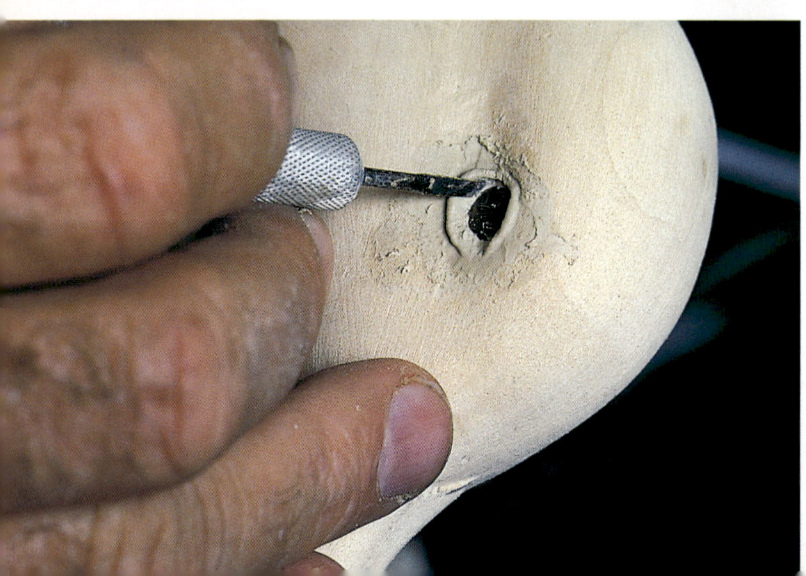

As the filler begins to set up, Jimmie shapes it into the membrane that surrounds the eye. This area will be smoothed later with sandpaper and shaped with the high-speed grinder.

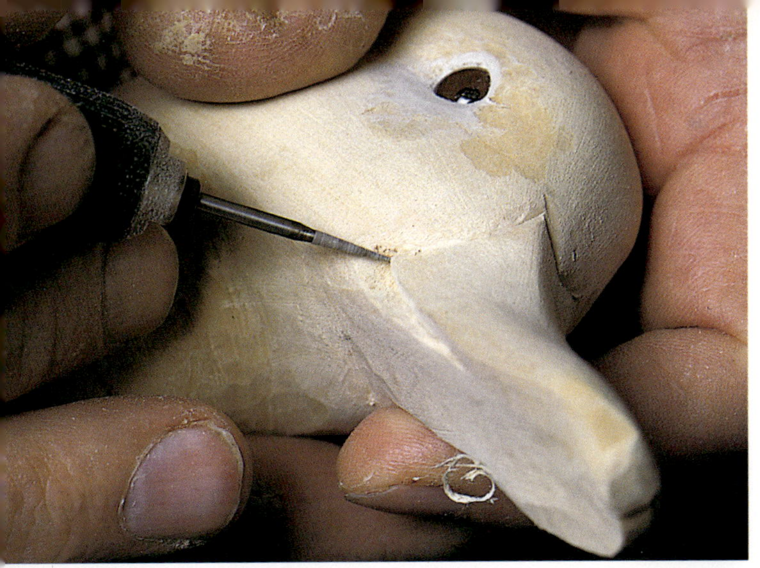

Before carving the area around the eyes, Jimmie details the area around the bill with a sharp tapered cutter on the high-speed grinder.

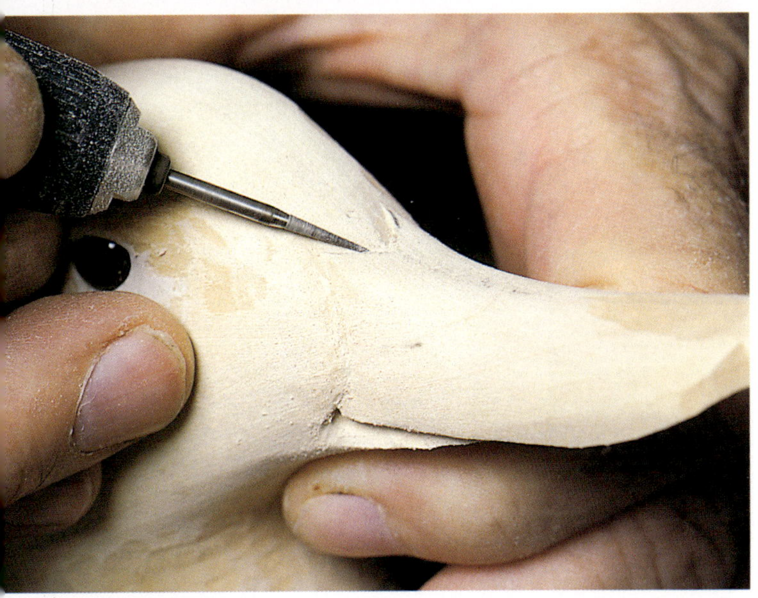

This step refines the lines carved with the knife prior to inserting the eyes. The tapered cutter softens the lines left by the knife cuts.

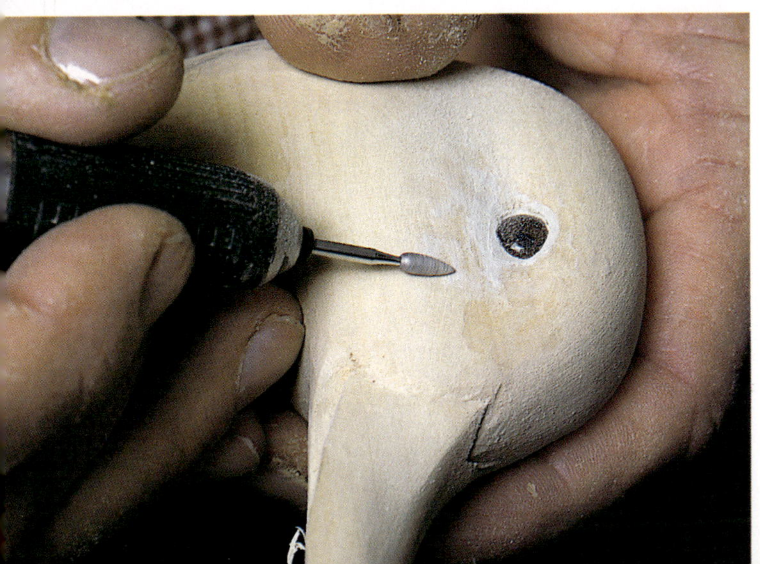

The area around the eye is carved with the high-speed grinder and a diamond stone. Jimmie carves in the direction of the feather flow, creating fine lines that will resemble feather detail in the final carving. Be sure the wood filler is completely dry before carving this area.

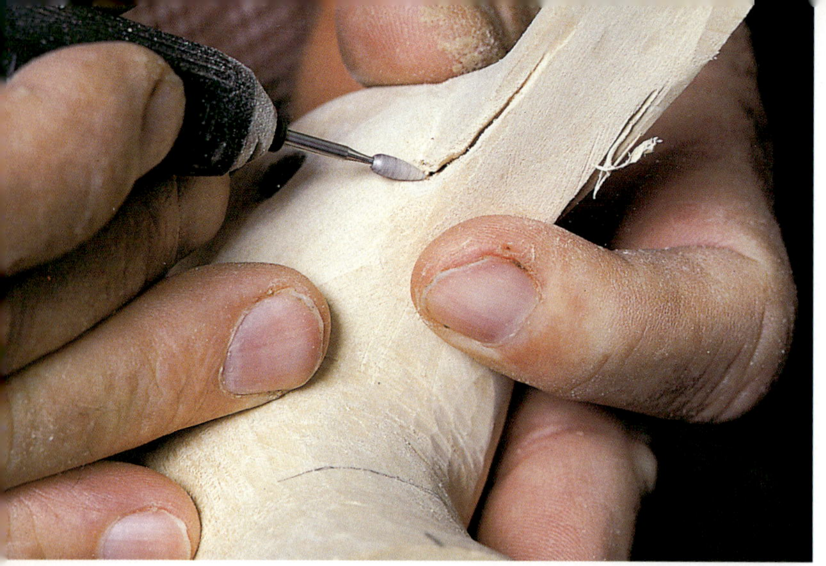

The same stone is used to soften the knife cuts separating the upper and lower mandibles. Jimmie uses the stone here almost as if he were sanding the wood, converting hard lines into soft ones.

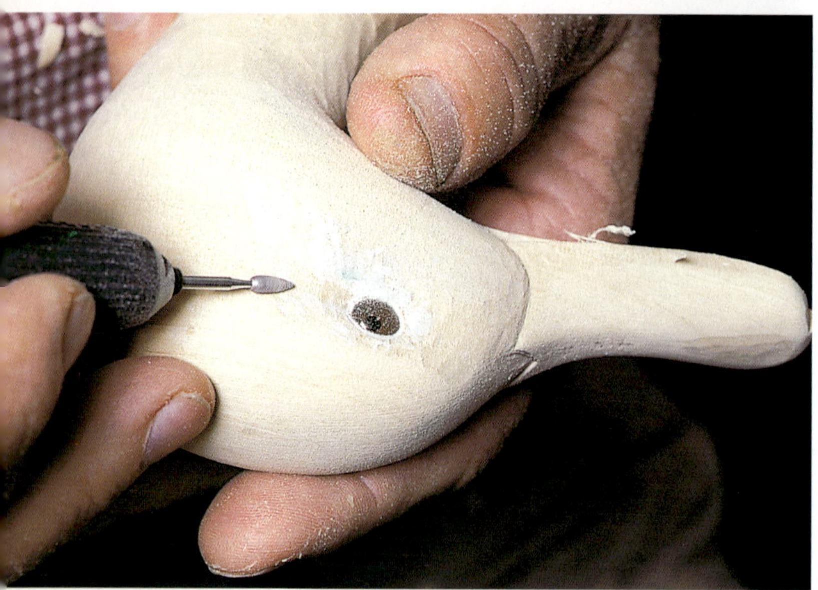

The eye membrane created by the wood filler is reduced, and the excess filler is removed from the eye channel by the stone.

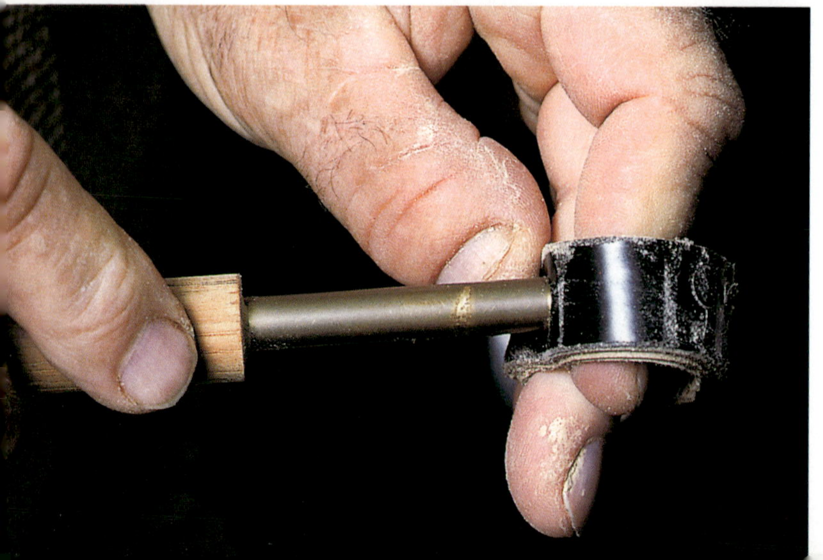

Jimmie is ready to give the head a final sanding, but first, to prevent the glass eyes from being scratched, he covers them with electrical tape. To do this, he uses the same 10-millimeter cylinder used to cut the eye holes, pressing it into a roll of tape.

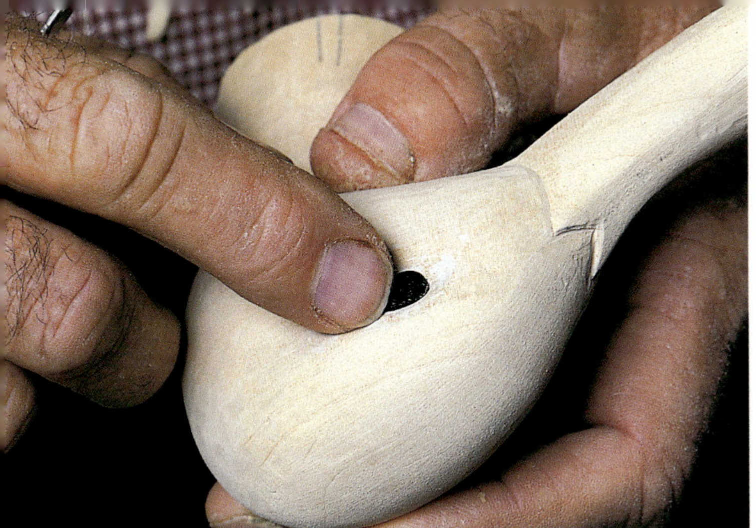

The 10-millimeter-diameter piece of tape is then carefully placed over the glass eye.

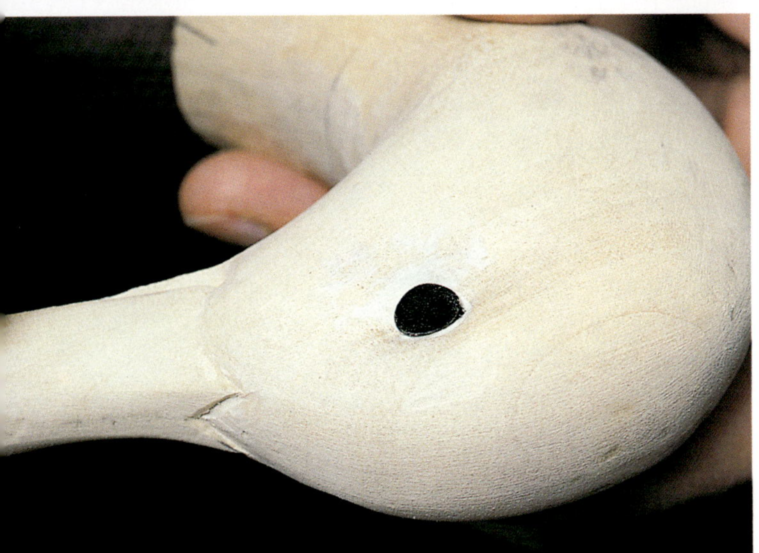

With the tape in place, Jimmie can sand right up to the perimeter of the eye without scratching it. If he were to scratch the eye at this point, it would have to be removed and the entire process of inserting the eye repeated.

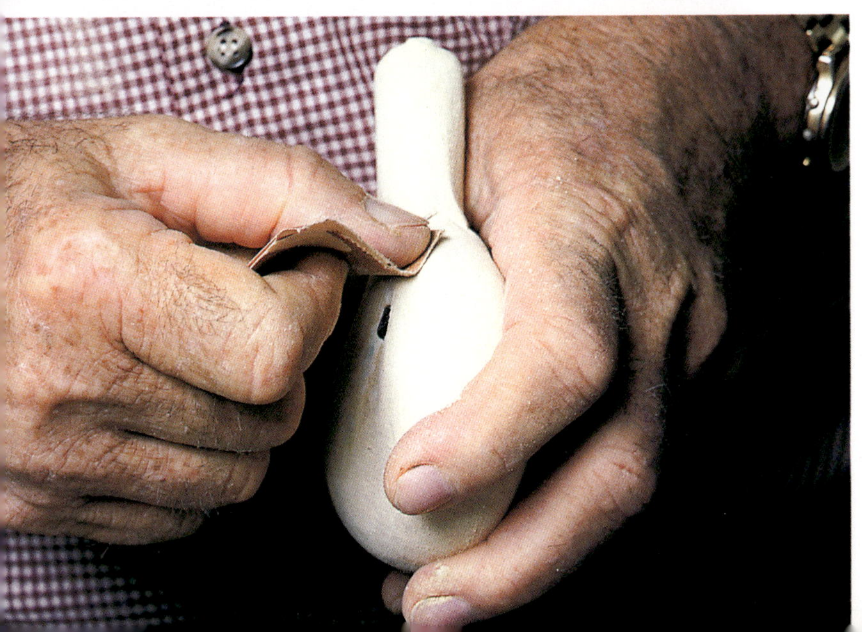

The head is sanded with 100-grit paper and is now ready to be placed permanently on the body.

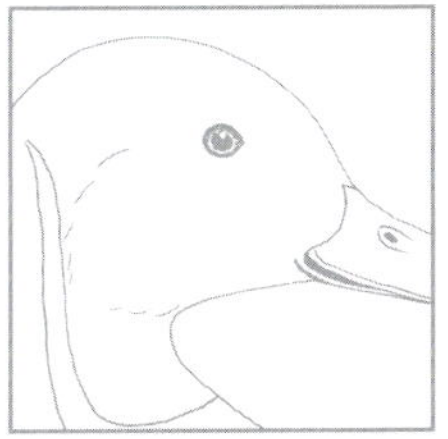

CHAPTER SIX

Preparing to Paint

If the pintail were a car, this is where the quality control station of the assembly line would go to work. At this stage, all the carving is done, but Jimmie checks the bird closely for accuracy and symmetry, and he uses the knife to do some final shaping, removing very thin slivers of wood until he is satisfied with the feel and the look of the bird.

The head goes back on, the pintail is sanded, and three coats of sealer are applied. The sealer is important for at least two reasons. First, it seals the surface of the wood and will not allow water to saturate the wood fibers. Should the decoy be hunted over or entered in a carving competition where birds are judged as they float in water, the importance of this step would be obvious. Also, sealer provides a uniform painting surface for the water-soluble acrylic colors that will soon be applied. So be sure to seal the wood, even if your pintail will never venture farther than the bookshelf in your den.

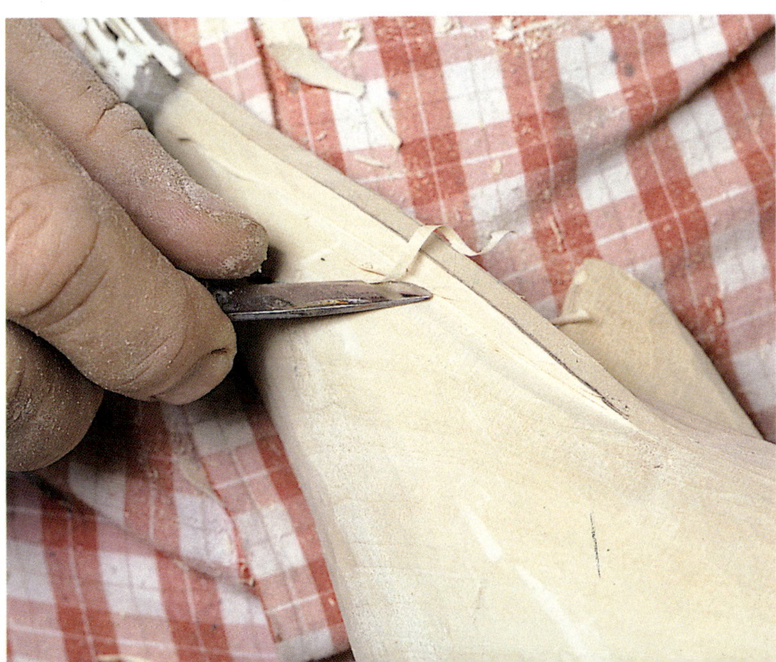

Jimmie uses the knife to smooth out the area on the tail where the PVC insert is in place. This is a general clean-up process in preparation for painting. The wood should be smooth and free of blemishes, and all detail should be accurate and complete.

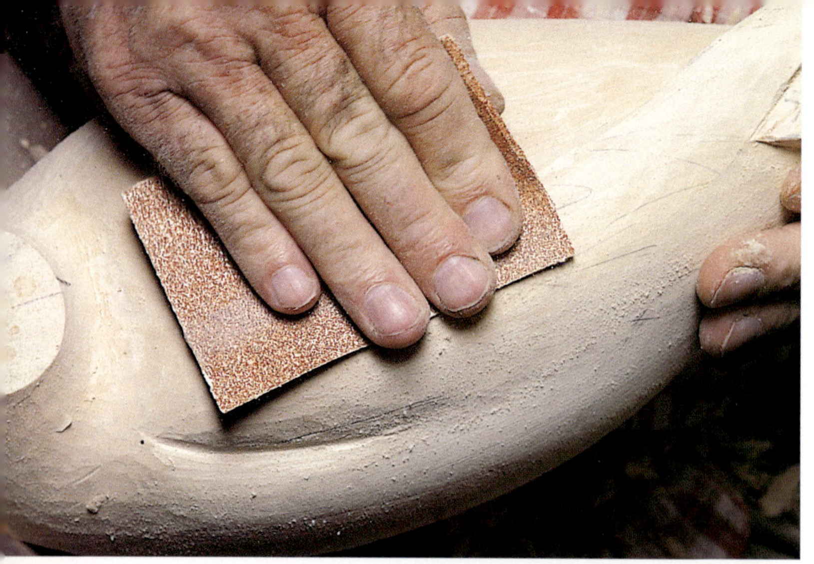

Jimmie uses 100-grit sandpaper to smooth the wood surface and remove any tool marks. The prime coat of paint will be stippled on, creating a stuccolike finish intended to prevent glare. This is, after all, a gunning decoy, and you wouldn't want the sunlight to reflect off it. The stippled base coat will help hide any small sandpaper marks. If this were a decorative decoy, the sanding would have to be much finer.

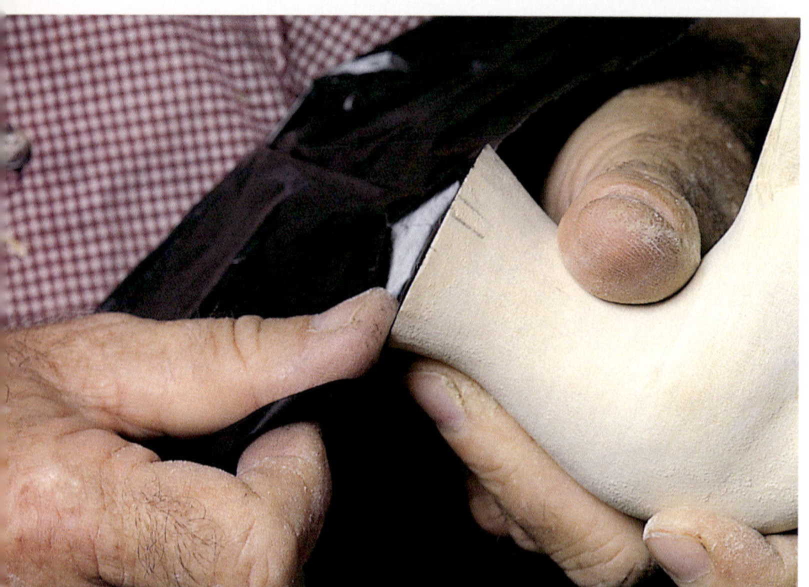

Jimmie is ready to reattach the head. To ensure a tight, seamless fit, he uses a sheet of carbon paper to blacken the surface of the neck where it meets the body.

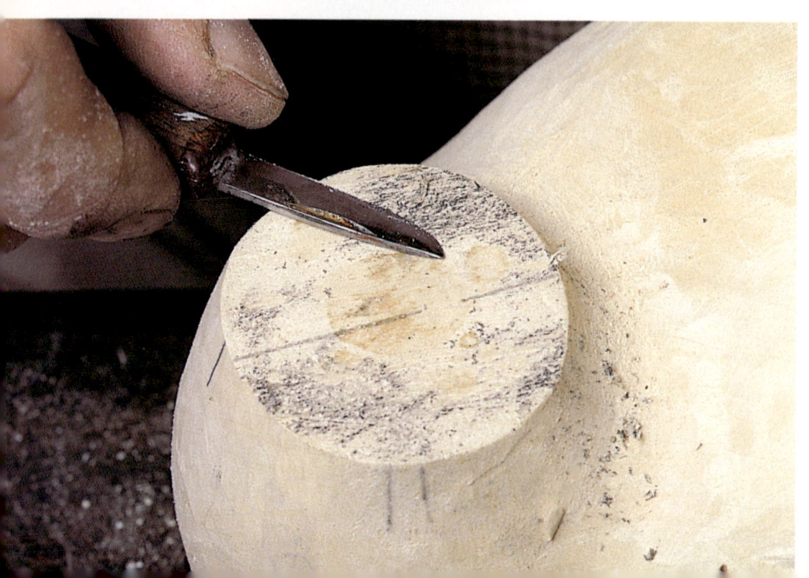

When the head is pressed into place and then removed, any high or low spots will be evident by the manner in which the carbon is transferred, or not transferred, to the mounting surface. Jimmie repeats the procedure several times to make sure of a perfect, seamless fit.

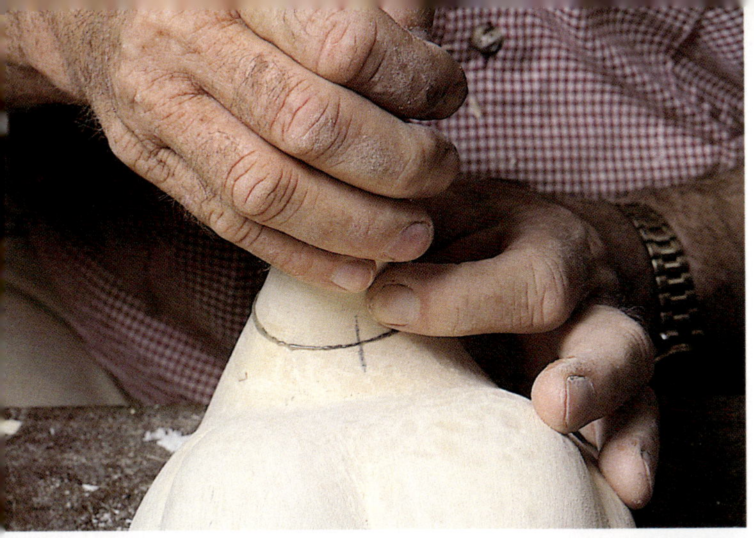

Two-part epoxy is applied to the neck area, and the head is pressed back into place, with the penciled registration marks in alignment.

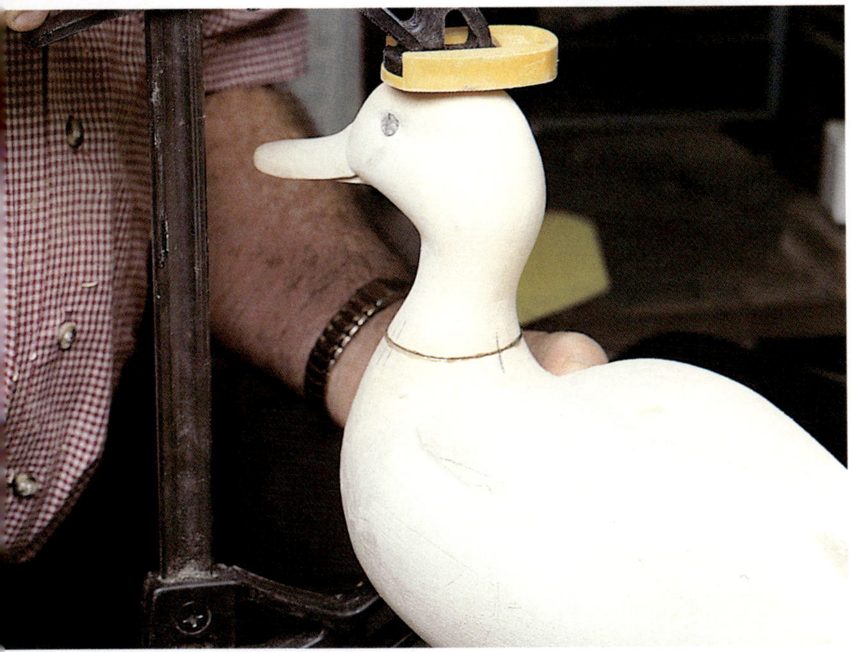

The head is tightly clamped to the body, and the carving is set aside while the epoxy cures.

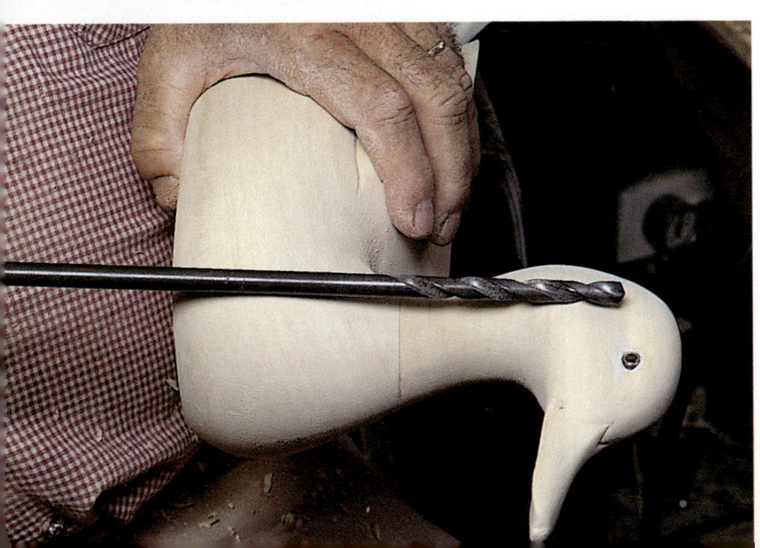

Although the epoxy will provide a good bond between the head and the body, an optional step, if the carving is to be a working decoy, would be to insert a dowel through the body of the bird into the neck and head area. Jimmie uses a hand drill and a long, 1/2-inch bit for this. It's a good idea to mark the bit at the proper depth before drilling; you don't want the bit to come through the top of the head.

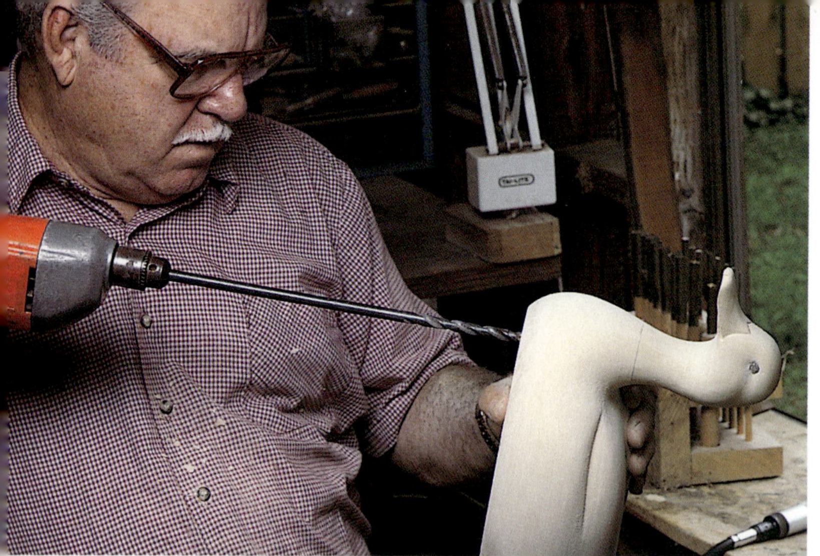

The hole is drilled, two-part epoxy is drizzled into the hole, and the dowel is inserted.

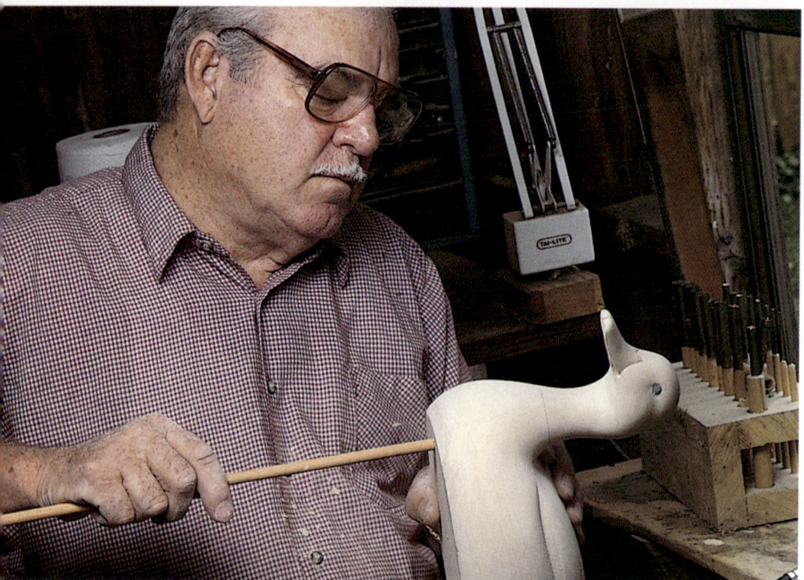

The dowel is pressed into place, and excess is cut off even with the surface of the bottom of the decoy.

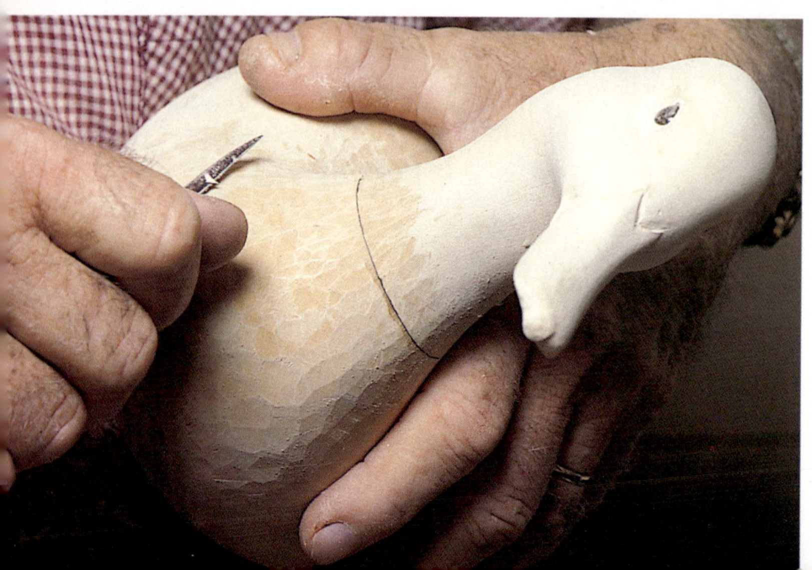

When the epoxy is dry, Jimmie gives the carving a final going-over. Here he does some final shaping to the breast and neck area. Most of the carving such as this is done with the knife, which Jimmie uses to remove extremely thin pieces of wood.

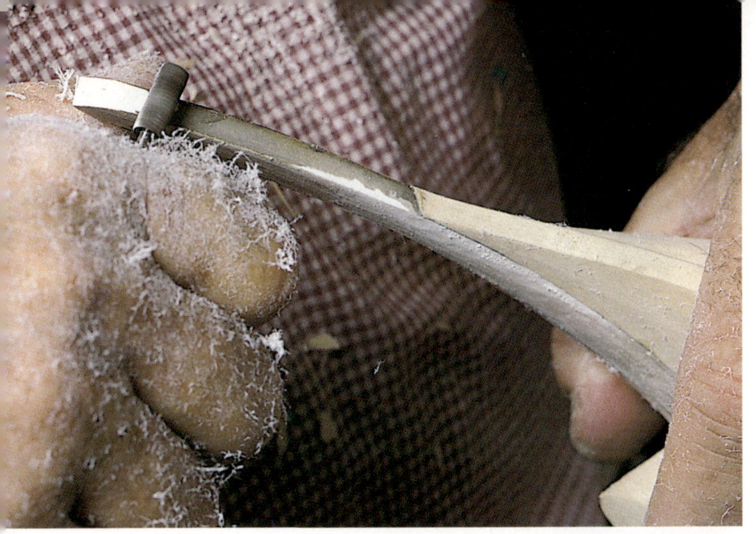

The tail is trimmed to shape and cut off with a cylinder bit mounted in the grinder. Jimmie doesn't measure the tail, but simply cuts it off at a length that looks good to him. He likes the look of a pintail with a long, upturned tail, so it may wind up somewhat longer than that of a real bird. The feathers of live birds vary, however, so don't be too worried about accuracy here.

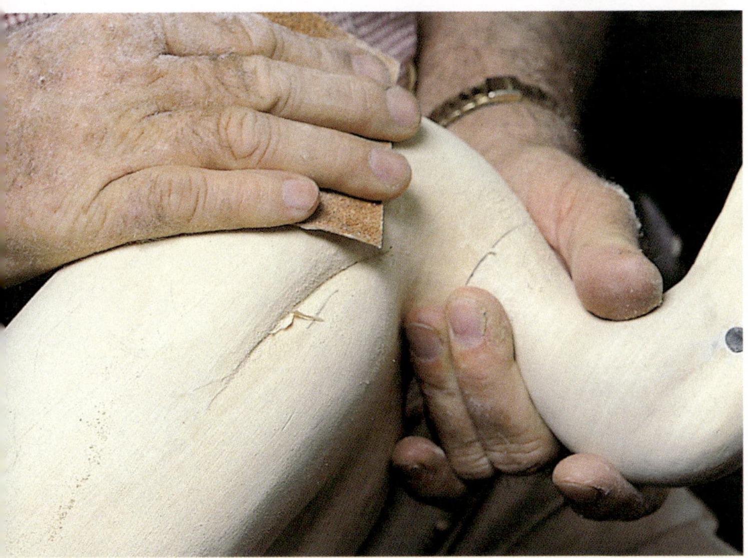

Jimmie gives the decoy a final sanding. He uses relatively coarse, 100-grit paper because the stippled base coat of paint will hide any sanding marks.

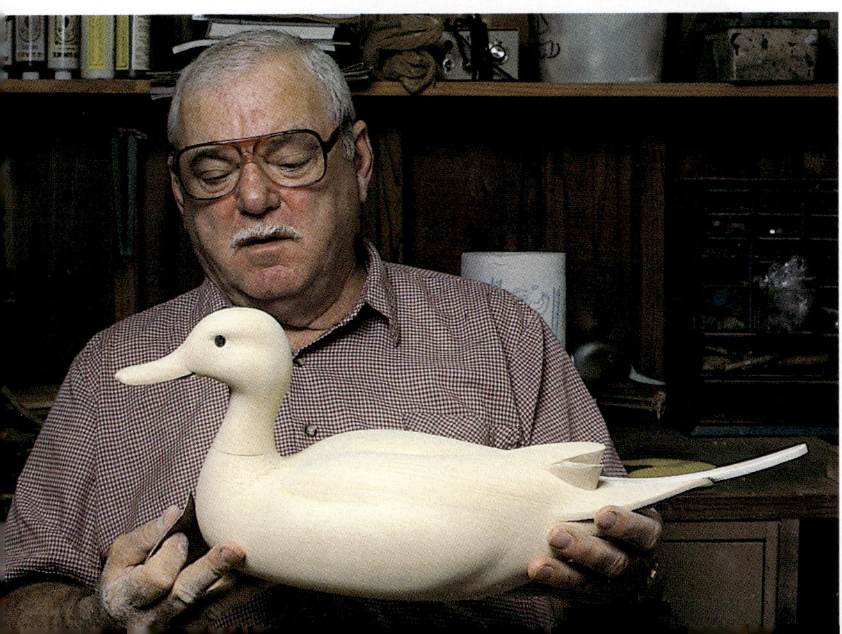

Before applying sealer, Jimmie examines the pintail from all angles, making sure the wings and sidepockets are symmetrical and accurate. "If you enter a bird in competition, the judges will look for little things that may be wrong," he says. "If you stop at this point and sand it down and study it carefully, mistakes can be picked up and corrected."

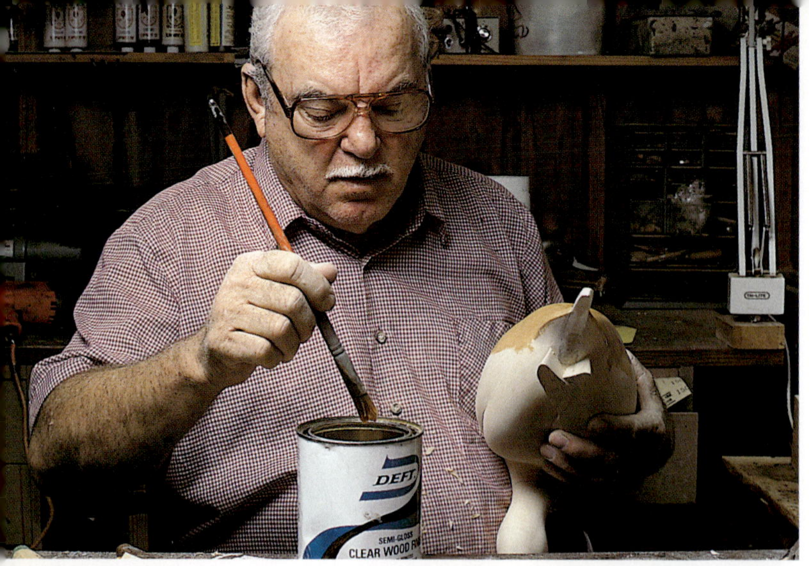

Jimmie seals the carving with three applications of Deft brand semigloss Clear Wood Finish. The sealer will provide a good, uniform painting surface for the acrylic colors that will be applied later, in addition to making the wood waterproof. If you plan to paint the decoy in the same area where you carved it, be sure to vacuum up the dust and other small wood particles before beginning the painting process.

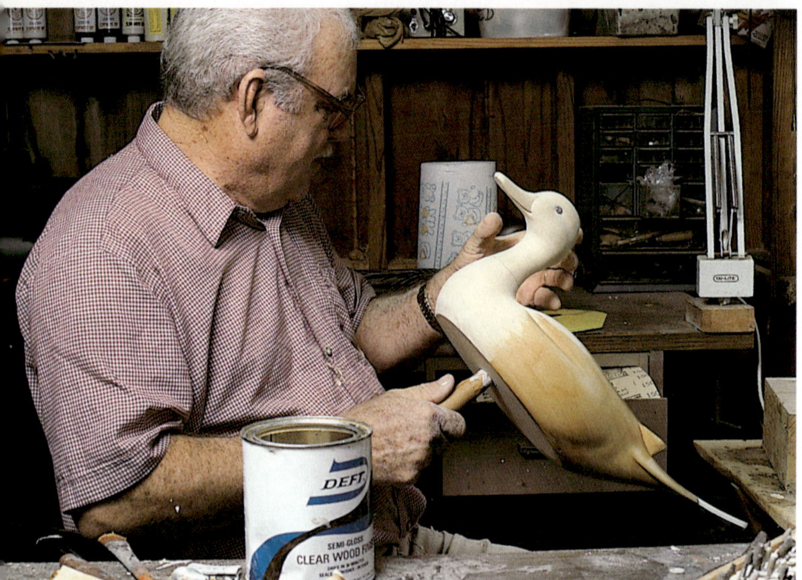

Jimmie uses a section of a wooden dowel as a handle when painting the decoy. A screw is epoxied into the handle with the threads exposed, and the handle is temporarily attached to the carving. The screw hole will later be filled and covered with the keel.

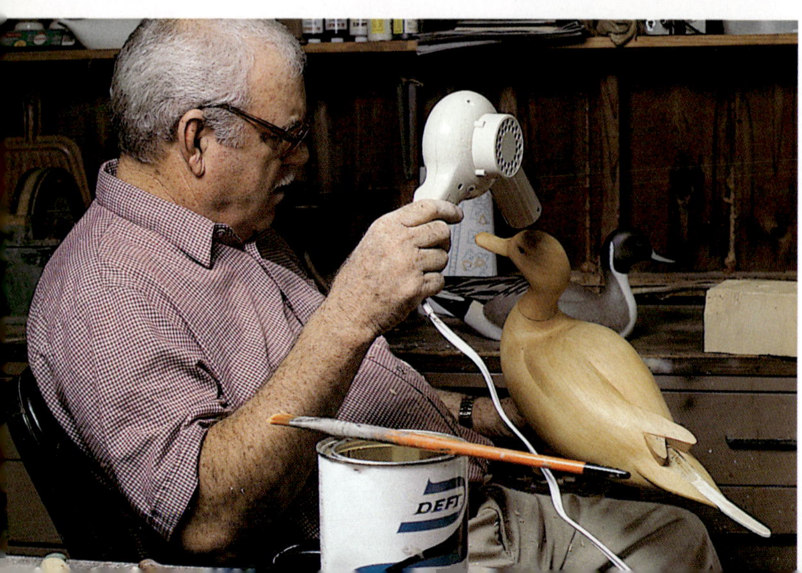

Three coats of sealer produce a hard, uniform surface. Jimmie dries each coat with a hair dryer between applications. When the third coat is dry, the carving is ready for the base coats of color.

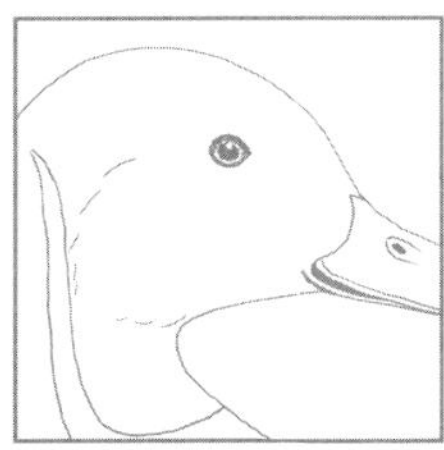

CHAPTER SEVEN

Applying the Base Colors

Jimmie paints the pintail in two basic procedures. First he applies base coats, which on the pintail drake consist of four colors. Later, over the base colors, he will add fine detail such as individual feathers, splits in feathers, and folds. For example, the intricate vermiculated lines on the feathers of the sides and back will be painted in the next chapter, but the gray background color that shows between those lines will go on now.

The four base colors are as follows: brown for the head; black for the bill, rump, tail, and tips of the primaries; gray for the back, sidepockets, and behind the neck; and off-white for the breast, neck, and flanks. All are Jo Sonja acrylic colors. Jimmie mixes a large quantity of the base colors and keeps them in airtight containers, using them for numerous carvings.

The brown is made of raw umber and raw sienna, with slightly more raw sienna in the mix. The base black is straight black tinted with phthalo blue, phthalo green, and burnt umber, with a small amount of varnish added. "Black out of the tube is flat and doesn't look right," says Jimmie, "so you need just enough tint to take away that dull look."

The base gray is smoke pearl or nimbus gray tinted with raw umber. Because the gray will later be covered by vermiculation and will thus appear darker, Jimmie keeps the value of the color on the light side. The base white can be either titanium or warm white tinted with raw umber to get a warmer, slightly darkened white. A small amount of blue would produce a cooler white. Untinted white feather edges will be applied on the off-white areas, and the different values of white will make them visible, although subtly so.

The base colors will be applied with a Raphael number 10 brush, and a number 2 brush will be used for fine detail such as the feather groupings on the wings. Jimmie uses an airbrush to blend areas where base colors meet.

Before putting on the base colors, Jimmie coats the carving—except for the bill—with a thick application of textured gesso. Gesso, like sealer, provides a uniform painting surface, and the texture makes sure this gunning bird will not reflect light. The gesso is stippled on. Jimmie first applies a thick coat with a large brush, then dabs at the paint with a series of dry brushes until a uniform texture is achieved.

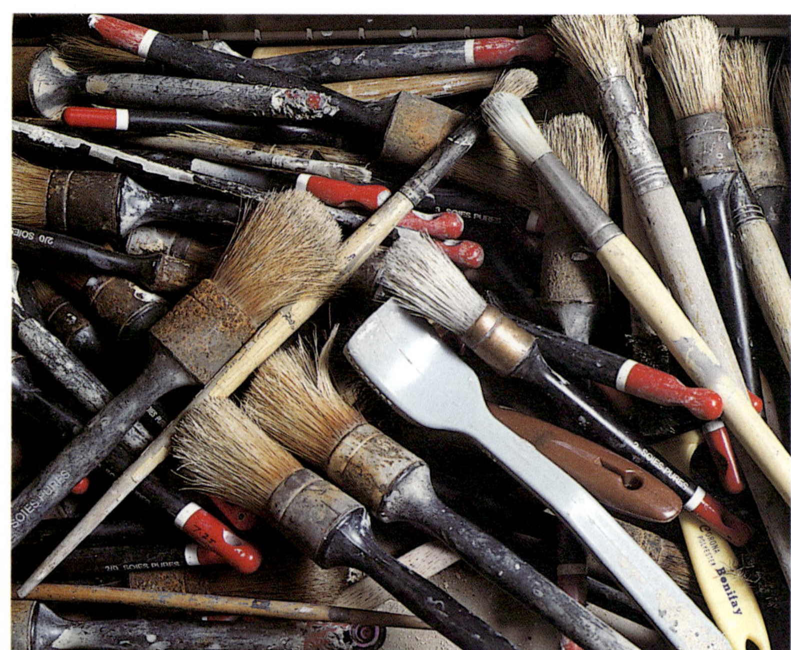

Jimmie uses a great number of brushes, especially for the stippling process, which involves putting on a thick coat of paint and then stippling it with dry brushes until it has a uniform textured appearance. This brush drawer in his studio holds a few dozen stippling brushes.

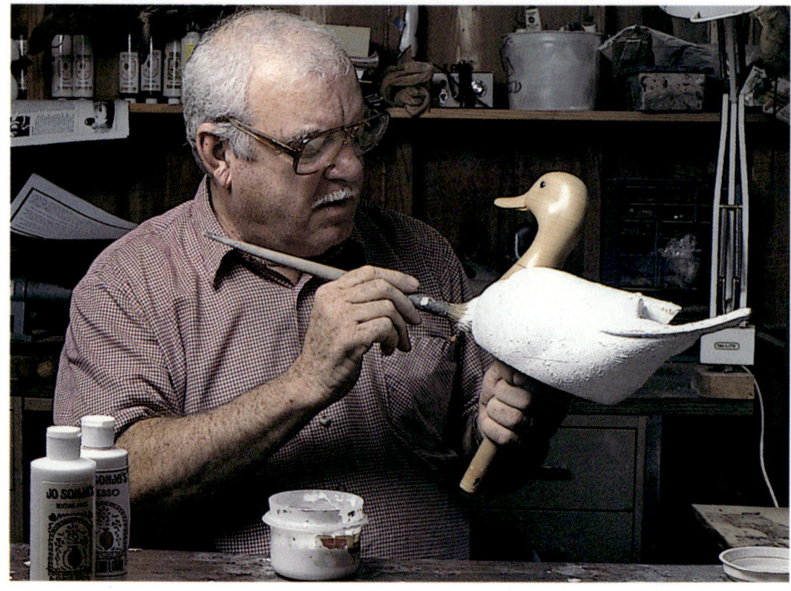

Before adding the base colors, Jimmie applies two coats of textured gesso to all of the bird except the bill. He uses Jo Sonja white gesso mixed with texture paste at about a fifty-fifty ratio. The gesso provides a uniform painting surface for the colors that will go on later.

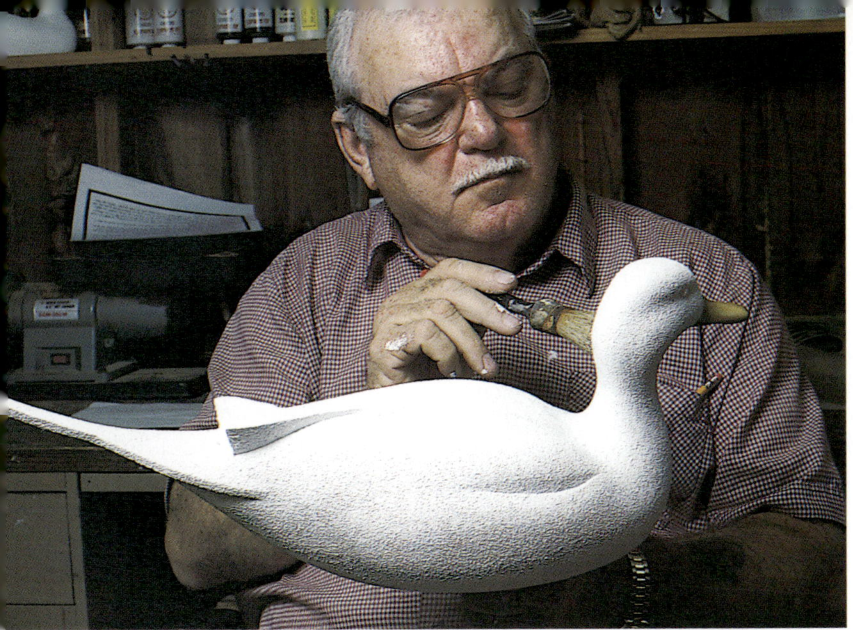

Jimmie dabs the textured gesso thickly onto the surface with a well-worn round brush. Then he uses several dry brushes to stipple it and make the surface uniform, putting them aside when they become saturated with paint.

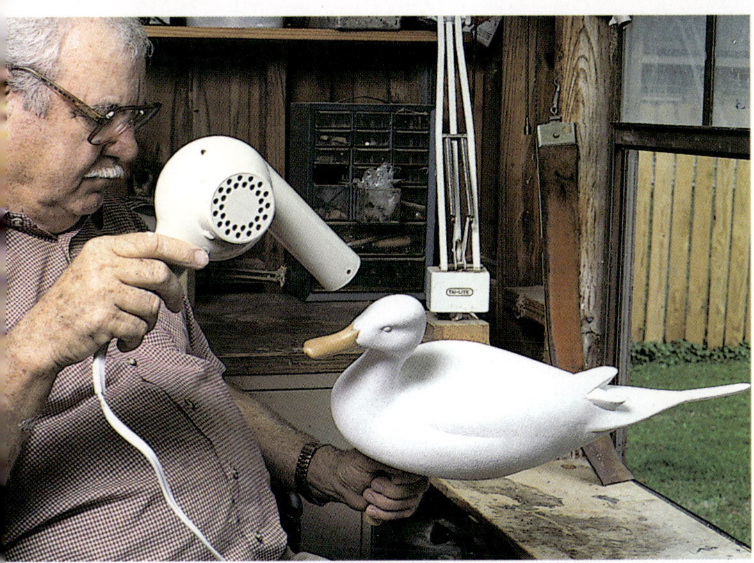

He puts on two coats of textured gesso, drying each coat with the hair dryer between applications.

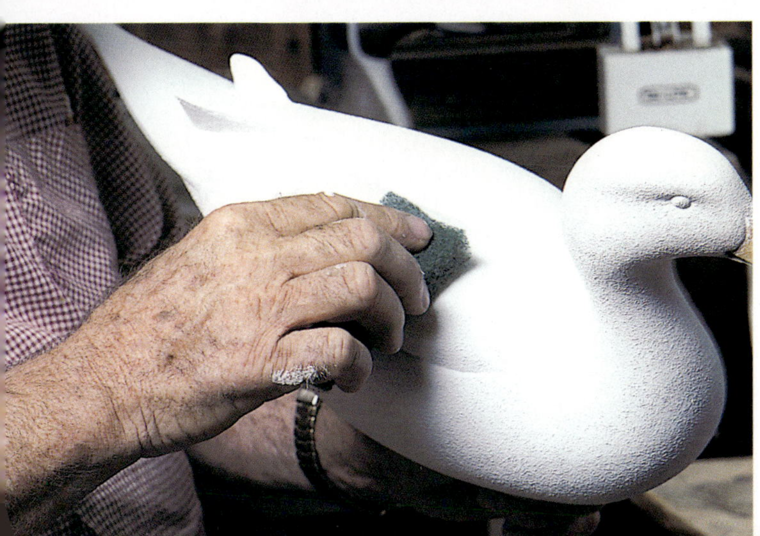

When the textured gesso has dried, Jimmie uses a pad of 3-M brand synthetic steel wool to remove the high spots and smooth the surface.

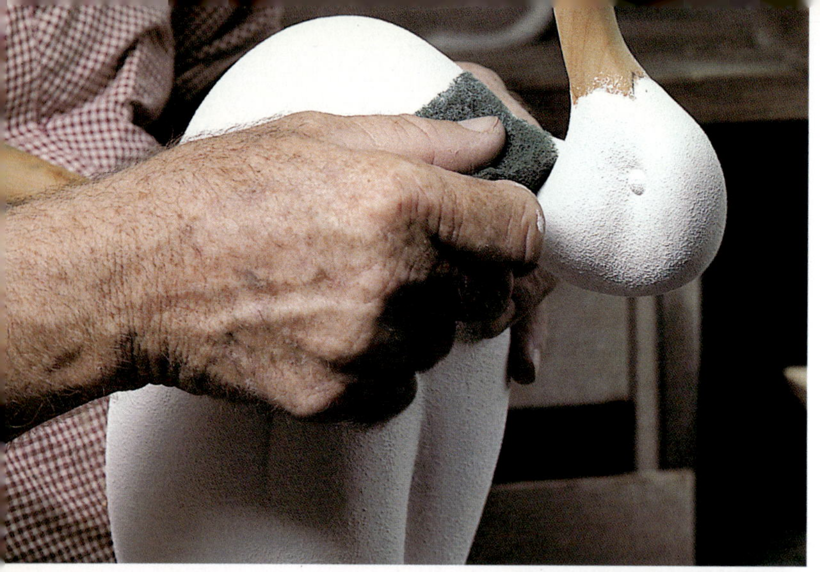

The pad is used to gingerly rub the surface of the paint. The gesso should have some texture, but the surface should not be as rough as a tennis ball.

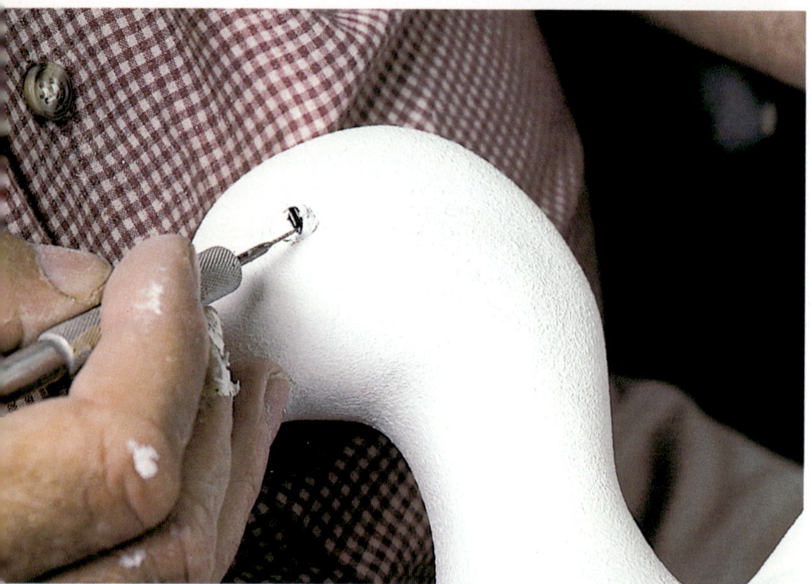

Jimmie uses a small pick to remove gesso from the glass eyes, being careful not to scratch the surface.

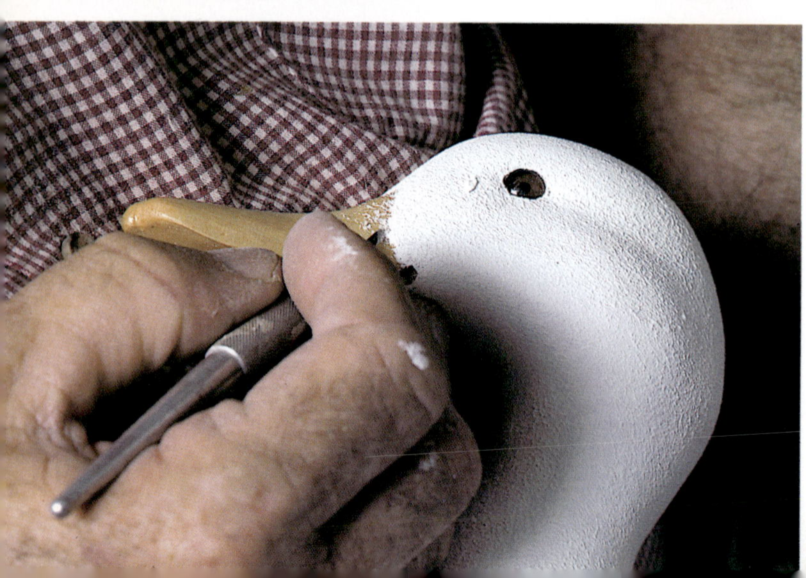

Any gesso that spilled onto the bill also is removed with the pick. While the body of the bird will have a textured finish to avoid glare, the bill will be smooth and leathery, so it's important to remove any gesso. Be careful not to scratch the surface of the sealer, or the wood will no longer be waterproof.

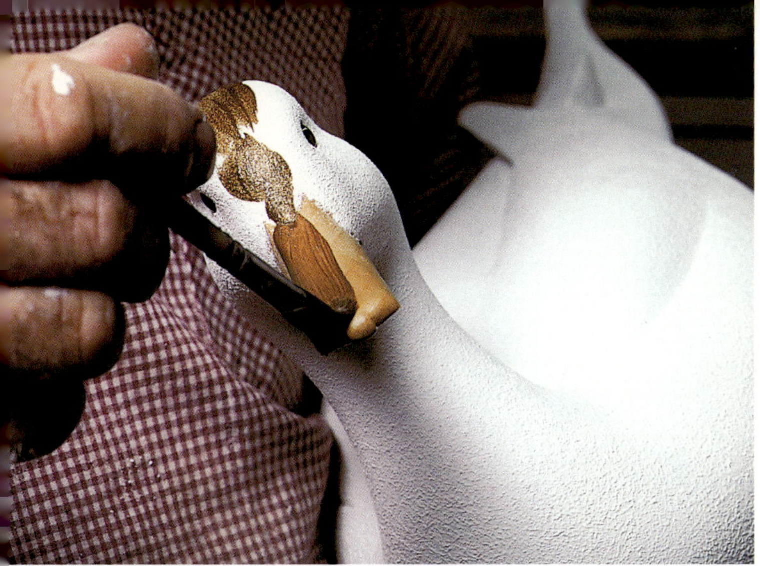

Jimmie applies a brown base coat, a mixture of raw umber and raw sienna, to the head and bill, putting on approximately three thin coats.

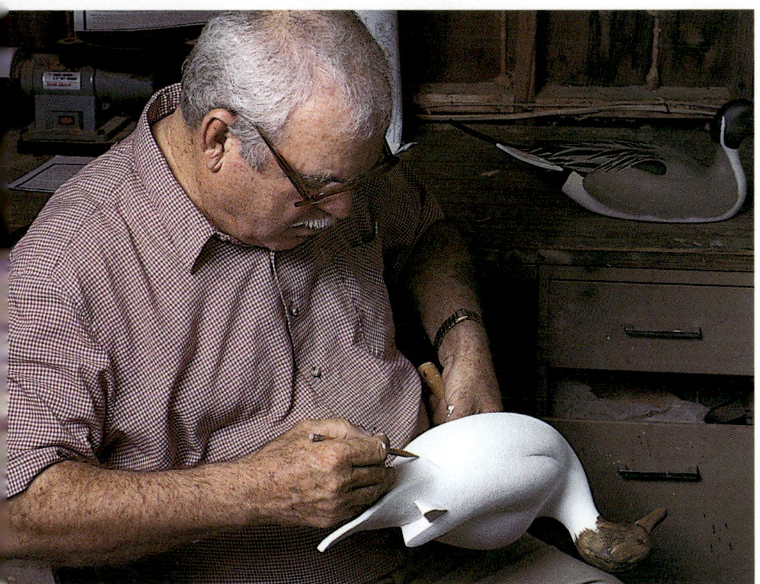

The rump will be painted black, but first Jimmie uses a pencil to outline the area to be painted. This ensures that the paint will be symmetrical on both sides of the rump. It's easier to work out the design in pencil than to try to make adjustments when painting.

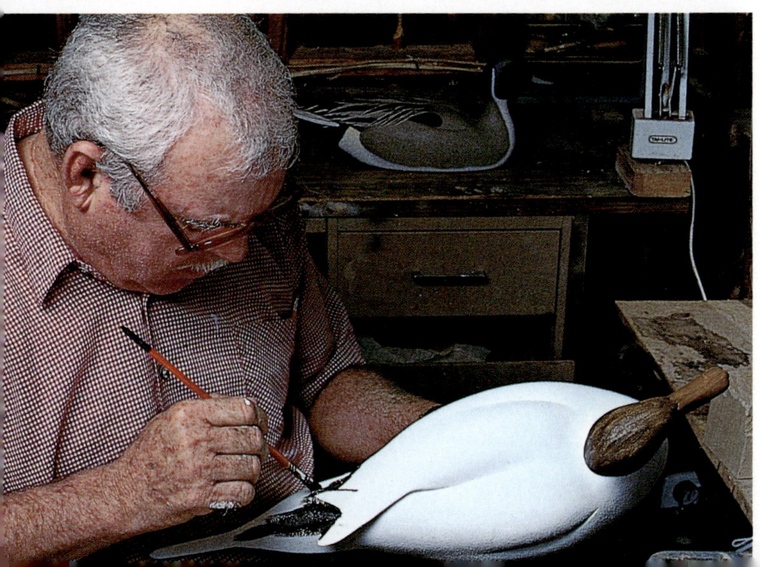

The black paint goes on the rump and on the tips of the primary feathers. The edges of the rump should be feathered a bit, as the next photo shows. Jimmie uses Jo Sonja black tinted with a small amount of phthalo blue, phthalo green, and burnt umber, with a little varnish added.

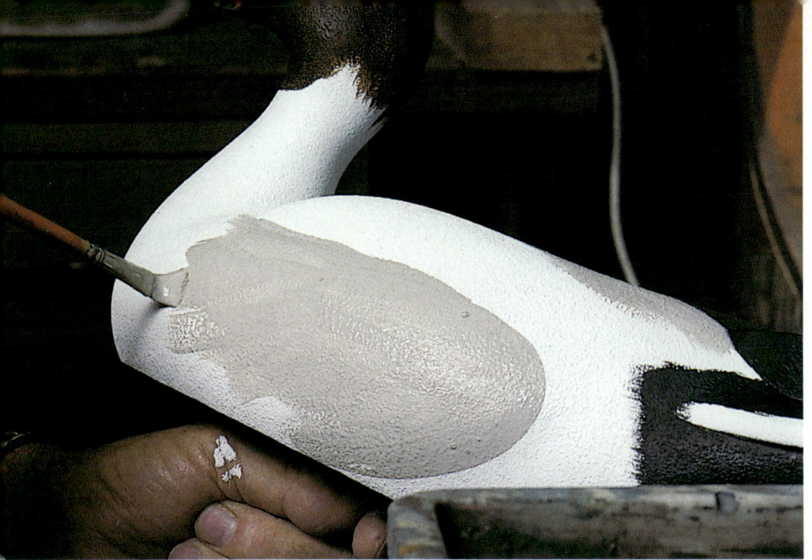

The base gray goes on the sides and back. It will serve as the background color for the vermiculation that goes on later. Note that the gray does not extend all the way to the belly of the bird, but stops in an irregular line about 1 inch from the bottom of the carving. This line will be softened later with an airbrush.

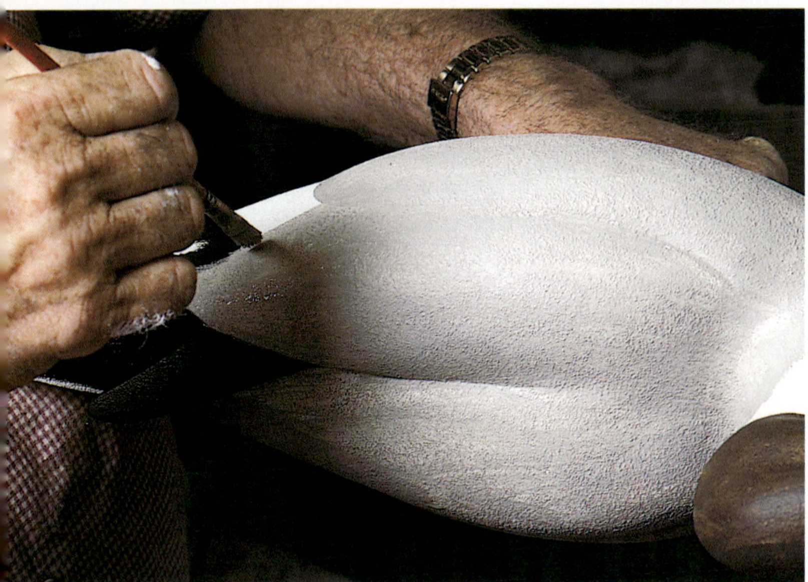

The gray base color meets the black of the rump. Your work doesn't have to be too fine at this stage, as the base colors will later be covered with feather detail and washes. This gray is smoked pearl tinted with raw umber. Because the vermiculation will darken it, the base coat should be a bit light.

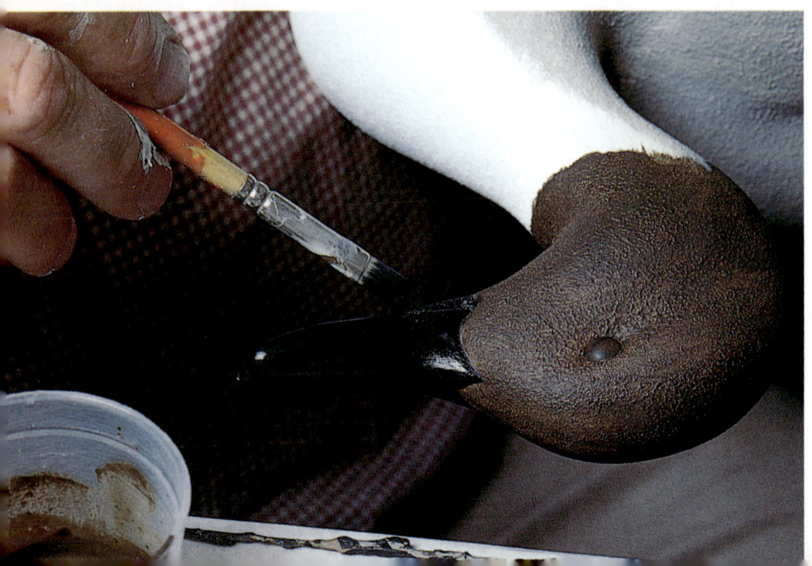

Black is applied to the bill, covering the underlying coat of brown.

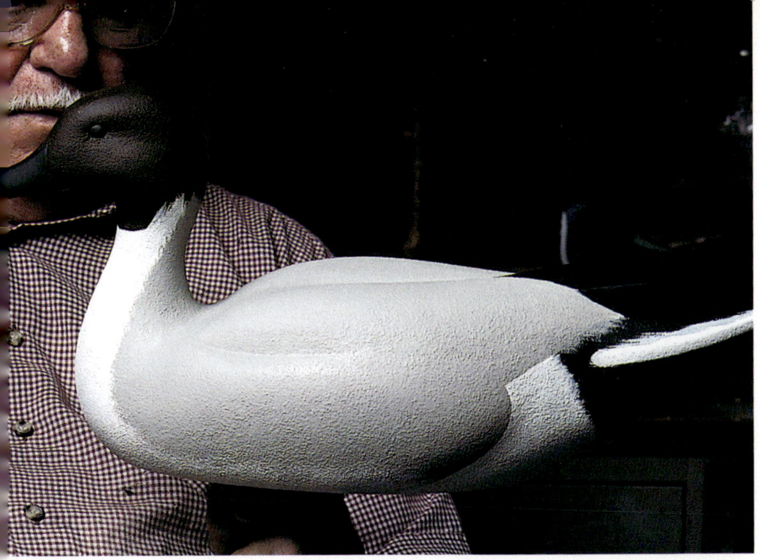

All but one of the base colors have now been applied, and Jimmie checks to make sure various areas are symmetrical on both sides.

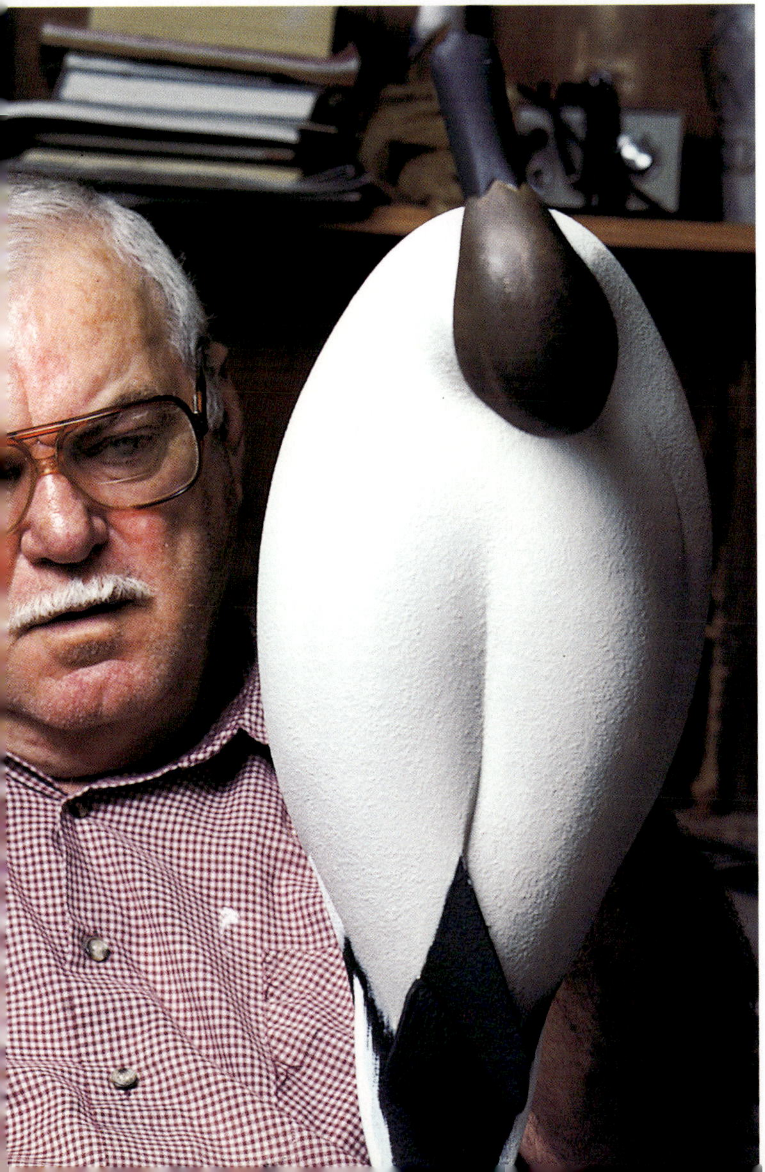

Note the pattern of base colors on the back, rump, head, and tail feathers. The base colors will provide a background for feather detail to be added in later steps. For example, irregular dark lines called vermiculation will cover much of the back and sides of the bird. The light gray base color will show through these lines. Yellow feather edges will be added to the head, and white, gray, and yellow feather detail will go on the rump and tail.

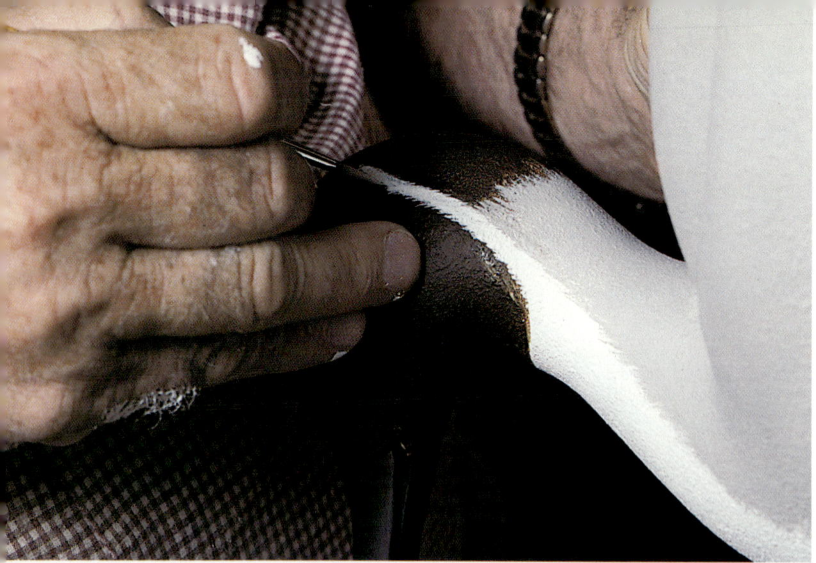

The final base color is off-white, made from titanium white toned with a bit of raw umber to produce a slightly warmer value. Here Jimmie paints the vertical stripe that extends up the sides of the head.

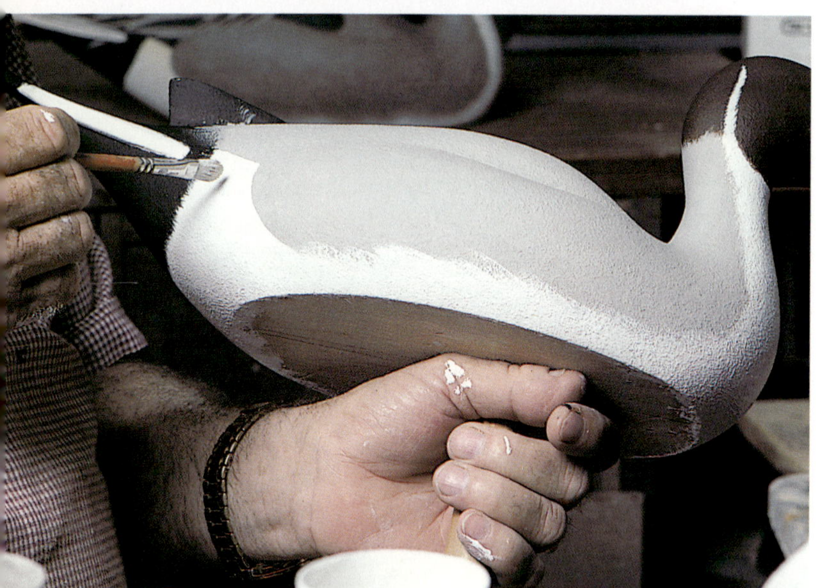

Off-white also goes on the breast, flanks, and rump of the pintail. Jimmie uses an off-white base because he will later apply feather edges of straight titanium white, which will show up nicely against the toned white.

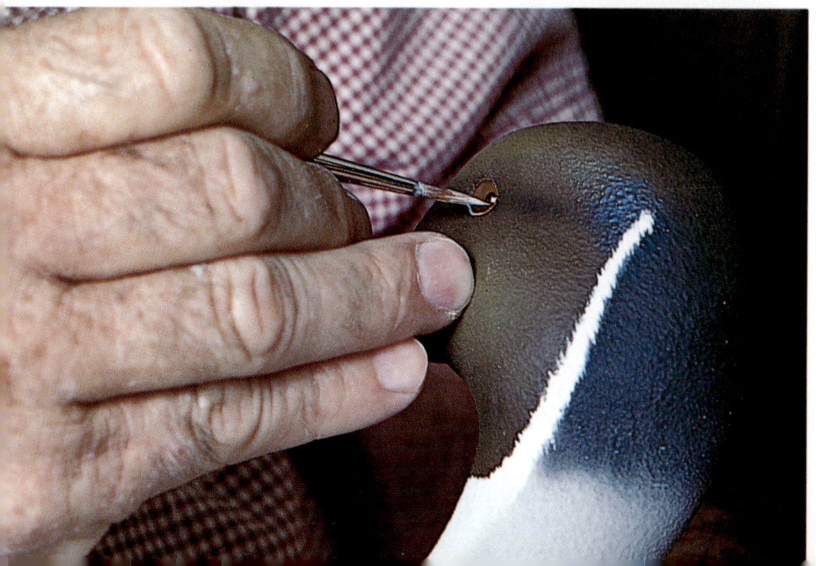

Jimmie also uses the off-white base color to paint the membrane around the eyes.

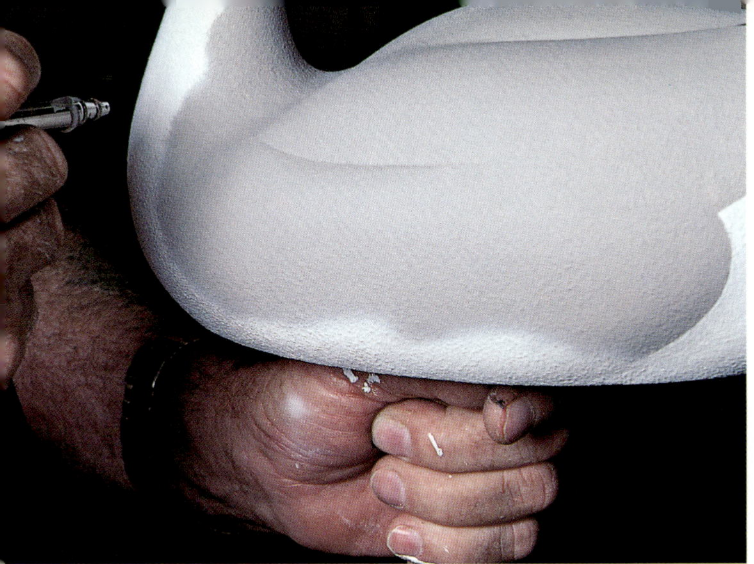

A final step in painting the base colors is to blend the edges where the colors meet. This can be done with a brush, using a paint-to-water technique to produce a soft edge, but Jimmie prefers to use the airbrush. Here he applies off-white to the edge between the breast and side.

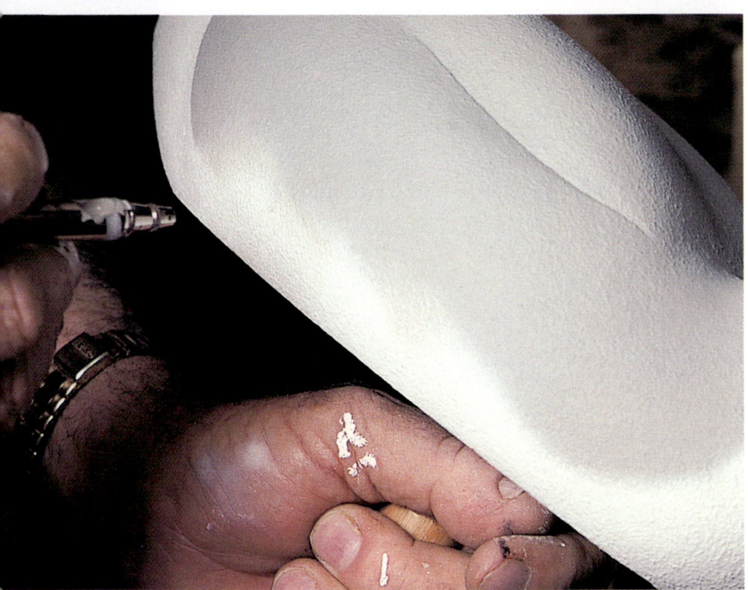

The flank area is softened by airbrushing off-white over the white gesso, extending the color into the gray somewhat to provide a soft edge.

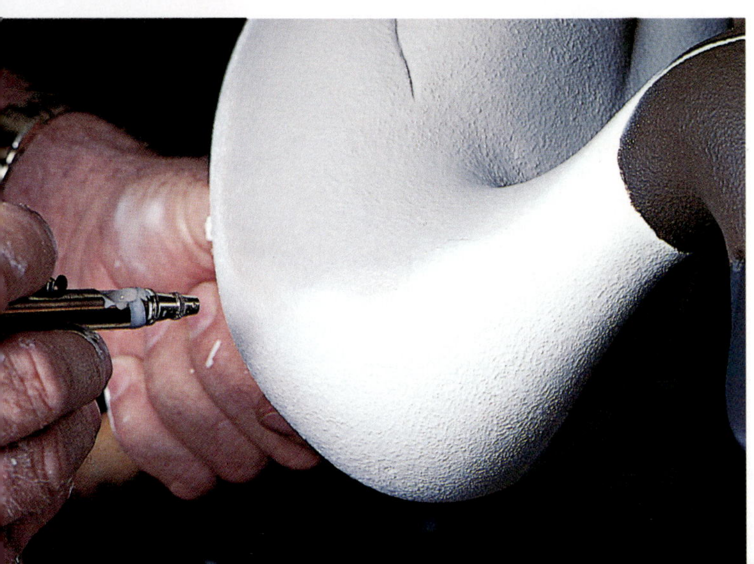

The same technique is used on the breast, creating a soft edge between the gray and white. The carving is now ready for some feathers and texture.

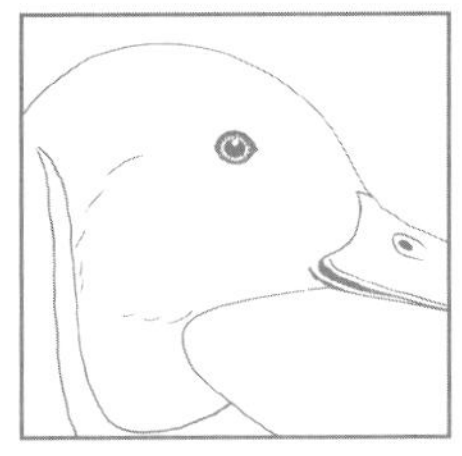

CHAPTER EIGHT

Painting Feathers and Fine Detail

On a decorative carving, feather detail is carved into the wood, but on a gunning-style bird such as this one, it is painted on. A highly detailed decorative carving, such as the green-winged teal done by Jim Sprankle for this series of carving books, has every quill and feather barb well defined. On this carving, only a few individual feathers are shown; most are merely hinted at. It's the difference between a literal interpretation of a bird and a more impressionistic one; if a gunning bird is well made—and this one certainly is—you don't have to show each feather for the viewer to know they're there.

Whether a carver chooses to make decorative birds or gunning decoys is a matter of preference. Jimmie learned to carve from a father and uncle who made gunning decoys, so this approach to the art of bird carving is a part of his life, his family tradition. He has made decorative birds, one of which was featured at the Easton Waterfowl Festival recently, but he prefers the gunning style.

The pintail drake fits nicely with the gunning-style interpretation. It is, first of all, a graceful bird, with gentle lines, a slim neck, and a long tail feather that mirrors the curve of the neck. The folded wings, painted in Jimmie's style, are strongly graphic, a mosaic of sweeping lines in black and white. Though this is considered a gunning-style bird, it obviously is not intended to go to work in a duck blind. But it does follow the tradition of detail being hinted at rather than stated outright. With Jimmie, it's an artistic decision, but for the decoy makers of a generation or two ago, it was a practical matter. Decoys had to be made quickly, and there was no reason to carve each feather. The function of a bird was to lure real ducks to shotgun range, so attitude—the way the bird floated and looked from a distance—was most important.

But gunning decoys became more detailed in the 1970s, through the use of tools such as high-speed grinders and pyrographic instruments. And with the popularity of carving competitions in North America, artists vied to see who could make the most lifelike duck. So the best gunning decoys today look roughly like the decorative birds in the 1970s.

On this pintail, Jimmie has carved the overlapping primary feathers, but the others will be painted on. Fine detail such as feather edges and splits also will be painted. Elements like these probably would not have shown up on traditional gunning decoys. So what we have is a highly detailed and realistic decoy carved and painted in the gunning decoy tradition.

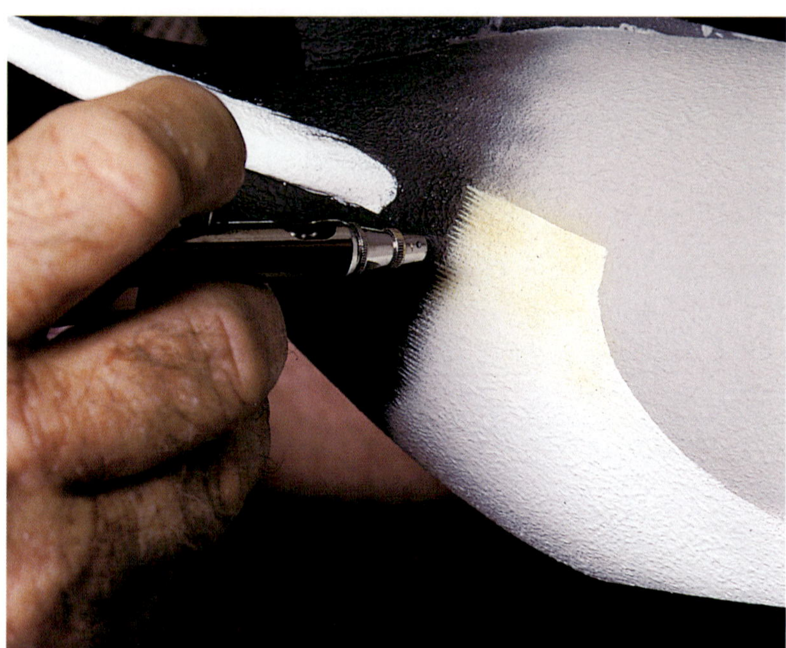

A mixture of cadmium yellow and raw sienna is airbrushed onto the flanks between the gray side-pocket color and the black rump. The yellow is applied lightly, with the outer margin blending to white.

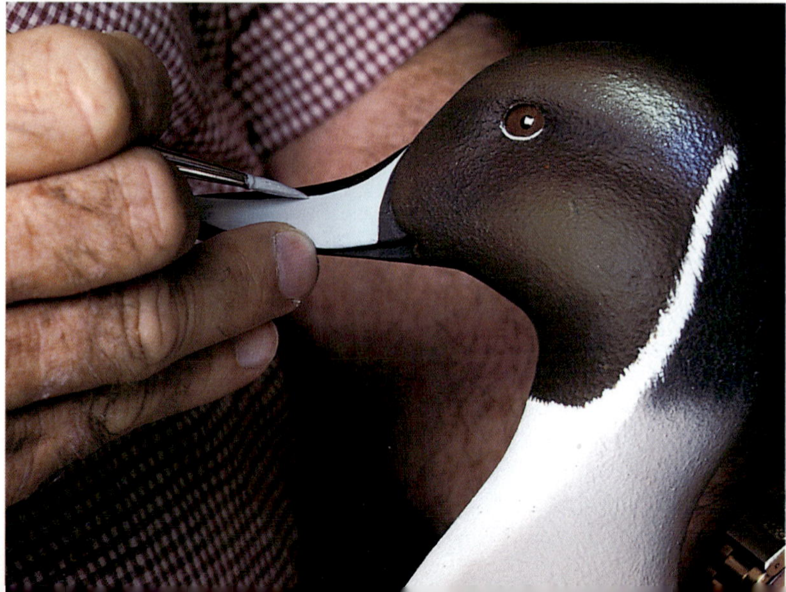

The top sides of the bill are painted light blue. Jimmie uses either cobalt blue or phthalo blue, lightening the color with smoked pearl. The blue should have a well-defined edge, and Jimmie applies the paint with a number 2 brush rather than the airbrush.

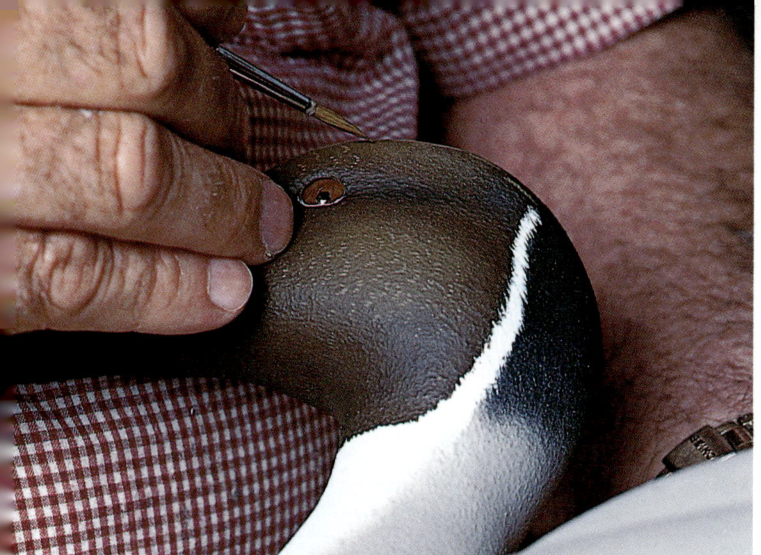

Tiny feather edges are painted on the head using the number 2 brush. Jimmie uses the yellow color earlier airbrushed onto the flank, darkened slightly with some raw umber.

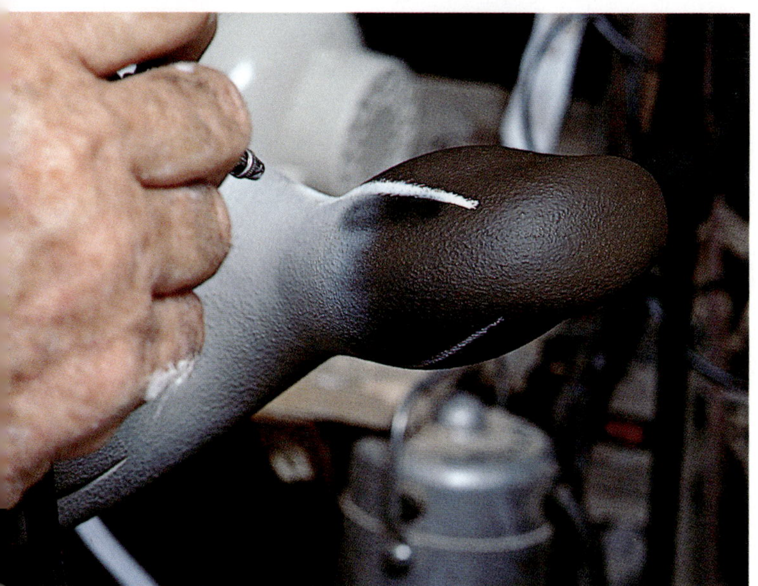

The airbrush is used to darken the back of the head with black. The crown is darkened by airbrushing with a mix of burnt umber and black. This blends into the black on the back of the head and gives the head a rounded, three-dimensional appearance.

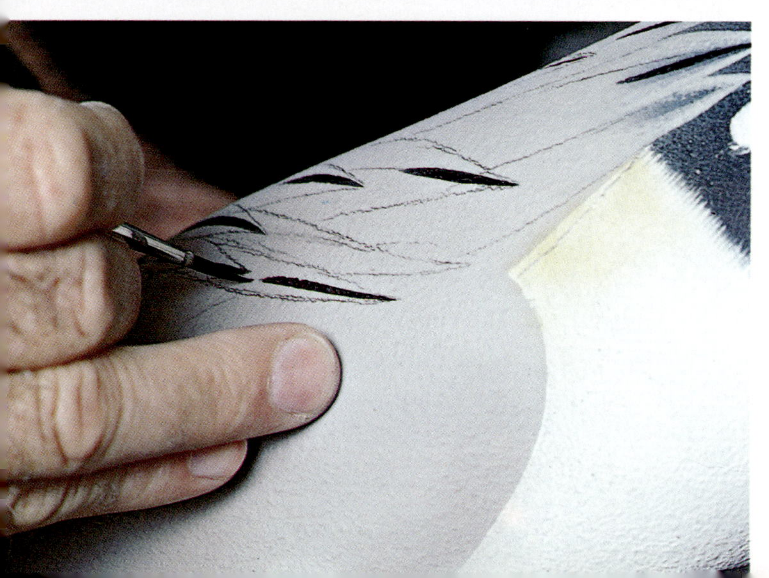

Jimmie is ready now to paint the wing feathers, but first he uses a pencil to lay them out, making sure that the sketched detail is accurate. He then uses the black mix to detail the feathers. Before painting these feathers, study your reference material carefully, paying particular attention to how the scapular feathers cascade down the sides and across the flanks of the bird.

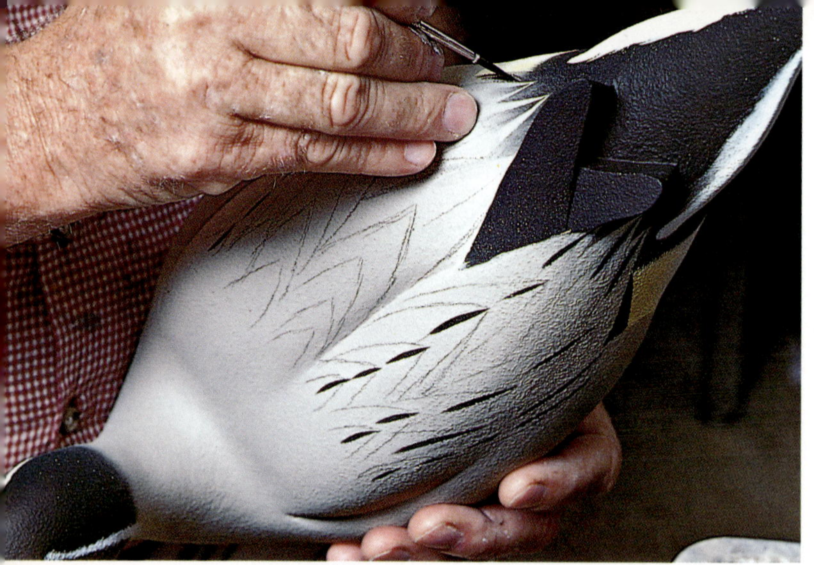

This shows the sketched diagram Jimmie uses when laying out the wing feathers. The black is Jimmie's standard mix of Jo Sonja black toned with phthalo green, phthalo blue, burnt umber, and a small amount of varnish.

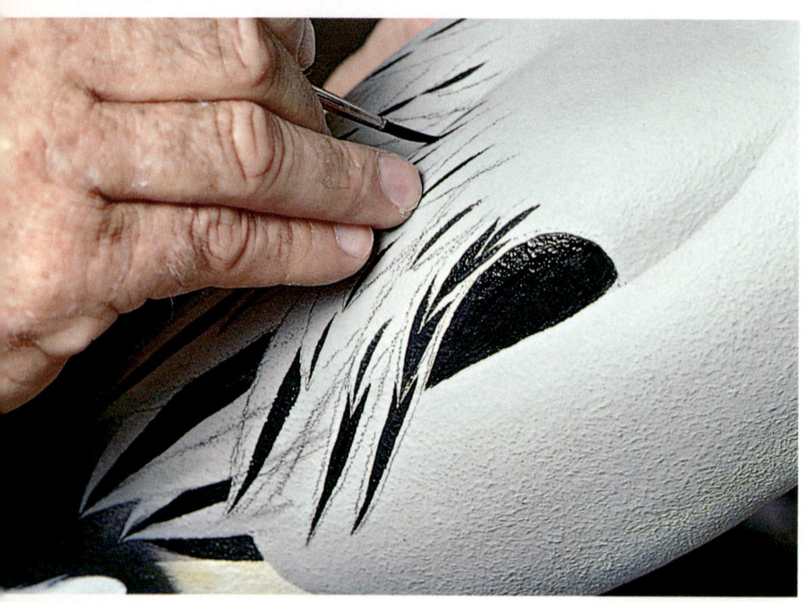

The flowing scapular feathers are shown clearly here, providing a good look at the relationship between carving and painting. When carving the sidepockets, Jimmie left the area where the feathers drape down smooth. If he had continued the ledge all the way back, the long, cascading scapular feathers would have had a very unrealistic bend in them.

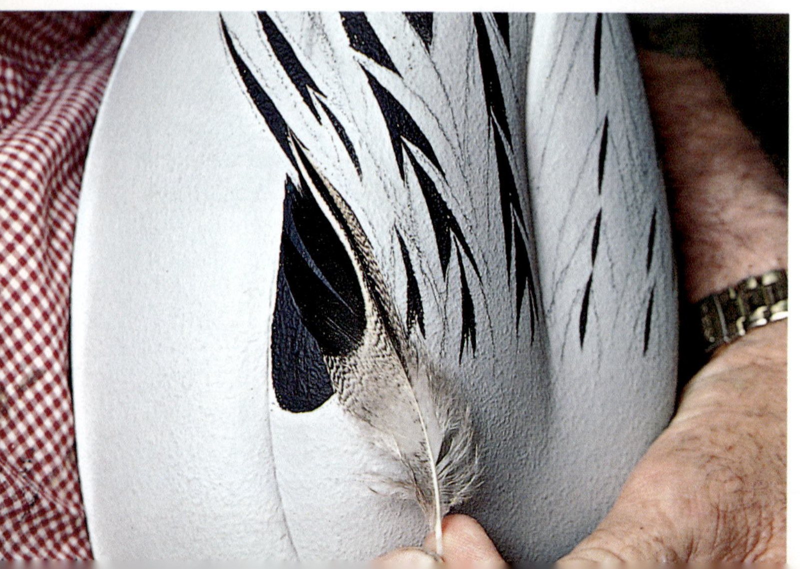

The best way to learn feather detail is to study the real thing. Here Jimmie compares the painted detail on the right wing with a real pintail feather.

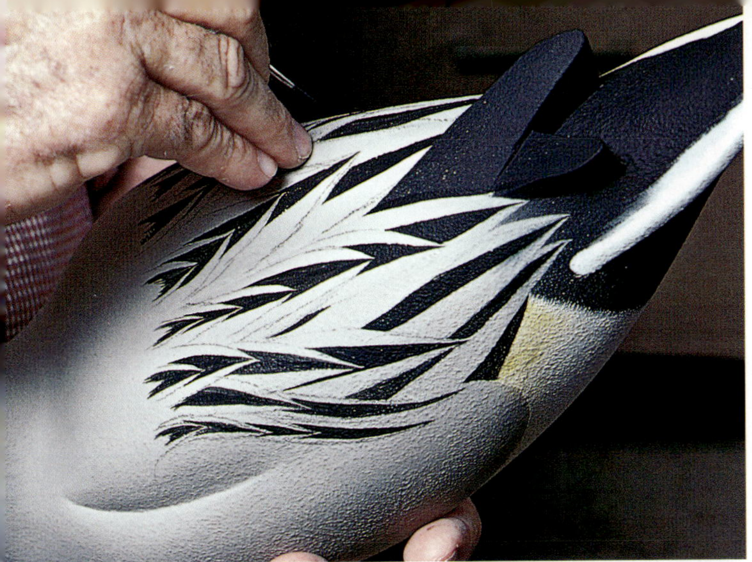

Jimmie paints the center portions of the flight feathers black, using a bird he bagged last hunting season as reference. The black feather marks of the pintail are very graphic and have a great deal to do with the visual attractiveness of the bird.

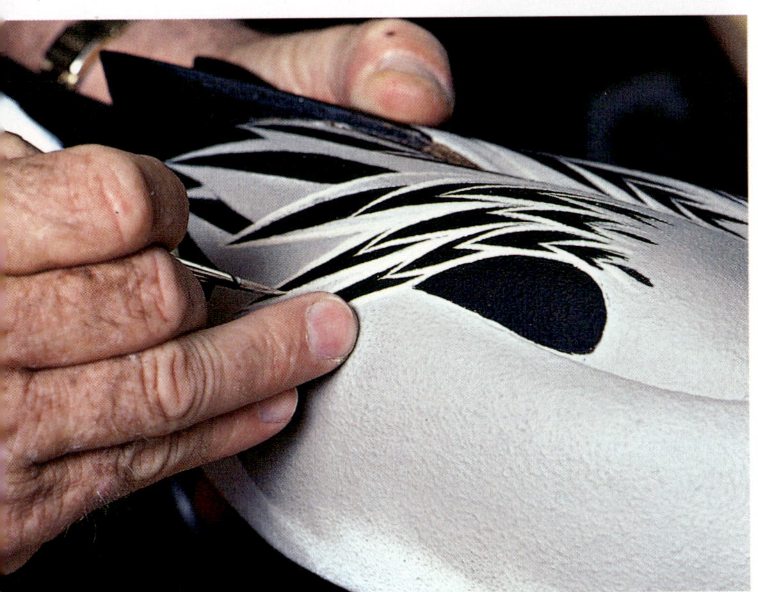

The outside edges of the feathers are a cream color. Jimmie uses a combination of smoked pearl, raw sienna, and a small amount of raw umber to create this color. He does not mix colors by formula, but rather experiments with colors on his palette until they look right.

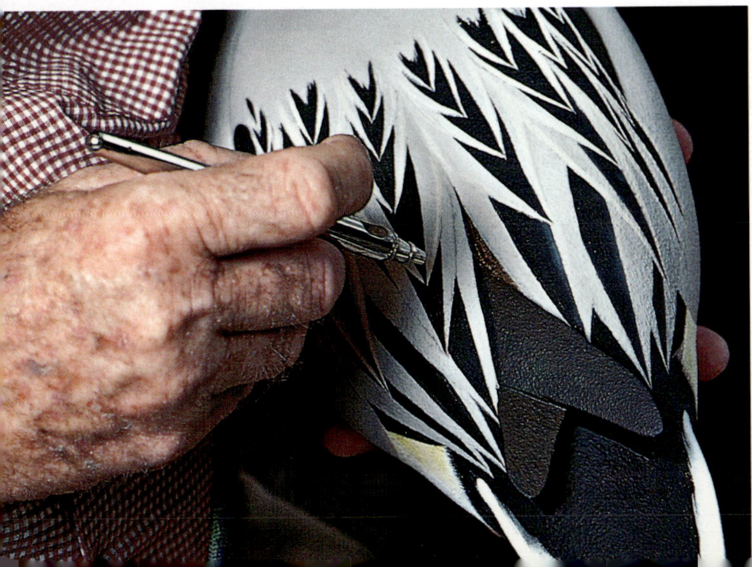

The airbrush can be used in this procedure; Jimmie uses it to soften the edges of the black feathers.

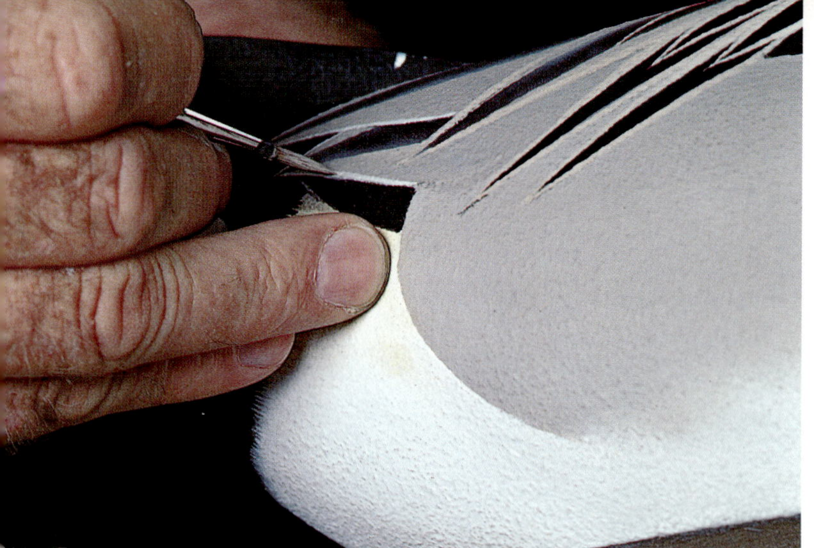

A light gray, the basic smoked pearl, raw sienna, and raw umber mix, is used to define the feather margins where the flight feathers lie over the rump.

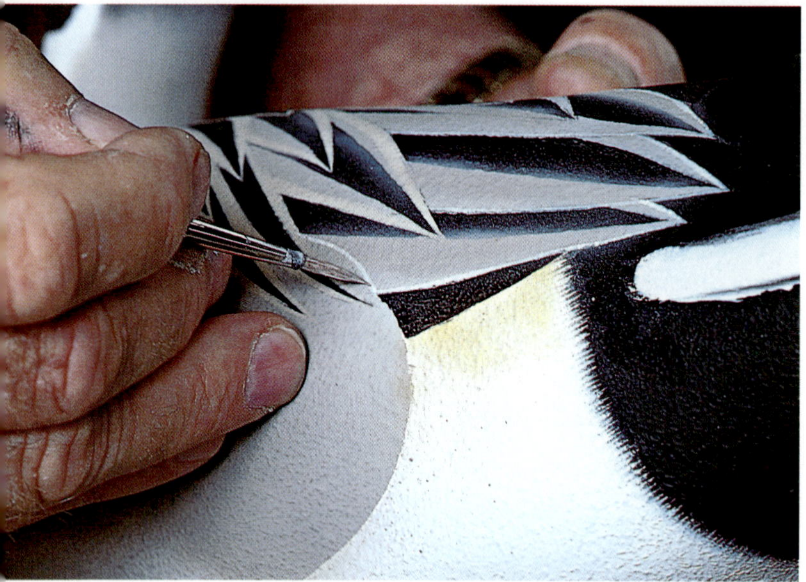

These gray lines create the impression of individual secondary feathers. Because the feathers are not individually carved, painted detail such as this is important in creating the illusion of realism.

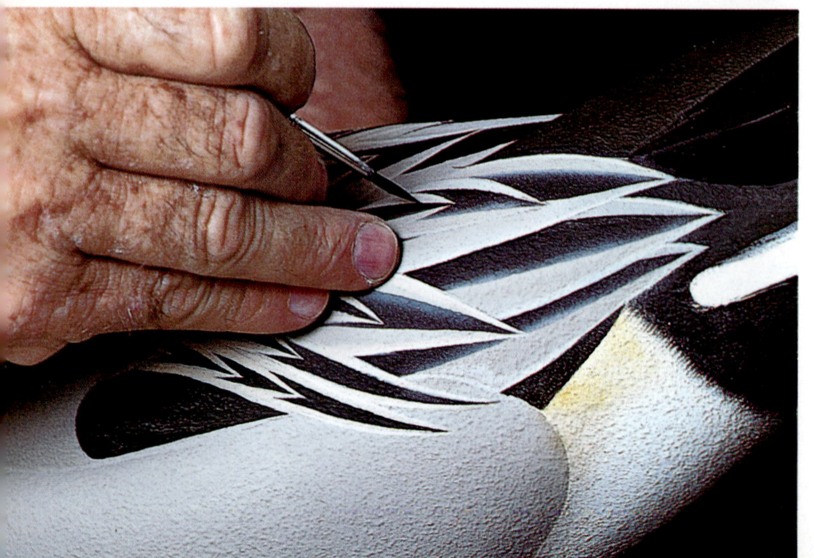

The center portions of the feathers are darkened by adding a bit of black.

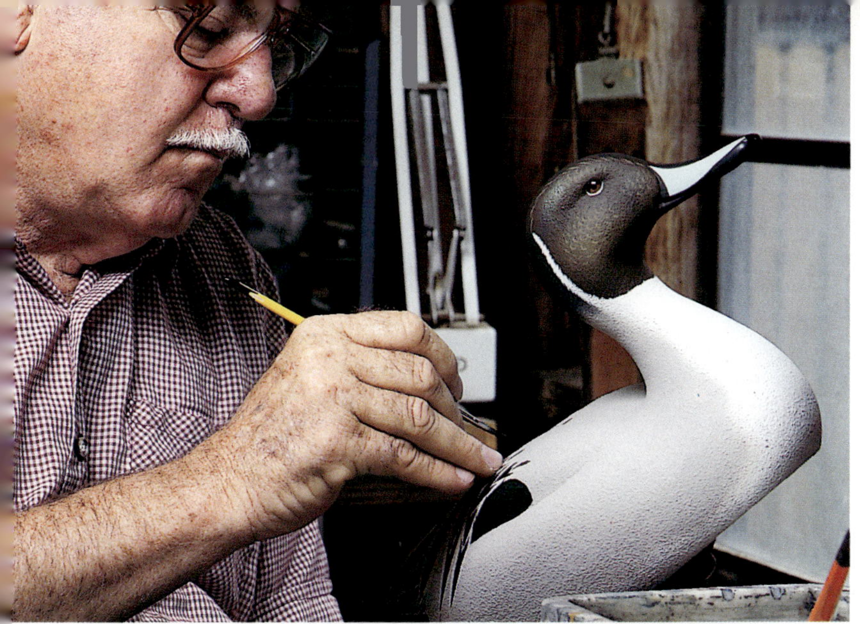

Jimmie uses a number 2 Raphael brush for painting fine detail such as this. He uses one or two fingers as an anchor, keeping his hand steady while only the fingers holding the brush move.

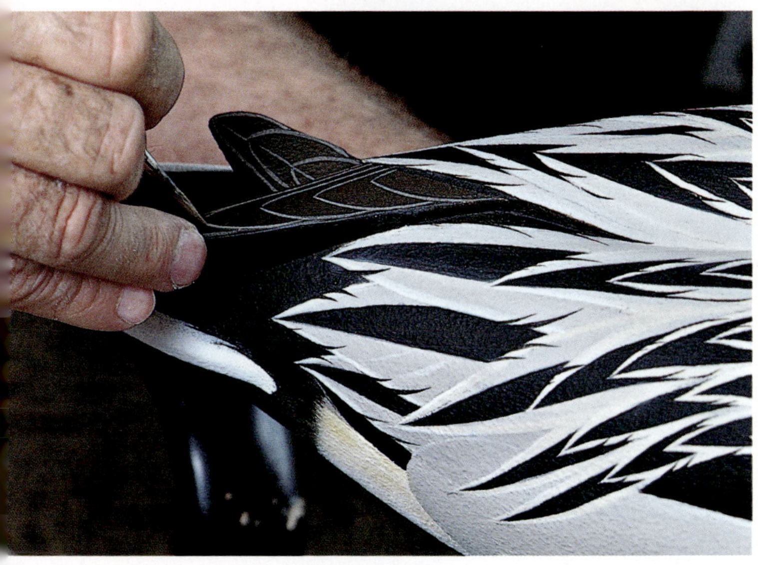

The gray mix is used to outline feathers on the black tips of the primary feathers where they cross over the rump.

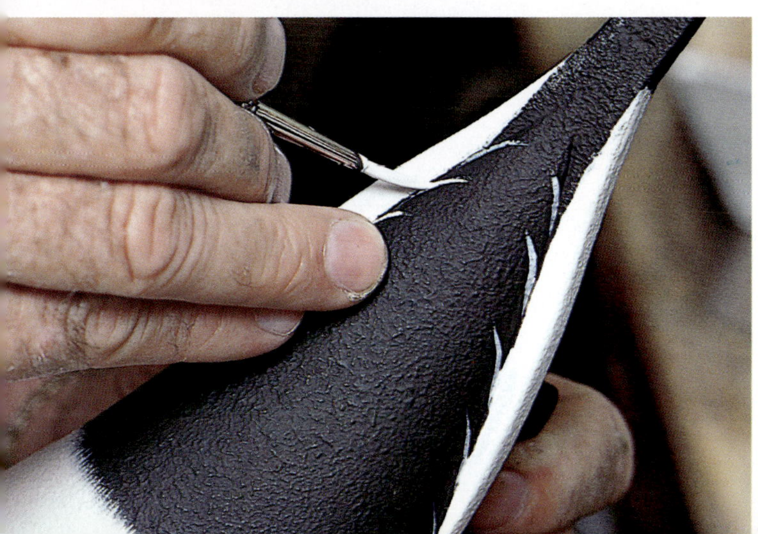

White edges are added to the black tail feathers.

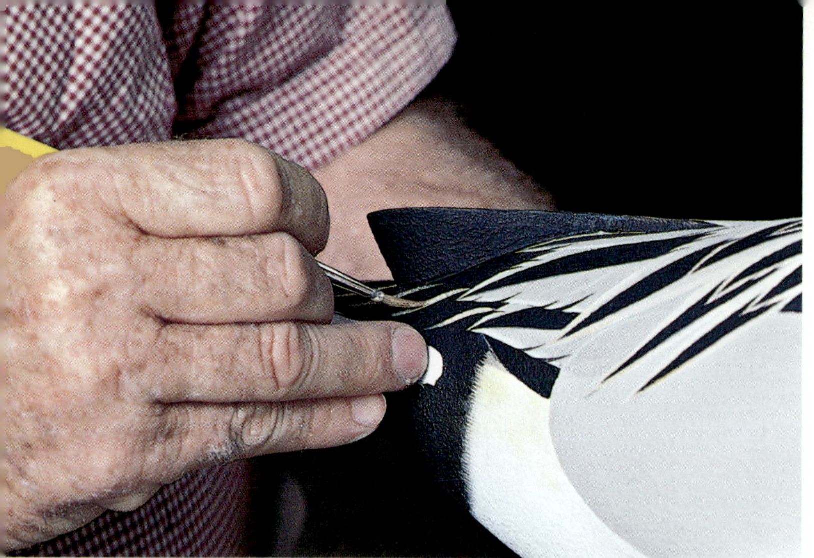

Jimmie creates feather edges on the tail with the yellow mix used earlier on the flanks.

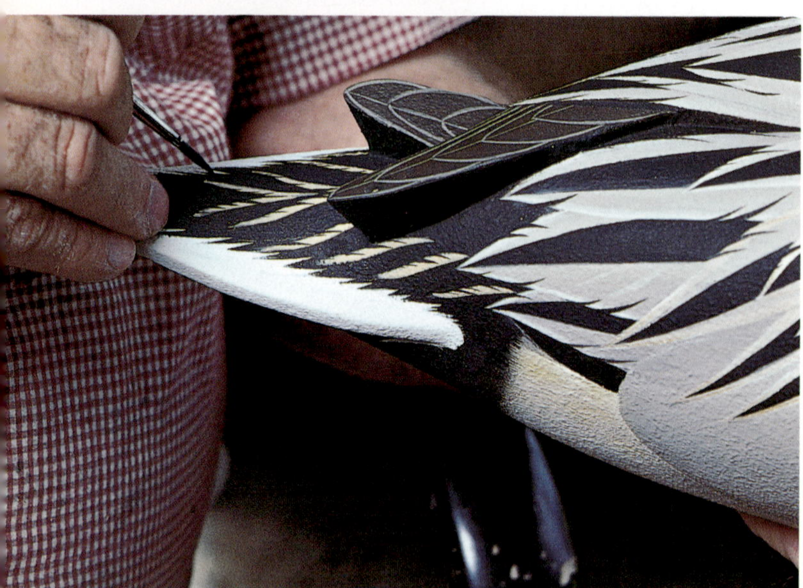

Once the yellow feather edges have dried, Jimmie uses the number 2 brush with black paint to add a few splits in the feathers.

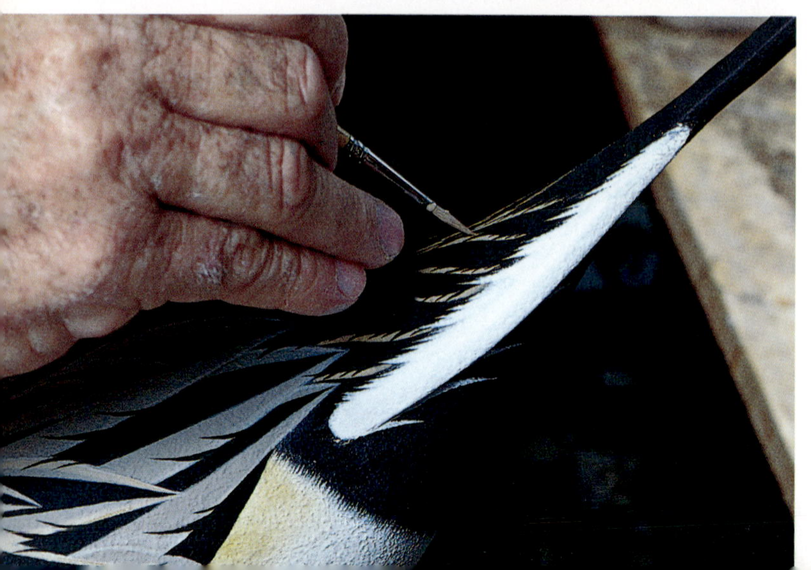

Breaking up these lines adds visual interest to the design of the bird, and they also provide a bit of realism.

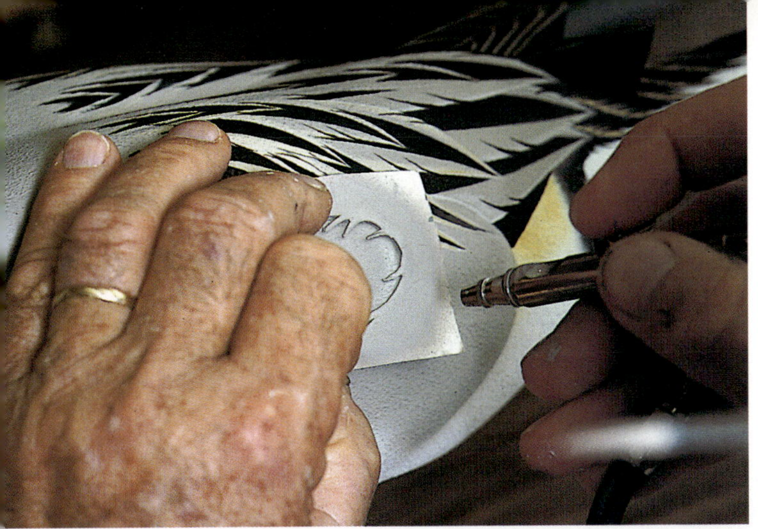

Jimmie will paint vermiculated lines on the sides and back of the pintail, but before he begins, he will add some gray feather edges on the sidepockets. To do so, he uses a paper template cut out in the shape of a feather, and he sprays on a darker version of the gray base color, deepened in value with phthalo blue and raw umber.

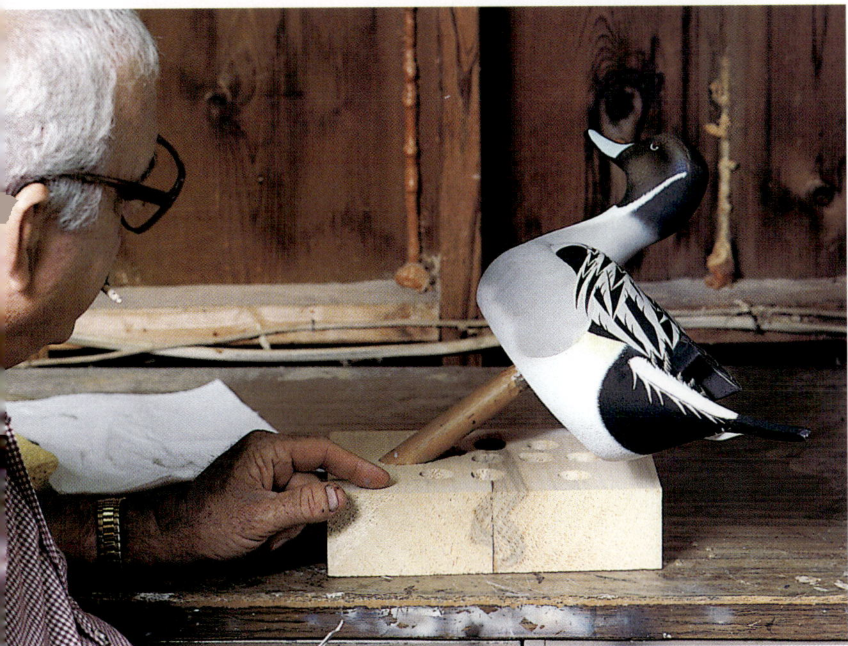

Jimmie checks the look of the sidepockets. The effect should be very subtle; when covered with vermiculation, the feather edges will be just barely visible but will add some depth to the sides. Jimmie's mounting system supports the carving at various angles while he paints it.

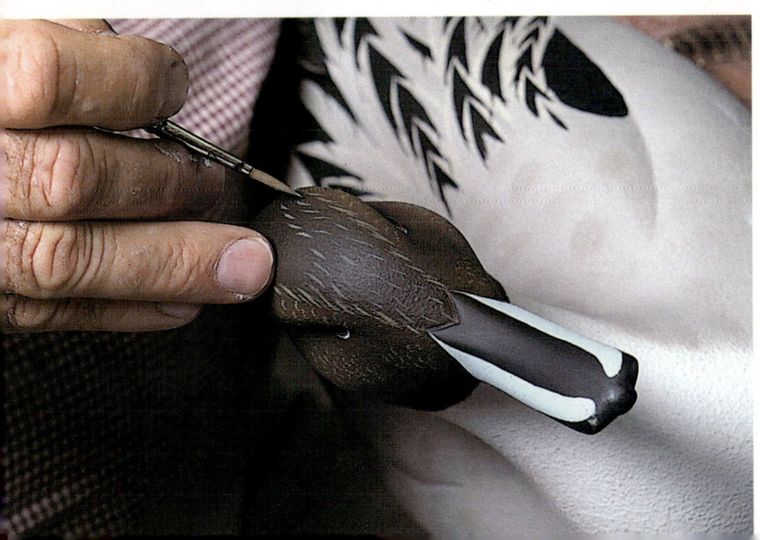

The crown of the pintail gets a few feather edges too. These are painted with the number 2 brush loaded with the gray-blue mix used for the feather edges on the sides.

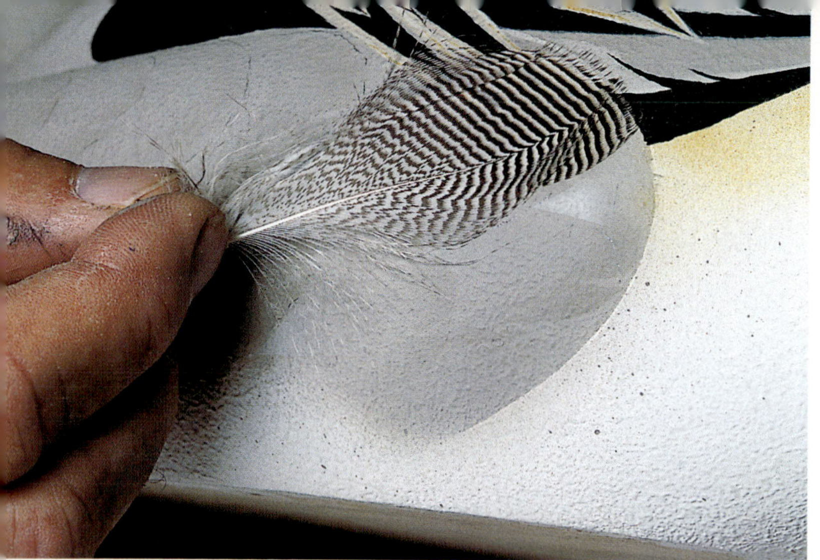

From a distance, the vermiculation appears to be a series of random, connected lines. But a close look at this pintail feather indicates that the lines actually are made of a series of very short, vertical lines placed close together. That's the effect Jimmie will attempt to give his carving.

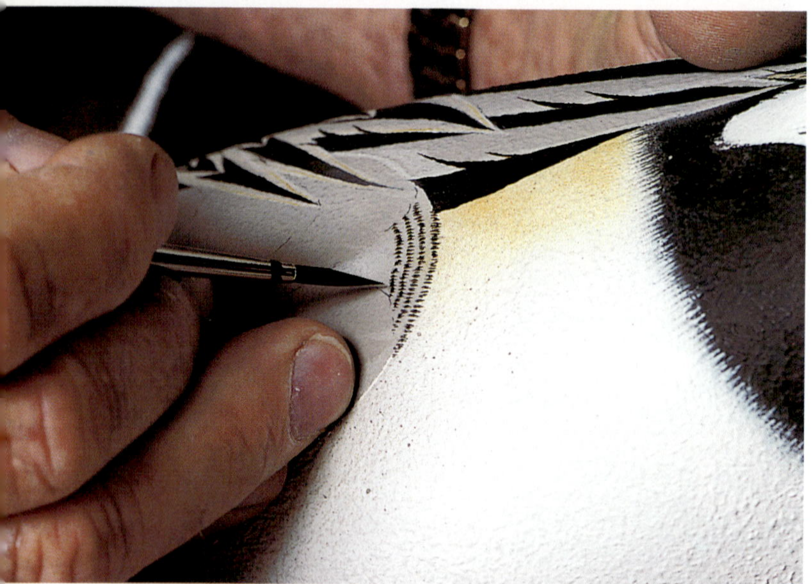

He begins at the rear of the left sidepocket, painting the lines with a number 2 brush loaded with the same black used earlier.

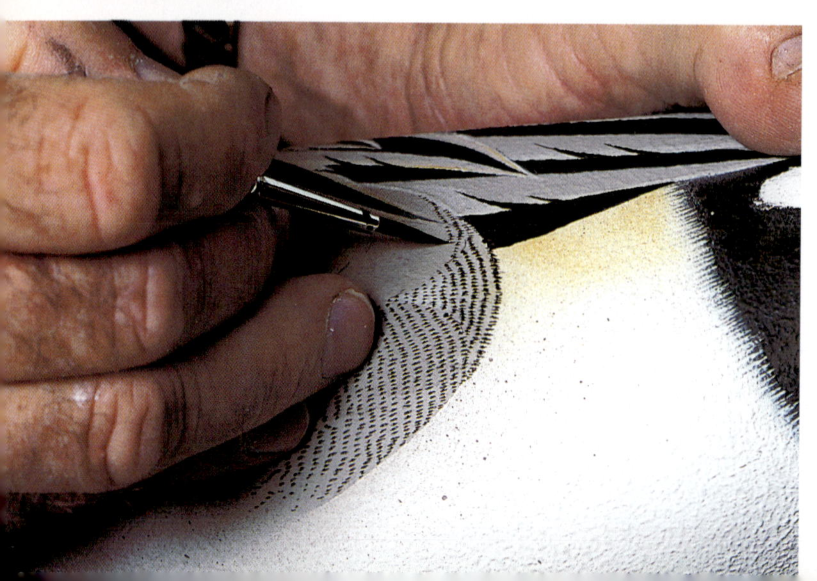

Work progresses from back to front. Jimmie likes to use an old number 2 brush whose point has become somewhat rounded rather than sharp. Vermiculation is a time-consuming process, but it's an important one.

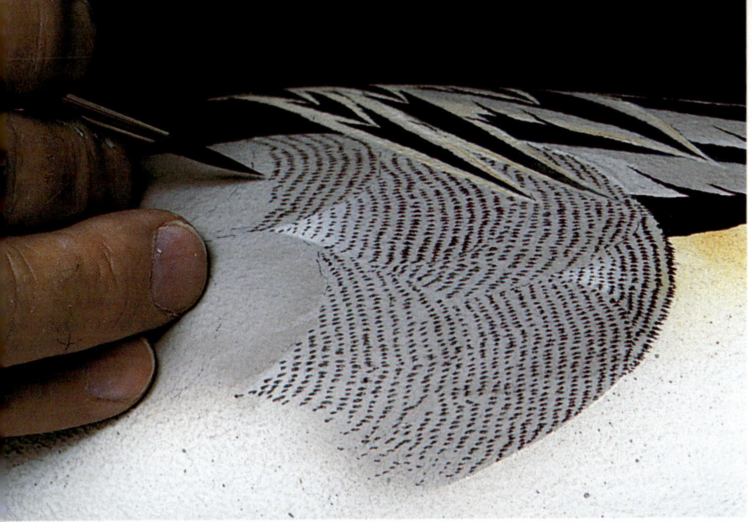

"Vermiculating is a matter of building up rhythm," says Jimmie. "It's like golf. Your first few swings should be practice swings. I begin working at a slow pace and pick up speed as I go along."

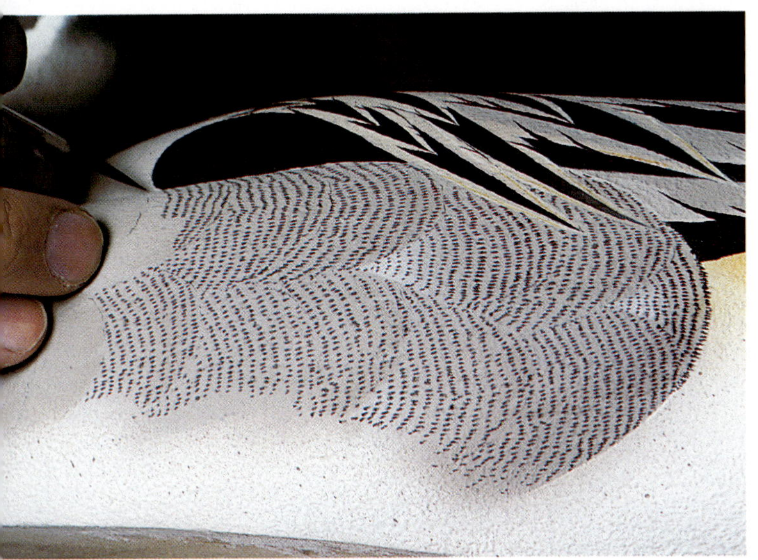

Jimmie paints a series of elongated dots that make up an obvious line. After vermiculating the sides and back, Jimmie will use a wash of very thin black paint to darken the area. Note that the vermiculation does not extend into the white of the belly; Jimmie will later blend the edge where these two areas meet.

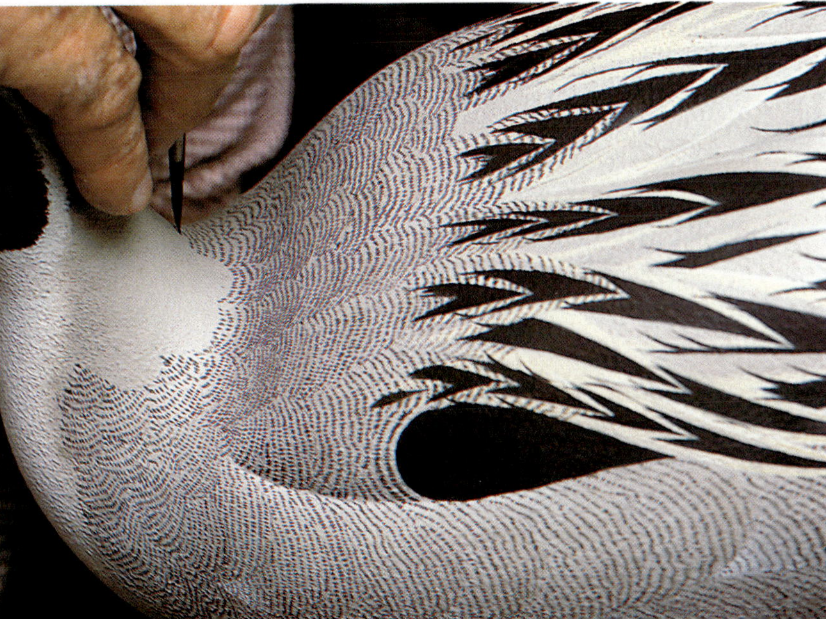

The vermiculation extends along the sides, over the back, and up the neck.

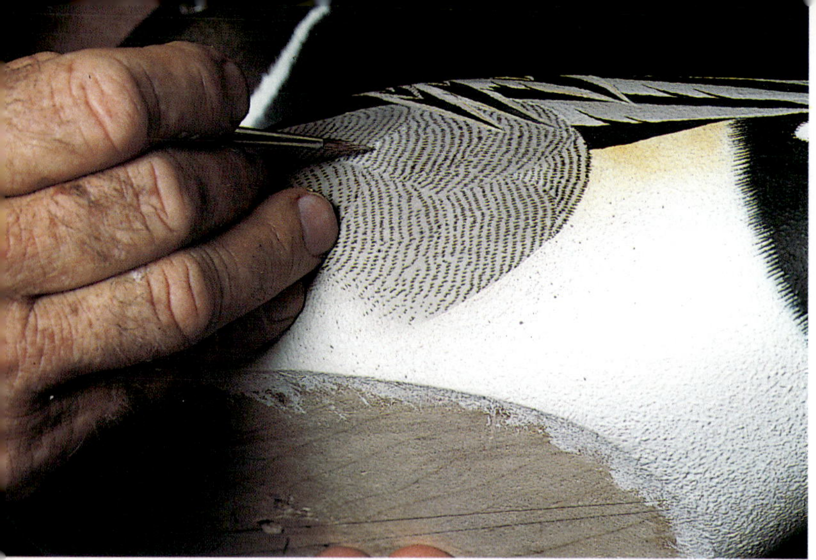

Some feather folds are created on the sides by lightening a few selected feathers. This creates highlights, areas where it appears that the outer feathers have parted, exposing the lighter ones below.

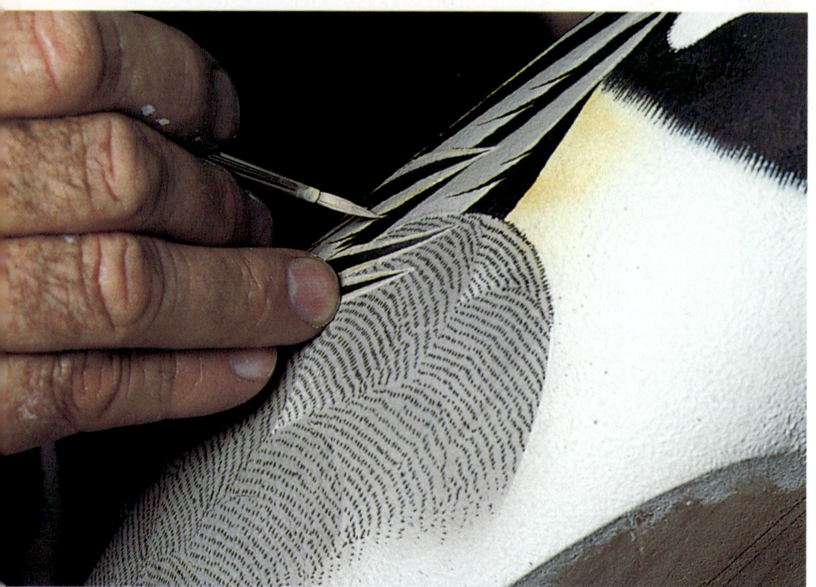

Two folds are visible in the rear of the left sidepocket. Jimmie uses the white paint to add a few splits to the black parts of the scapular feathers.

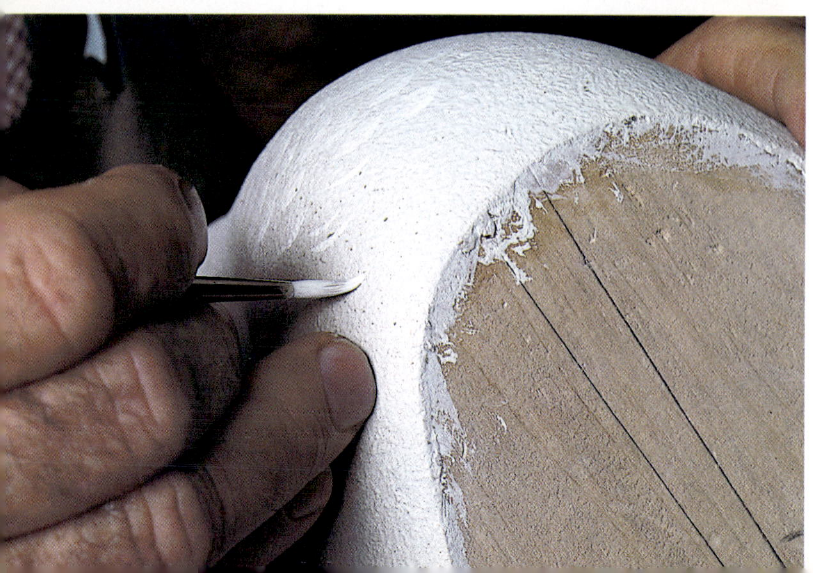

Feather edges are painted on the breast and belly using a white-on-white technique. The base color of titanium white was tinted with raw umber to produce a slightly warm off-white. Thus, the feather edges of straight white added now will show up. This process adds to the illusion of depth and softness.

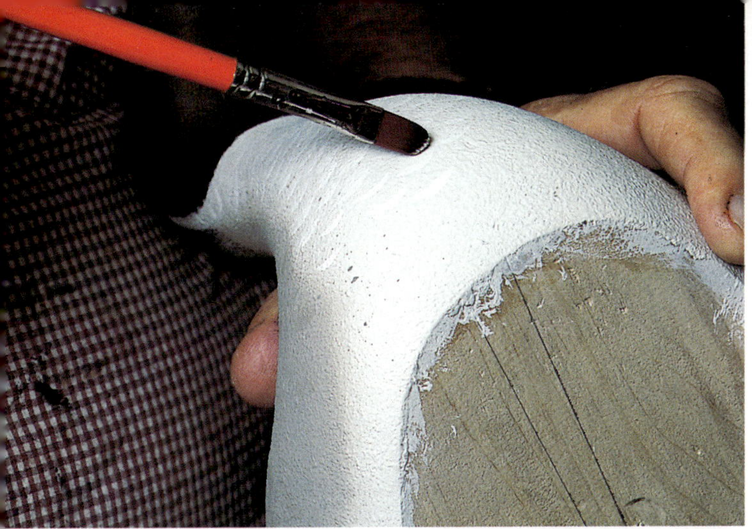

Jimmie paints the feather edges with a number 2 brush, then uses a number 8 brush with a curved tip to pull the paint back somewhat, softening the inside while leaving the outside edge well defined.

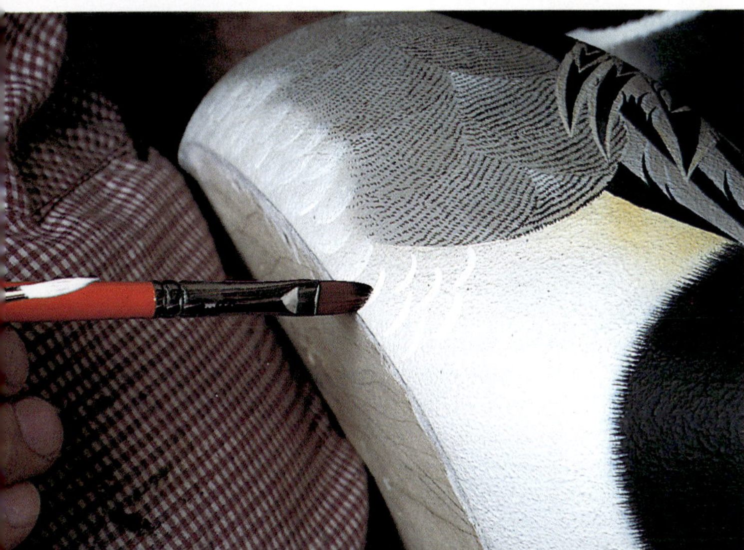

Jimmie uses the larger brush to spread the white paint slightly. He leaves the outside edge of the feather as it is, touching the white paint on the inside portion only. The idea is to create the illusion of a soft inner edge.

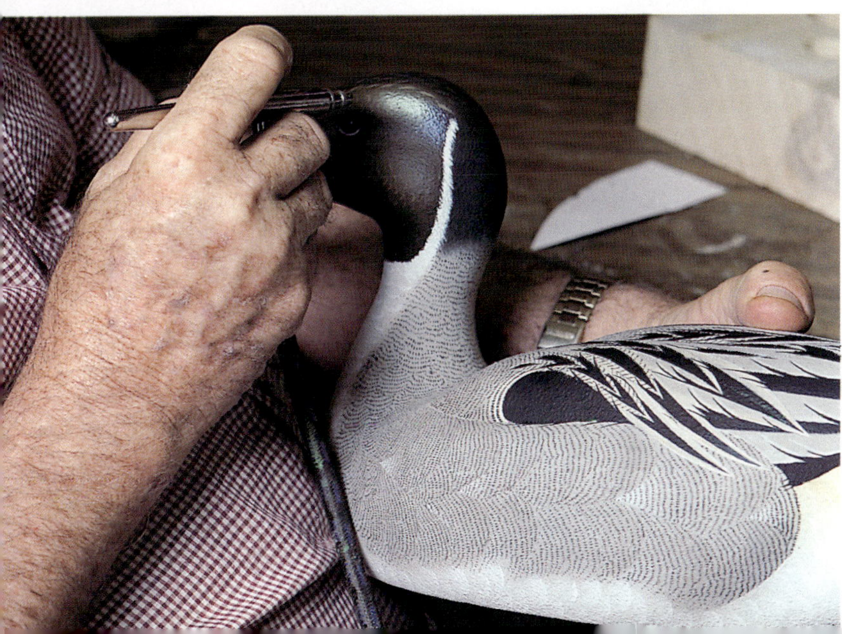

The crown of the pintail's head is given a little color with the airbrush by applying successive thin washes of iridescent blue and iridescent green. A little green also goes on the rump and the tertial feathers.

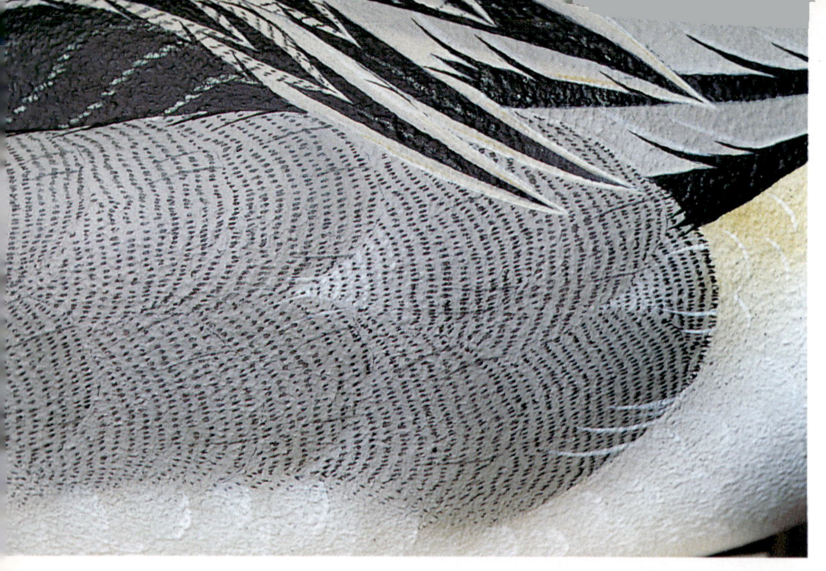

A thin wash of black has darkened the sidepockets somewhat. Note the manner in which Jimmie ended the vermiculation where it meets the belly, increasing the distance between the black lines and making them smaller. This, in effect, blends the vermiculated area into the white of the belly.

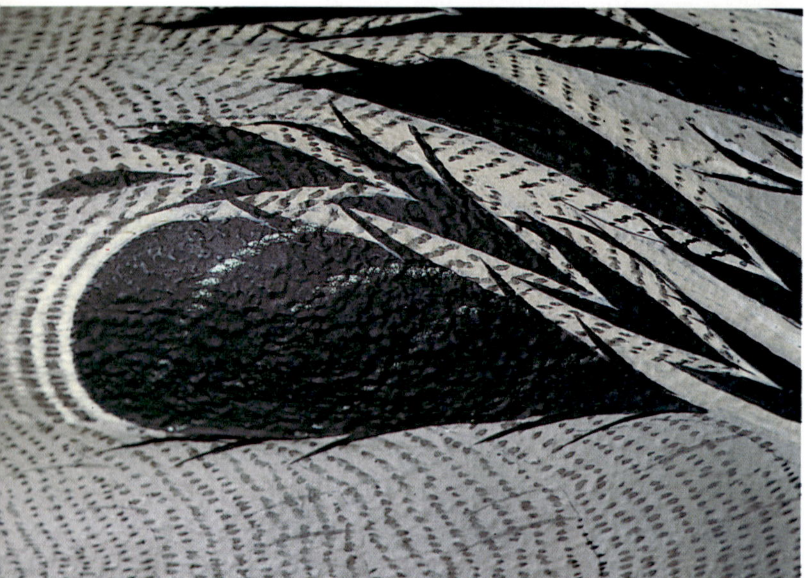

This close-up shows the scapular feathers as they drape down over the sidepockets. Jimmie has put some iridescent green feather edges on the large black area of the tertial feather.

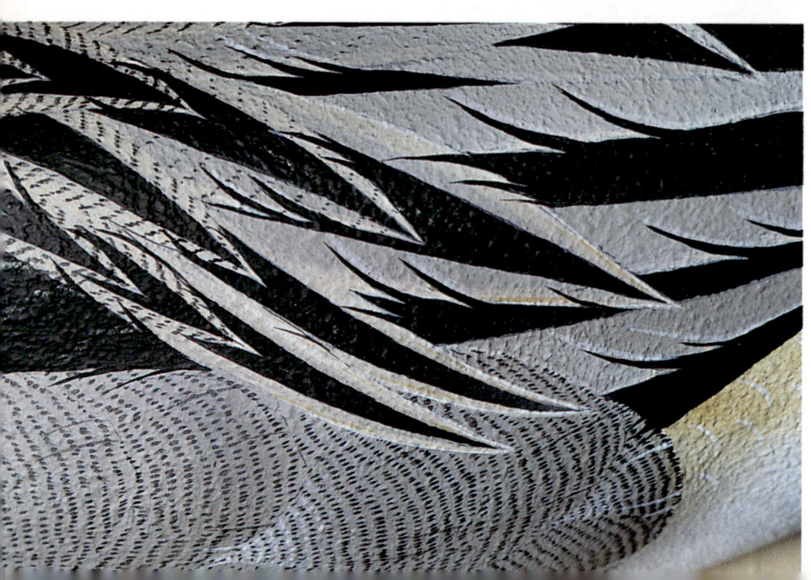

Detail shows the draping scapular feathers and the highlights created by painting "folds" in the feathers by adding white lines to the vermiculation. These folds can be placed anywhere in the vermiculation, but Jimmie warns not to overdo it.

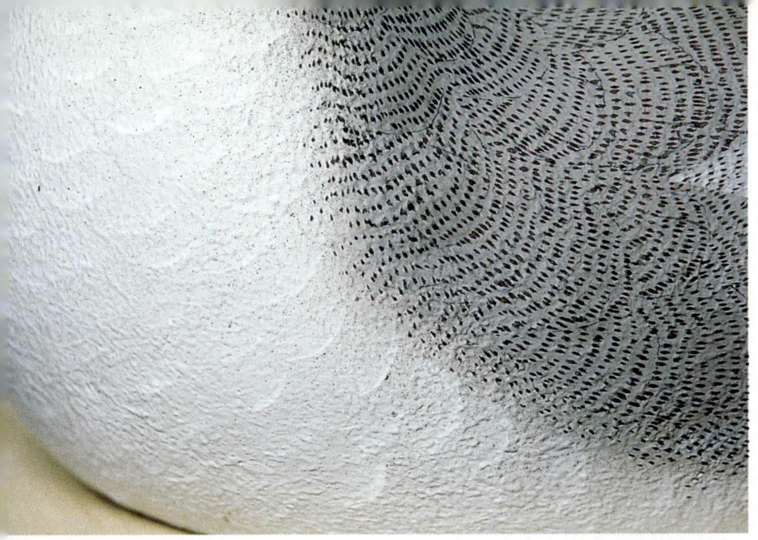

This close-up shows the white feather edges of the breast and belly. They should be visible but should not call attention to themselves. The idea is to create the illusion of softness and depth.

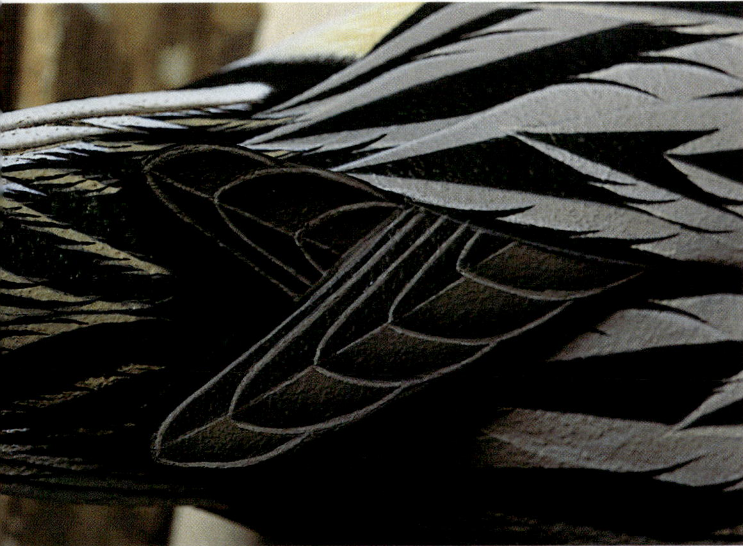

The primary flight feathers cross over the rump of the pintail. Note the painted feather edges and the black feather splits.

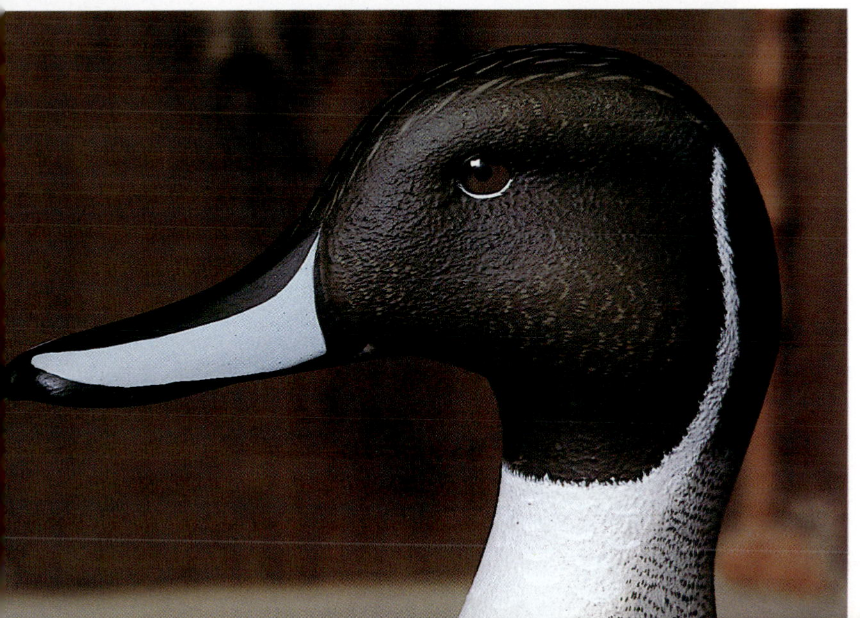

Detail of the head shows the subtle feather edges in the brown and the manner in which Jimmie feathered the edge of the brown paint. Note that Jimmie did not carve nostrils for this gunning-style bird.

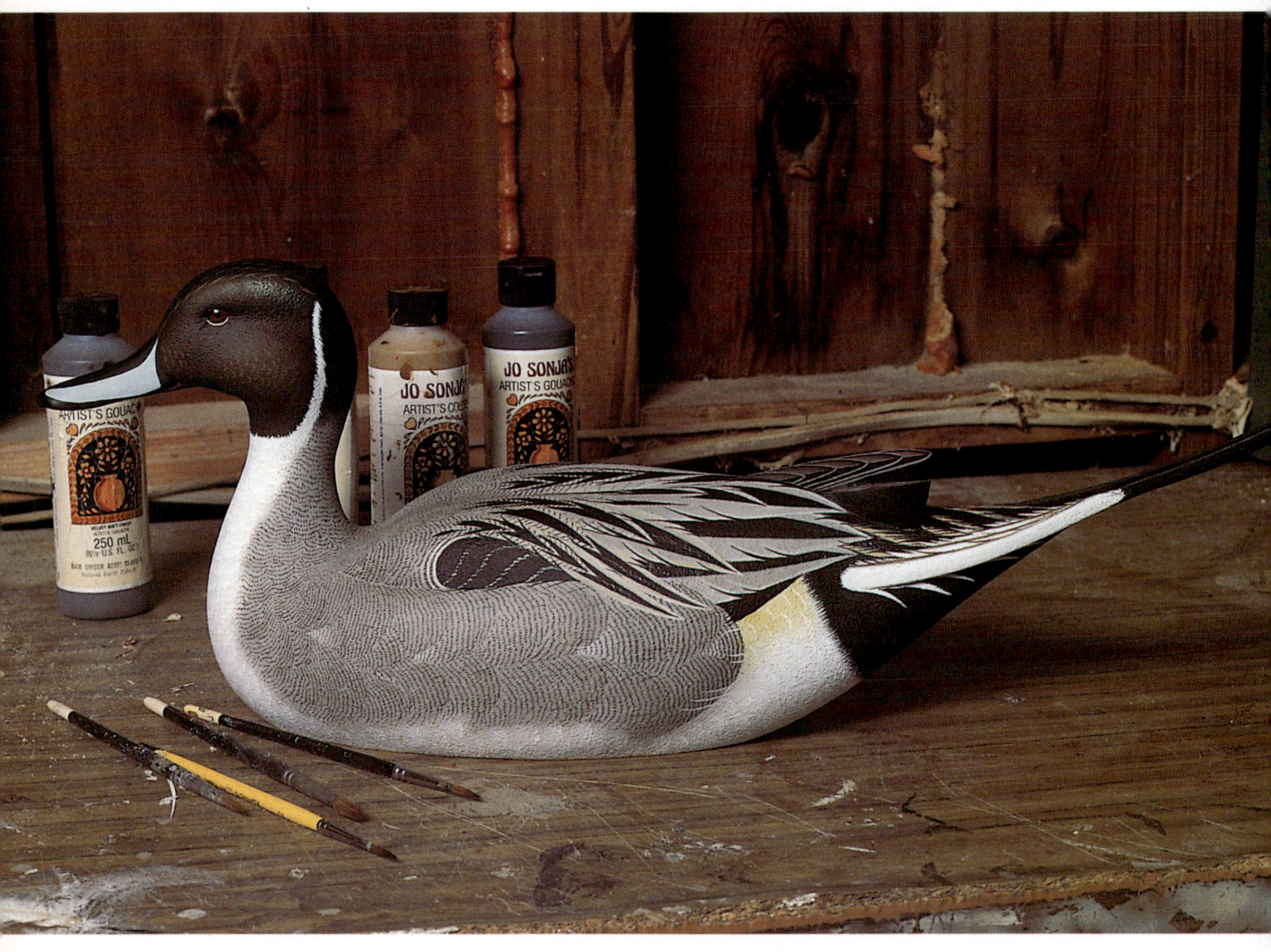

The completed pintail on Jimmie's workbench. The final step, if you want a decoy to hunt with or to enter in competitions, would be to add a weighted keel that would enable the decoy to self-right on the water and float in a natural manner. The keel is optional, however. If you simply want a bird to put on the mantel, you can sign and date it, varnish the bottom, and go on to your next carving project.

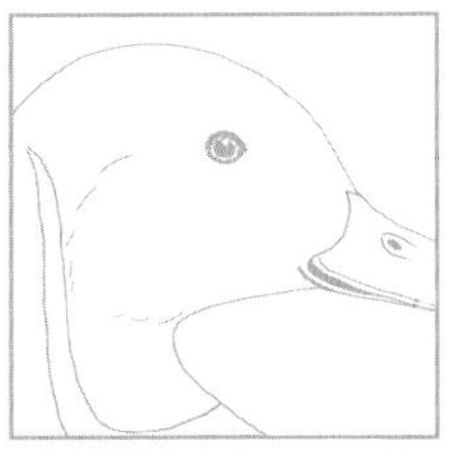

CHAPTER NINE

Making and Attaching the Keel

Jimmie makes the keel out of a piece of Spanish cedar cut to the length of the body. He drills holes in the keel and will pour molten lead into them to create ballast, helping the bird to self-right. After drilling the holes, he uses a knife to remove wood between them and make the opening slightly wider at the bottom, so that the lead will not fall out after it has hardened.

The lead will go toward the front of the bird because the front tends to float higher and needs to be weighted down. The keel can also be shifted left or right to correct a list. Tupelo will sometimes be denser on one side than the other, causing the decoy to float at a slight angle. Moving the weight to one side makes the opposite side float higher.

Jimmie carefully pours the hot lead into the keel a little at a time, allowing the lead to cool in between. If he poured all the lead in at once, it could scorch the wood.

If the lead is too heavy, causing the front to float too low, some of it can be removed with the drill press. If the addition of the keel is not sufficient to pull the front down, more weight can be added by removing the keel, drilling holes into the body of the bird under the keel, and adding more lead to those holes.

Gunning birds must float realistically to function well in a hunting situation, but even if the decoy will never be shot over, it still must float properly if it will be entered in a carving competition, where the entries are traditionally judged as they float in water. A hole for the decoy anchor line should be drilled in the front of the keel.

The keel is attached with 2-inch wood screws that are countersunk about 1/2 inch. Jimmie typically uses two or three screws to hold the keel in place. Holes for the screws can be drilled through the lead. Finally, the keel is lightly sanded and is sealed with the same clear Deft varnish applied to the bottom.

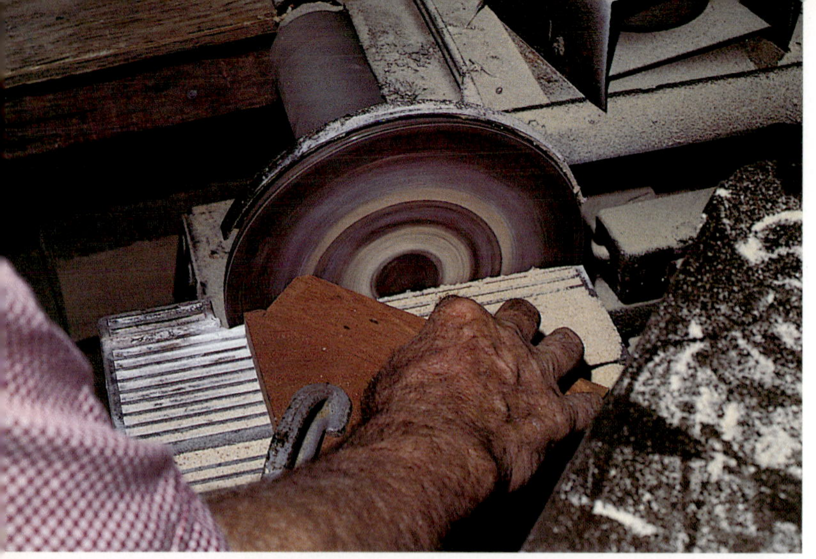

The keel is made of Spanish cedar cut slightly shorter than the bottom of the decoy. Here Jimmie bevels the bottom edges of the cedar with a jig he made to fit his sanding machine.

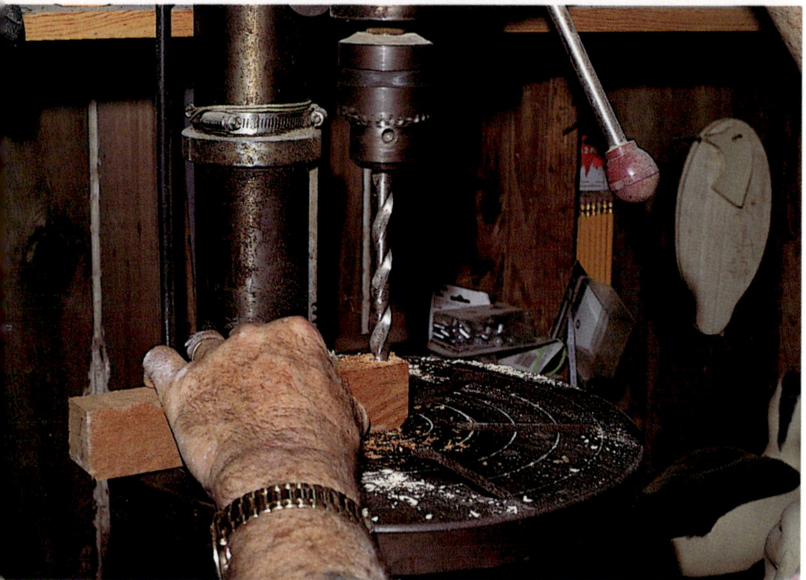

The keel is hollowed out on a drill press, then a knife is used to remove wood between the drilled holes.

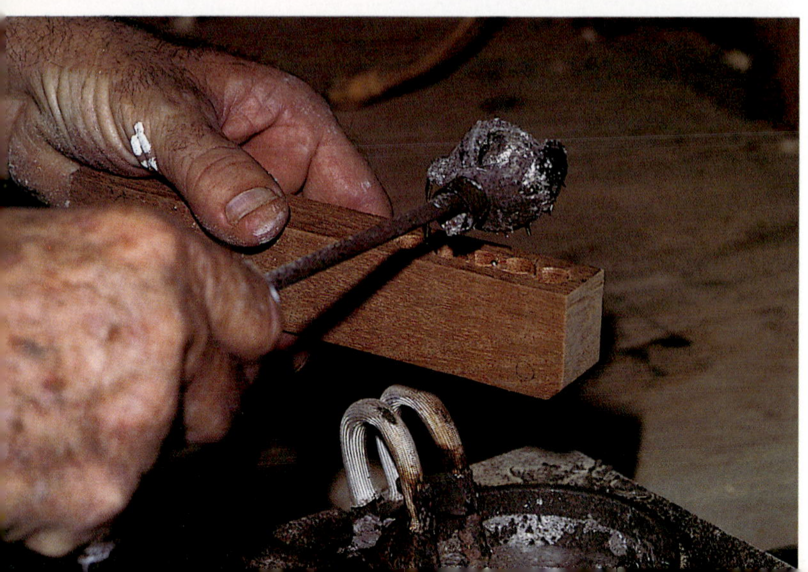

Lead is melted in a lead pot and is slowly poured into the opening in the keel. A small amount is poured at a time to avoid scorching the wood. Be sure to heat and pour the lead in a well-ventilated area to avoid breathing the fumes, and take care to avoid contact with the hot lead.

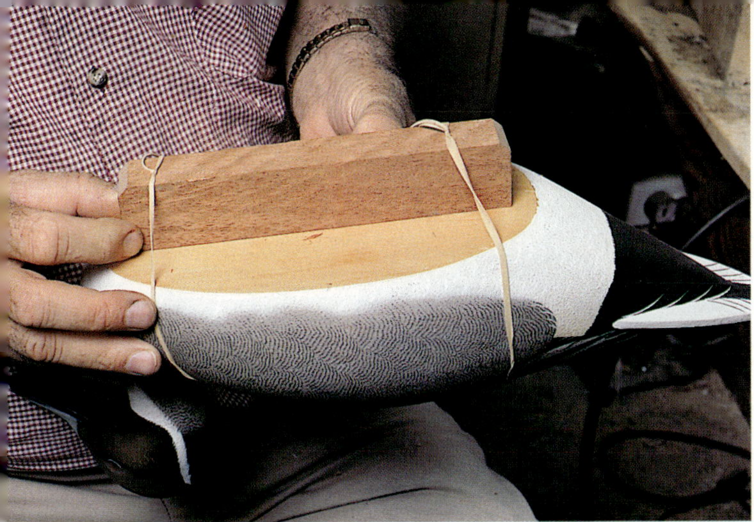

The keel is temporarily attached to the decoy with rubber bands. The decoy is then floated, and the keel is moved front to back and side to side to correct any unnatural tilt.

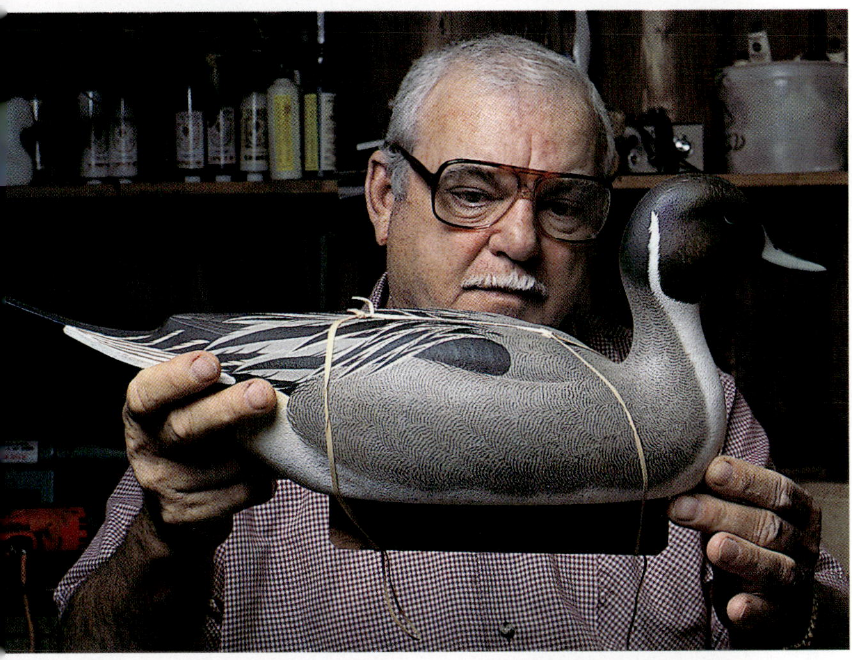

When Jimmie has the keel positioned where he wants it, he marks the location, varnishes the keel, and attaches it to the decoy.

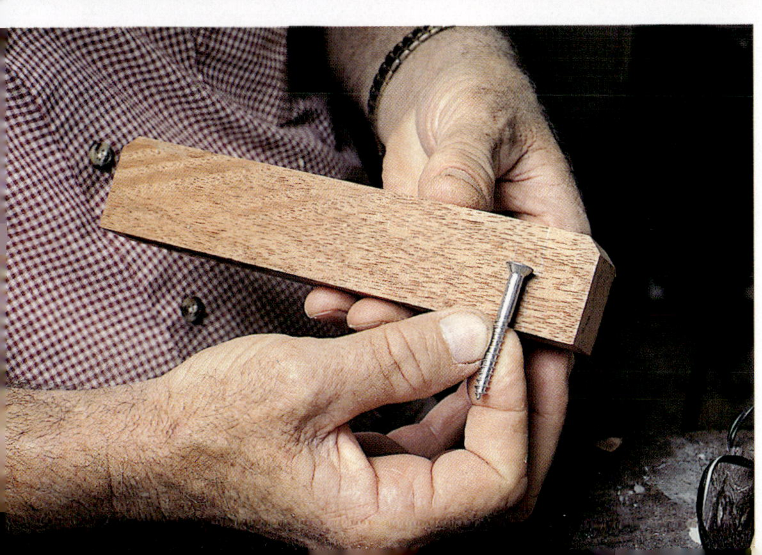

The keel is attached with counter-sunk wood screws, as shown. A hole should be drilled in the front of the keel for attaching an anchor line.

The Finished Carving

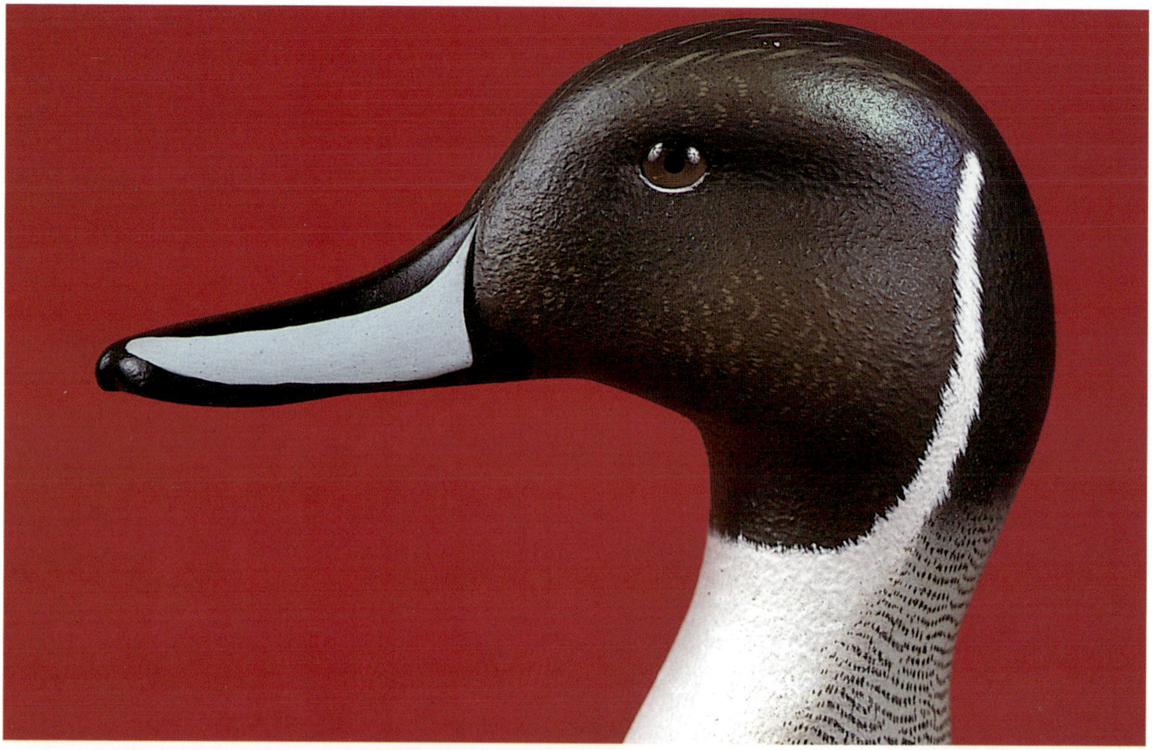

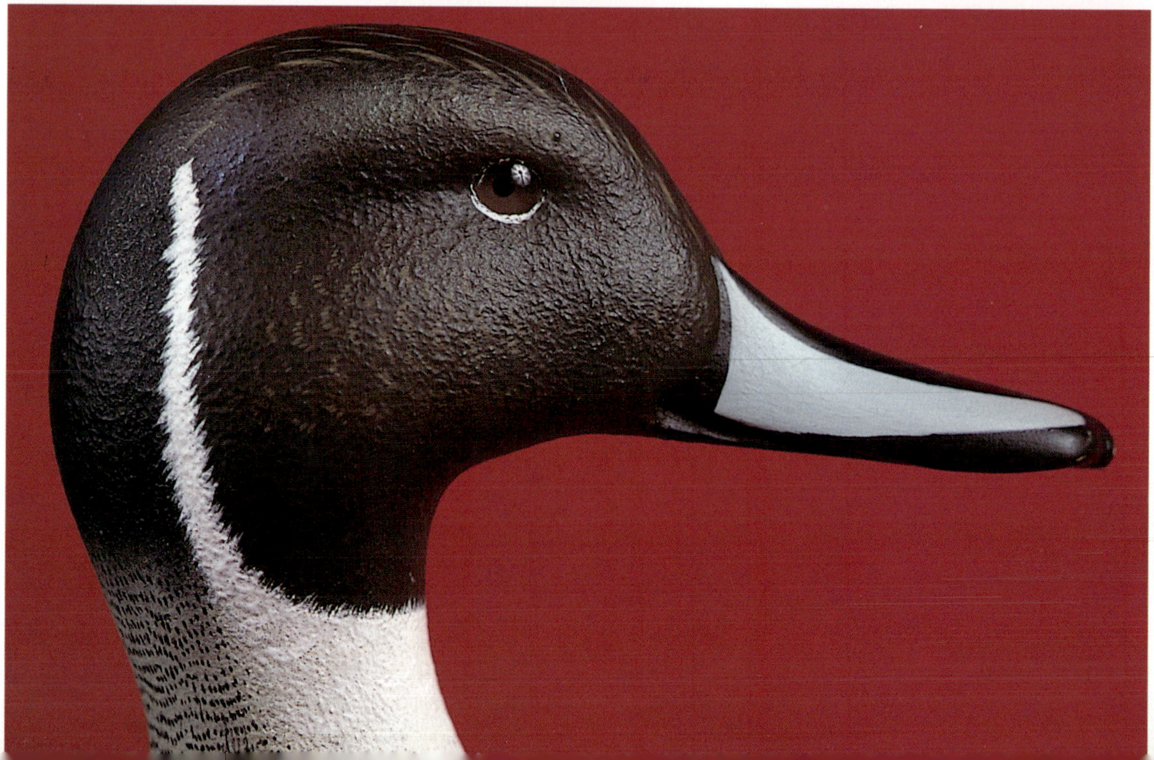

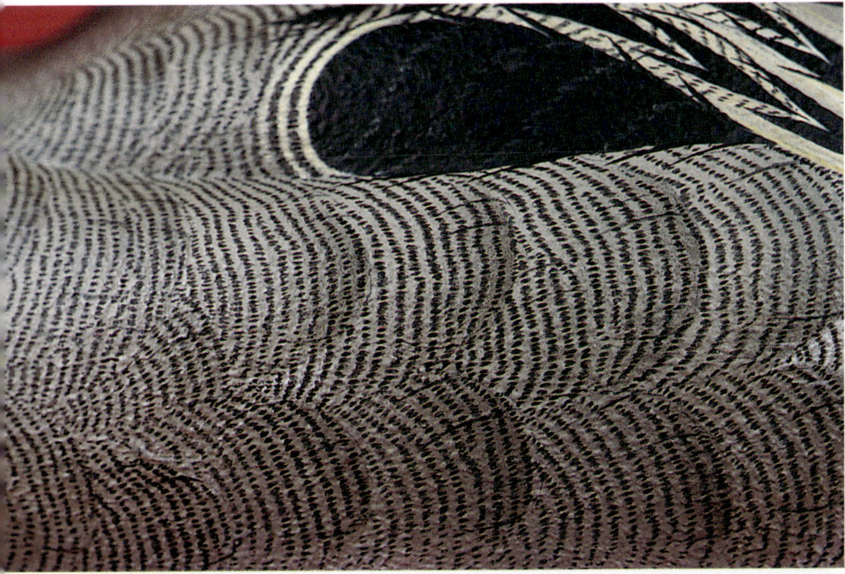

The dark, irregular lines along the flanks of the pintail are called vermiculation. A close look reveals that they are not solid lines, but a series of short strokes of paint placed closely together. Jimmie uses a number 2 brush for this purpose.

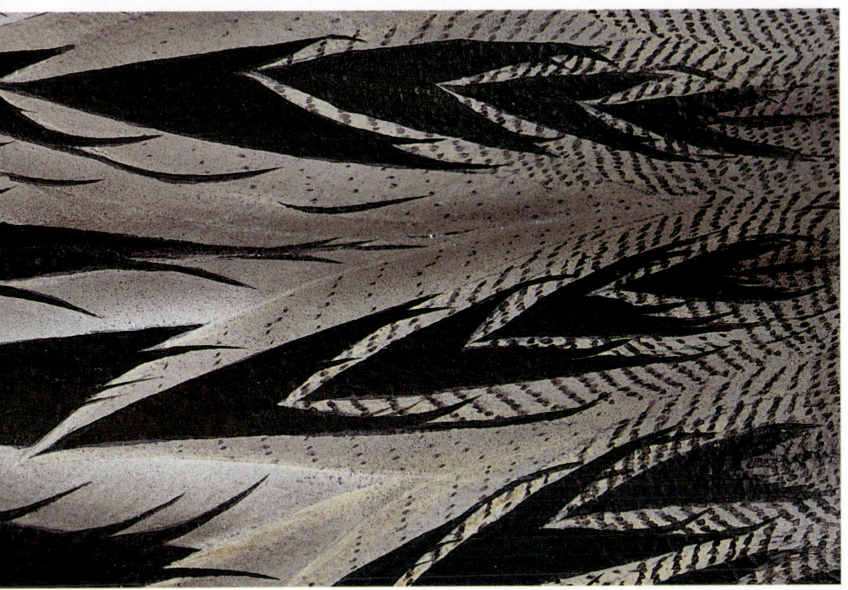

This closeup of the flight feathers shows how graphic they are and how they add visual interest to the bird. Note how the various splits in the feathers add realism to the carving.

Opposite, top: The blue sides of the pintail bill have a clearly defined edge. Jimmie makes the light blue color by mixing smoked pearl with either cobalt blue or phthalo blue.

Opposite, bottom: The neck stripe of the pintail should not have a hard edge. Jimmie uses a small brush to create an irregular edge, giving the impression of brown and white feathers overlapping.

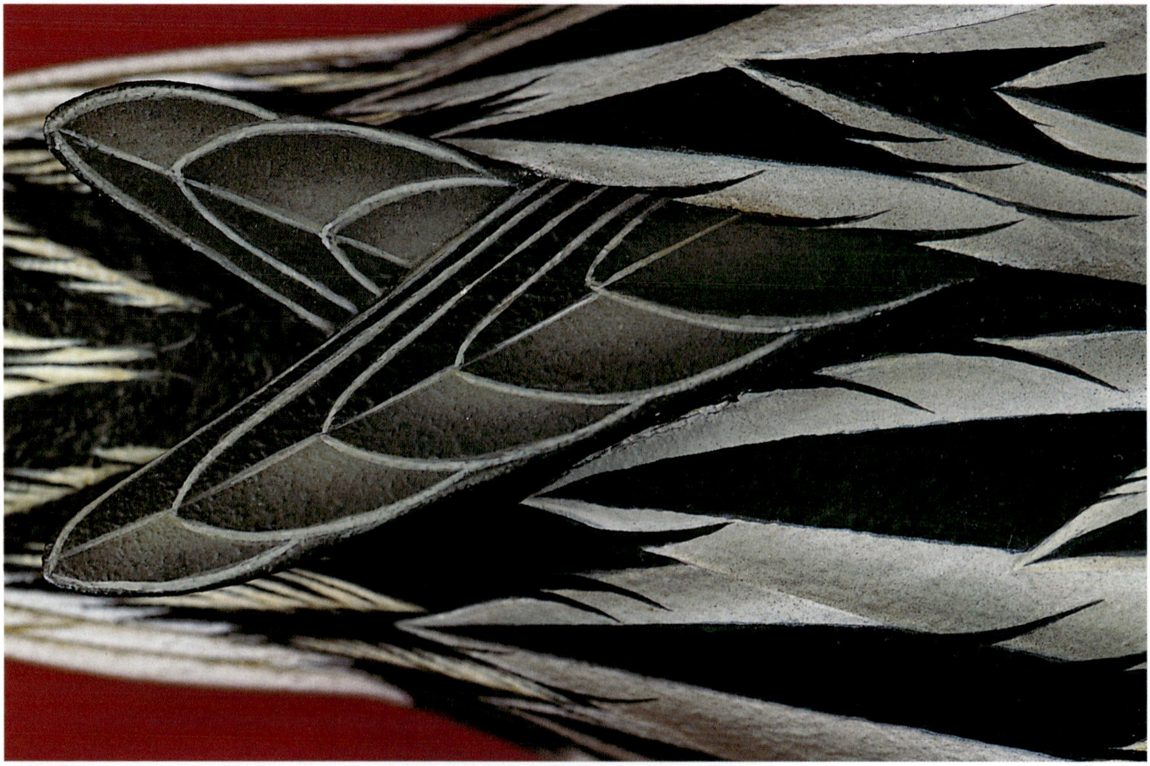

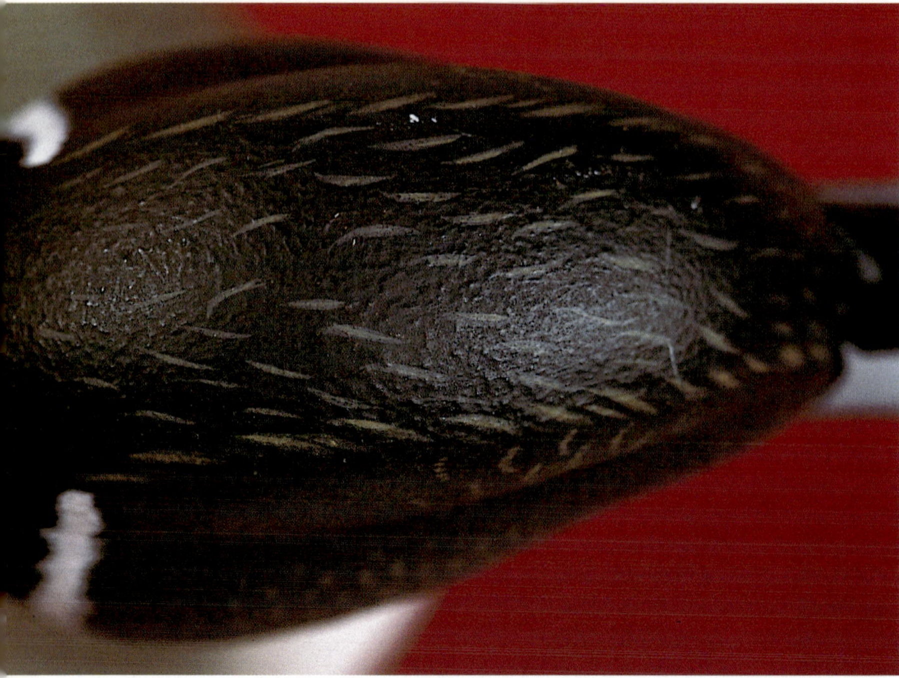

The primary flight feathers are raised, with the left feathers overlapping the right. These feathers are outlined in gray, and each feather has a subtle highlight in the larger sector. Jimmie often uses an airbrush do to this.

This closeup of the top of the head shows the feather edges Jimmie paints with a small brush and also the gray-blue mix he uses for painting feather edges on the sides of the bird. Details such as these are not vital in a hunting decoy, but since this is a decorative bird in the hunting style, they add to the visual interest.

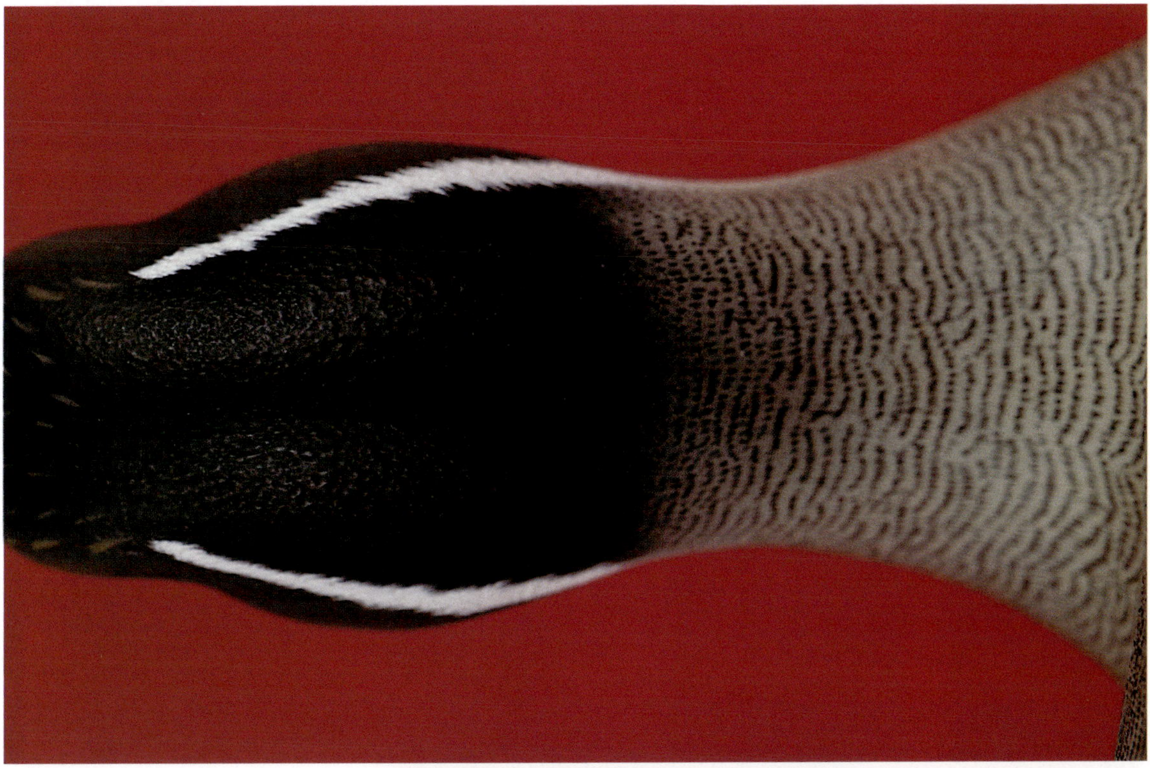

The vermiculation runs up the back of the pintail and onto the neck, gradually fading into the brown of the head. Note that the white vertical neck lines are not identical but are fairly symmetrical. One should not be more dominant than the other.

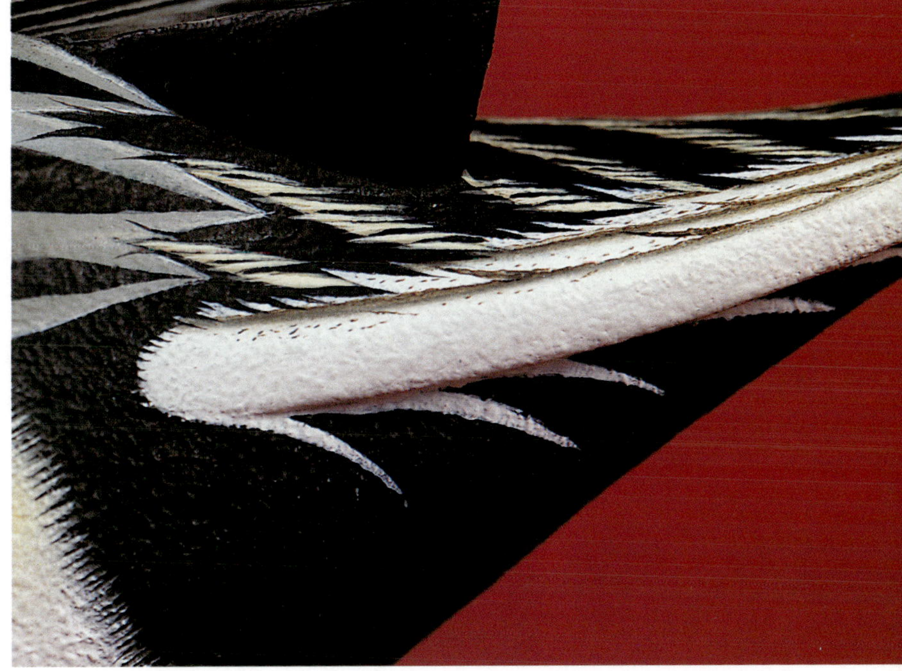

The rump also adds to the graphic qualities of the pintail, with the white-on-black coloration. The rump is slightly upswept, beginning a gentle curve that will continue with the long pintail.

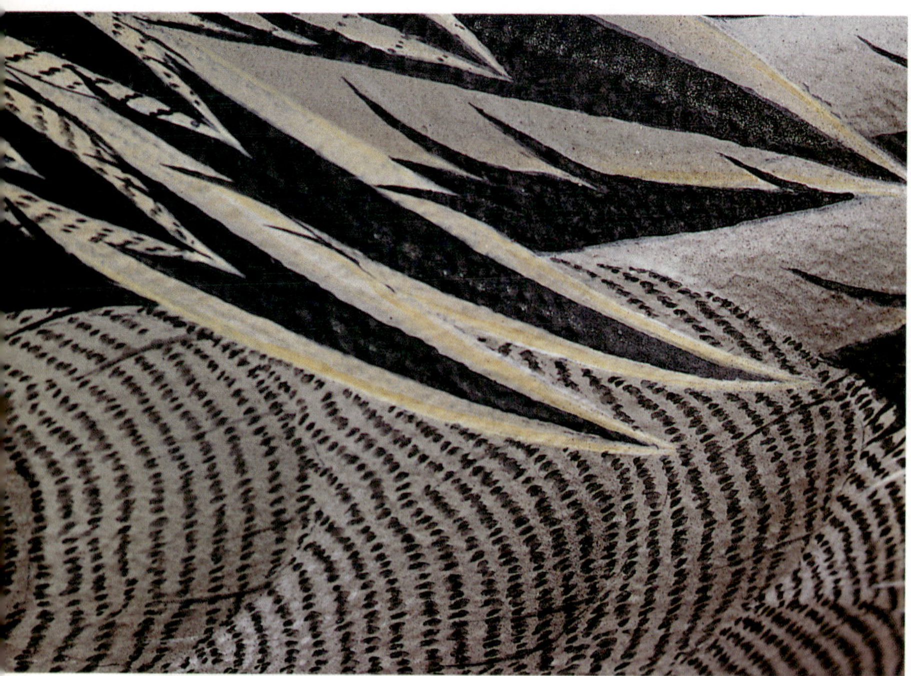

The graceful flow of the scapular feathers across the side pockets of the pintail add a great deal to the design of the carving. The subtle curve and the fairly intricate design can best be studied by using a real feather. Jimmie uses as reference ducks bagged during hunting trips.

The cobalt blue edges of the bill extend slightly to the front. The blue areas should be fairly symmetrical, so one will not dominate the other. Note the carved nail at the tip of the bill.

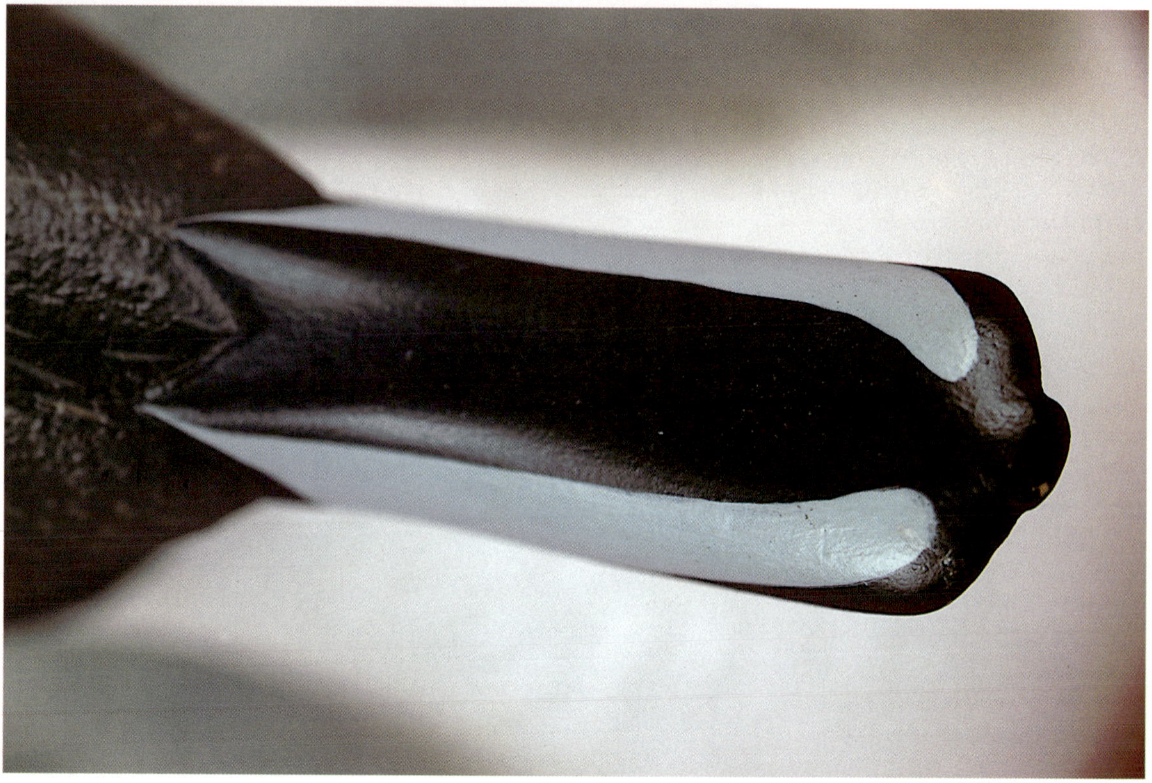

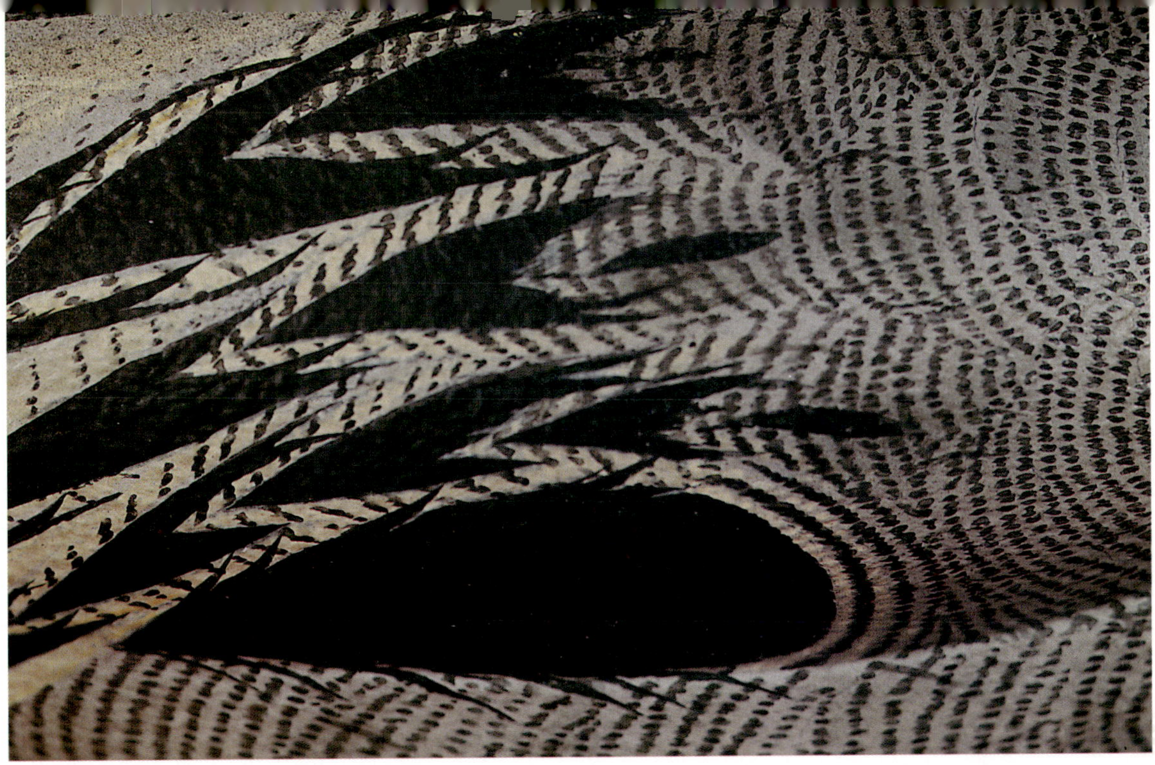

This closeup shows how the scapular feathers flow around the wing and onto the side pockets. The cream-colored edges of the feathers are a mix of smoked pearl, raw sienna, and raw umber. Jimmie mixes the color on his easel until it looks right, using a real feather as reference.

A closeup of the scapular feathers along the back of the bird shows where they blend into the vermiculation of the upper back (right). The vermiculation covers the cream-colored scapulars in this area.

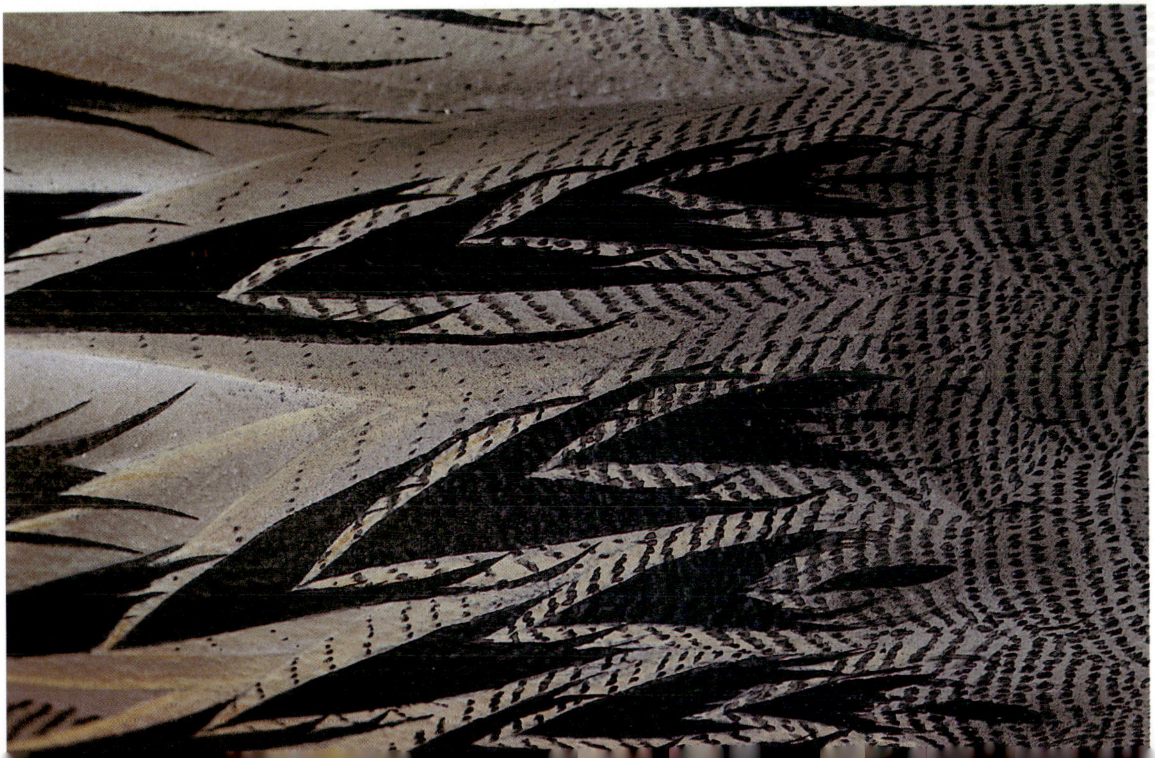

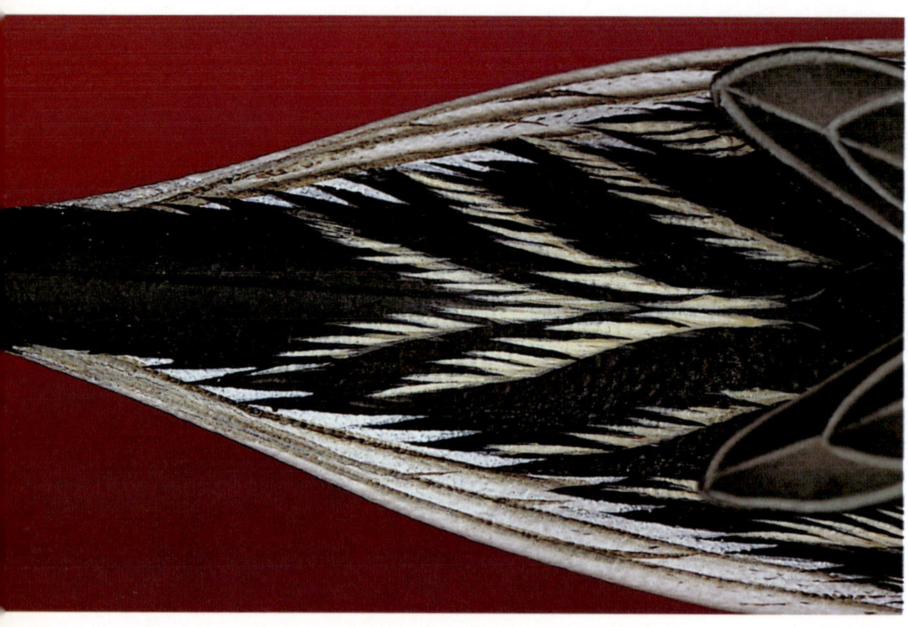

The feather markings on the top of the rump continue the graphic approach to painting this bird. The black tail feathers have white edges, while those on top of the rump have yellow edges.

A side view of the entire bird shows how all these visual elements come together to create a pleasing whole. The vermiculated area has a soft, subtle edge, the scapulars drape gracefully down the sides, and the slightly upswept tail provides an elegant curving line.

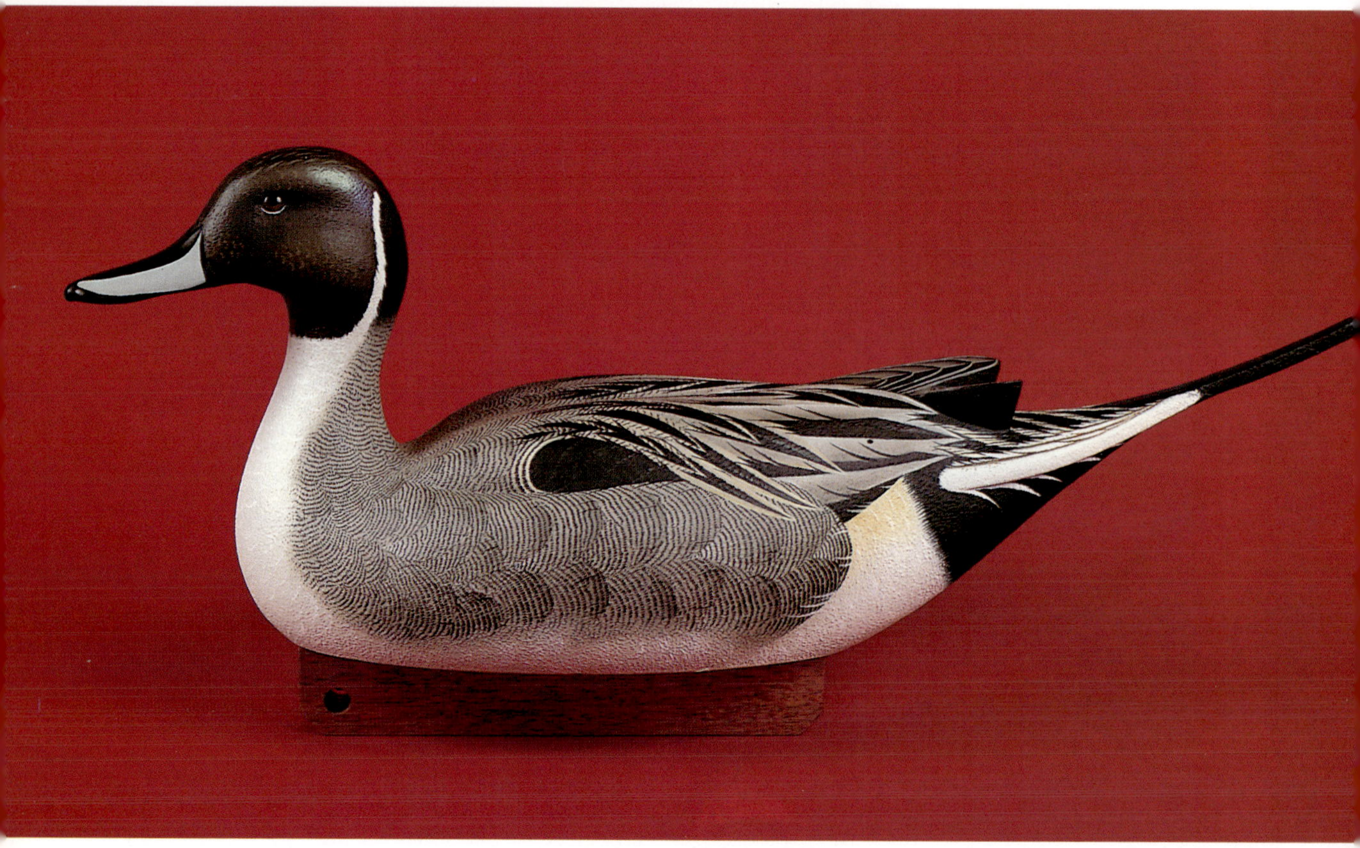

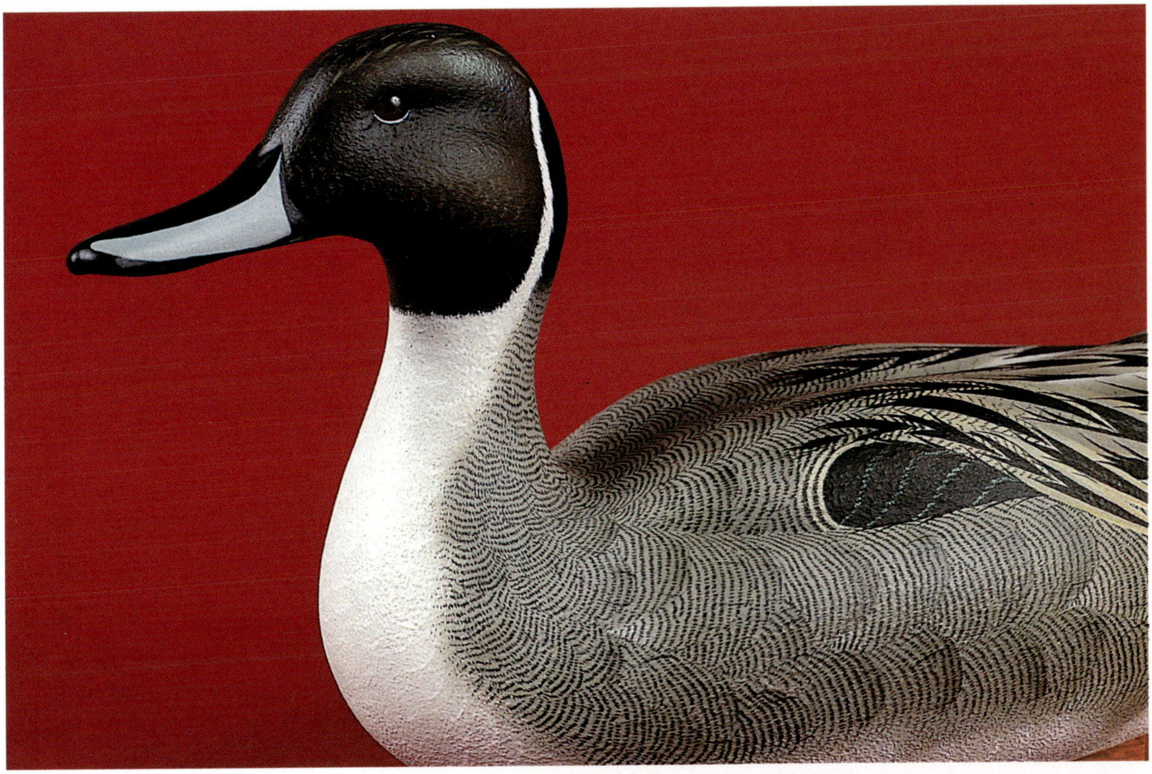

The manner in which Jimmie painted the vermiculation along the sides and back can be seen here. The slight texture is created by stippling textured gesso onto the bird as a base coat.

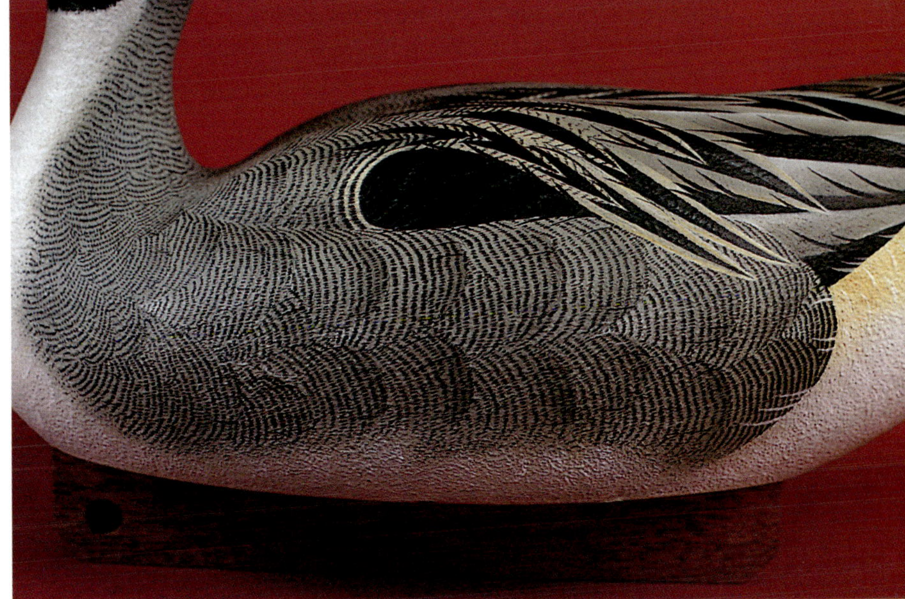

The vermiculation on the sides of the pintail ends just before joining the breast of the bird. A few feather splits have been added toward the rear for the sake of realism.

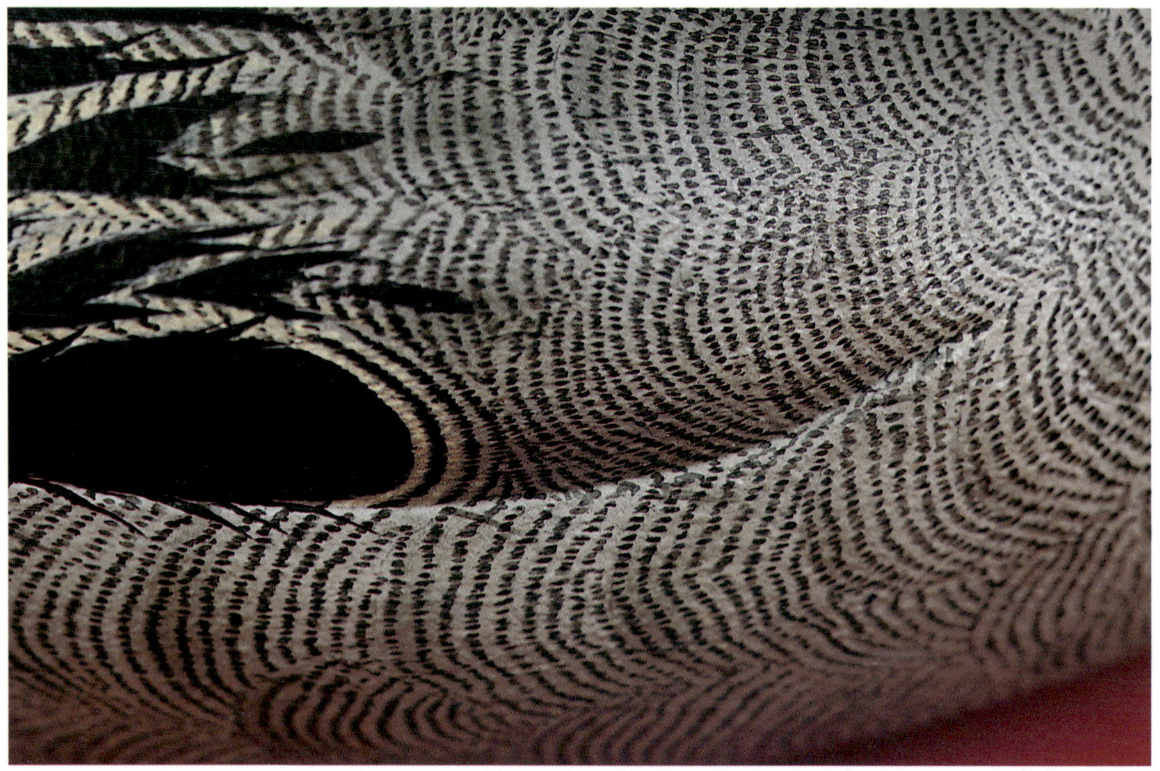

The groove separating the wings and sides of the pintail illustrates how carving and painting complement each other. This groove is omitted, however, where the scapulars flow over the sides, covering the ledge.